The Complete Book of Coin Collecting

Also by Joseph Coffin

COIN COLLECTING

COINS OF THE POPES

OUR AMERICAN MONEY

THE COMPLETE BOOK OF

Coin Collecting

BY JOSEPH COFFIN

Illustrated with Photographs

SECOND REVISED EDITION

Coward-McCann, Inc. New York

Library of Congress Catalog

Card Number: 59-11009

Second Revised Edition, 1967

PRINTED IN THE UNITED STATES OF AMERICA

VAN REES PRESS • NEW YORK

Preface

THIS BOOK is for the purpose of introducing the fascinating subject of coin collecting to those who know little or nothing about it. At the same time it is hoped that there may be some information for even those who have already begun to collect seriously. It is not a book on any specific field of coin collecting. There are already legions of books on every aspect of ancient and modern coins, mostly of a highly specialized character. These books range from catalogues or lists to very scholarly studies of the coins of many different and little-known countries. Some of these works are of such a scholarly nature in fact that they are apt to discourage potential collectors and keep them from enjoying a fine pursuit. The lists, of course, are necessary and often indispensable as we look for coins of any particular country. However, they are undoubtedly dull reading for anyone who is not looking for a certain coin.

Therefore, the principal object of *The Complete Book of Coin Collecting* is to point out in, we hope, an interesting manner the many fine aspects of the collecting of coins of all countries and times.

I would like to extend my special thanks here to the numismatic firm of Stack's, of New York City, for the loan of most of the coin photographs.

JOSEPH COFFIN

Contents

Sixteen pages of illustrations will be found following page 126.

The Complete Book of Coin Collecting

CHAPTER ONE

The Beginning of a Coin Collection

THE COLLECTING of coins, paper money, or any of the allied objects embraced in the general subject of numismatics, such as tokens and medals, should be considered almost as a good artisan considers his profession. Starting at the bottom with a solid foundation is a sensible plan in any field. In this way a working knowledge is obtained that will, later on, save time, money, and effort.

As we will hear a lot about numismatists and coin collectors, it is well to differentiate between the two terms. One can be a numismatist but not a collector, and vice versa; or, one can be both. A collector is just what the name implies, one who collects; a numismatist is a scholar, one who makes a study of coins, what they mean, where they are found, their historical significance, iconography, archaeological interest, and many other things.

These chapters are entirely in the interest of the coin collector and, we will assume, one who is at the very beginning of his collecting career. And we hope at the same time that the collector's objective is not simply to amass a great many more or less shiny objects to look at now and then with the satisfaction of a hoarder. In other words, it is hoped that he will derive his satisfaction from a greater knowledge of the world we live in, as it is and as it was far back in history. Only in this way will the collector some day feel justified in calling himself a numismatist as well as a coin collector.

Almost everyone has the beginnings of a coin collection. There are few who do not possess at least one or two old or odd-looking coins, a medal, token, or souvenir of a centennial celebration or world's fair. It will be our purpose to arouse the interest of those who have had no experience in coin collecting, to save them time in completing particular series, and to assist them in securing the maximum enjoyment at the least possible expense. At the same time, it is hoped that there will be an idea or two for those who have been at the game a long time and may possibly have overlooked a detail that might have helped them to get the most out of their collection.

Acquiring a collection of coins having interest and value, of course, is not a few weeks' work. Some people might wish to specialize from the beginning, and it might be well for them to purchase the penny, nickel, dime, quarter, or other boards which any hobby dealer sells. The popular expression "penny board" is used, because that is what they are generally called. As far as United States coinage is concerned, numismatists insist we have no penny; all we have is the cent. These boards contain spaces for each date of a series, such as Indian-head and copper-nickel (or "white") cents, Lincoln cents, or Liberty-head, buffalo, and Jefferson nickels, and so on. In filling these boards one at least becomes familiar with the various designs, the mint marks, the hard-to-get dates, and the importance of condition in making a worthwhile collection. Under this plan most of the recent cents, nickels, or other denominations could be taken from circulation with the possible exception of the very scarce ones such as 1909-S VDB, 1914 D and 1931 S cents, and a few others. At one time even these could be picked up in change, but with the increased popularity of collecting, the scarcer dates or mint marks are hard to find. Incidentally, until very few years ago it was possible to pick up a good many Indian-head cents, but these have virtually disappeared from circulation and would now have to be purchased.

On the other hand, for some people it is sometimes a good idea to start by collecting everything of a particular kind. That is, all coins, or all sorts of paper money, tokens, or medals. In this way you will sooner or later run across a series that, because of your own particular background, will intrigue you more than others.

The true collector is more or less independent and will naturally work out his own problems as he goes along. Nevertheless, there are certain features which take time to discover while working alone, and a short cut here and there may save much time for the busy man or woman. Among these features are the care and cleaning of coins, varieties of coins, tokens and paper money, common numismatic terms used by dealers and collectors, the comparative scarcity of some dates, and many other things which every collector learns for himself in due course but which he might have learned at less expense of time and money if he had had knowledge beforehand.

Coin collecting today is one of the most popular of all hobbies. It is also one of the most ancient. The old Romans collected Greek coins and thought highly of them for their beauty, while still collecting their own coins and those of other nations. Among comparatively modern collectors were the Popes of the thirteenth and fourteenth centuries, and during the Renaissance collecting coins was a favorite pastime of many Italian noblemen. In England and France collecting was in full swing during the sixteenth and seventeenth centuries. Some collections were dispersed during troublous times, by the Puritans in England and the Revolutionists in France. Some collections were preserved and rest in the universities and the British Museum and other institutions in the British Isles. Two latter-day collectors of royal persuasion were the late Victor Emmanuel III of Italy and the late King Farouk of Egypt. Victor Emmanuel was a numismatist of distinction who wrote many large volumes on the Italian coinage. The whereabouts of his collection since World War II is not known. Farouk owned a tremendous collection, containing a great many United States rarities as well as many others, which was sold at auction a few years ago.

We can separate the collecting possibilities very roughly into three, or possibly four, divisions. There is the collector of United States coins, the foreign coin collector, and the collector of ancient coins. There are also those who collect medieval coins. It seems simple on the surface, but it happens that each class can be subdivided into a great many others. In the United States field, for example, there is the Colonial period, private and territorial gold coins, regular issues, proofs only, patterns and trial pieces, commemorative coins, and the complete sets of any particular denomination. And there are also several additional series, comprising paper issues, fractional currency, Confederate money, and broken bank bills. There are collectors of large cents only, or Indian-heads or Lincoln cents, or dimes exclusively, or any other denomination. The foreign coin collector has a large field. Some specialize in the new issues of each country, others in nineteenth- or twentieth-century issues, proof coins, or specimen sets, as they are sometimes called in other countries. Again, anyone may choose his own special kind of collection. One man, a hatter by trade, is interested in coins with effigies wearing hats. There is also the female collector who has a large number of coins bearing figures of women, or issued in their honor, and there are a great many of these from early Greece and Rome to the present day.

While it is not always possible to form a collection of items pertaining to such popular vocations as typist, accountant, plumber, or carpenter, there are exceptions, such as the above-mentioned hatter. Some professions are more favored than others in this respect; there are many medical medals and books about them, and medals honoring musicians are legion. There are not many coins having to do with locomotives, or even automobiles; the few that do exist, however, can be well augmented by a collection of medals relating to such other vehicles as airplanes or balloons. On the other hand, there are many showing bridges, aqueducts and buildings, particularly churches. Most numerous seem to be those depicting ships of all types and ages. Ships are well represented on our own commemorative coins, starting with the Columbian half dollars of 1892 and 1893, and continuing with the Pilgrim half dollars of 1920 and 1921, the Huguenot-Walloon half dollar of 1924, the Hudson half dollar of 1935, the Long Island and Norfolk half dollars of 1936, and the Delaware half dollar of 1938. The Rhode Island half dollars of 1936 show a canoe, which according to our nautical friends is only a boat, but at least is seagoing or more properly water-going. The canoe, incidentally, is a popular theme on many Canadian silver dollars.

When a person's trade or calling does not determine his collecting specialty, his individual likes or special interests may. This is why a religious or Biblical collection of coins is always popular, and one which constantly brings forth new and interesting items. The literature on Biblical coins—those mentioned in the Bible or current in the days of the prophets—though not plentiful, is nevertheless adequate for any study of the subject. There are also many coins, both ancient and modern, showing animals, such as those of Ancient Greece and Rome and of Eire, or even birds and fishes, if this is what we are looking for. There have been studies and articles on hairdressing as depicted on ancient Greek and Roman coins, as well as on later specimens of European and Asian currency. Buildings are well represented, and there have been articles written about architectural features displayed on coins, particularly the ancient series. There is even a growing list of items issued by or honoring numismatists, among which may be included the hundreds issued over the years by coin dealers. We can see from all this that there is almost no end to what may be sought after in our collecting activities. The literature on any special series may not always be found in large quantities. However, there is always something bearing on our favorite subject.

In ancient times barter was the means of getting what one wanted in exchange for something one wanted less. Homer mentions exchanging wine for bronze, polished iron, skins, and cattle. The English word "barter" is derived from the old French *bareter,* meaning to cheat, which may have been a feature of this sort of trade on both sides. The word "money" is from the Latin *moneta,* which in turn came from *moneo,* to warn. In ancient Rome, Juno was the goddess of warning. In gratitude for her many warnings of impending dangers, the mint was placed in her temple and, as guardian of finances, she was called Juno Moneta. The word "coin" comes from the Latin *cuneus,* meaning wedge. This was because the dies that made pieces of money looked like wedges. Our word "dime" comes from *decimus,* meaning tenth, or tenth of a dollar, and "cent" from the Latin *centum,* or one hundredth, meaning that one hundred cents make a dollar. "Dollar" is from a European word *Joachimsthaler,* relating to the vale or valley of Joachim, where the first large silver coins were made early in the sixteenth century. The word has many variations, such as thaler, taler, tallero, daalder, and so on. The English word "pound" comes from the Latin *pondo* or *pendere,* meaning a weight. "Peso" and "lira" also have reference to weights. The English pound is designated £, since the full expression was *libra pondo,* "a pound by weight." The abbreviation for the English penny is "d," for *denarius,* a reminder that the Romans, who used this coin, once occupied Britain. The ox was an original form of money in ancient Greece, and the Latin word for ox, *pecus,* relating to cattle, has come down to us in such words as "pecuniary," meaning state of finances, "impecunious," impoverished or lacking money, and others. The Anglo-Saxon word *feoh* also meant cattle, and later money; we have a reminder of this derivation in the word "fee." Similarly, "capital" is a variation of the Latin *capita,* meaning heads of cattle.

There is no particular link between the crude iron or bronze bars of ancient times and the real authentic stamped coin. There are, however, many in-between media which could be called missing links; for example, the gold and copper ring money of ancient Egypt and the Celtic ring money. Swedish plate money is also considered coinage, since it bears stampings of authority.

Some collectors make a practice of collecting odd and curious money—quite successfully, since many things enter into such a collection. Tobacco has been used as money, also blocks of salt or tea, feathers, shells, beads, ivory, beaver skins, and dried codfish. Of course, various regions of the world govern the use of such material: shells in the South Seas, ivory in Africa, beaver skins in Canada, and codfish in Newfoundland. Other products, not as crude as some of these but just as odd, are the porcelain tokens used in Siam many years ago, mostly as gambling counters, and the playing cards that were once used in Canada.

The first metal coins were crude. While the identity of the originator of the stamped metal coin is very much in doubt, it is generally agreed that coins were first issued on one of the islands of Greece. These coins bore a face, or obverse, only, the reverse bearing simply a crossmark of the die. The Greeks, the Persians, and, finally, the Romans, minted coins of silver, gold and bronze.

Paper money came into use later, probably in China about 1400 A.D., although many archaeologists claim that Babylonian clay tablets made many centuries before were the real ancestors of paper money. This form of money is an adaptation of a draft, a promise to pay. Of itself it has no value, except as currently used in trade, and therefore differs from metal money, which often has a high intrinsic value. Nevertheless, old and obsolete paper money in good condition may command a high price from a collecting standpoint, according to its rarity. The collector who specializes in paper money has an infinite variety, which includes state bills, foreign and war bills, invasion and concentration camp currency, and other forms, all of which will be discussed later.

Instead of the more orthodox collections, some prefer an unusual assortment. It is fascinating to learn about unusual and interesting coins, and there are many of them, from a single coin or small set of coins (from two to a dozen or so) all the way to certain series that may take half a lifetime to satisfactorily complete. Among the single unusuals there is the Maria Theresa taler, or dollar. Named after the Empress of Austria, whose head they bear, these dollars of silver are all dated 1780, the year first issued, and have been used in certain countries in the Middle East and Africa, particularly those bordering on the Red Sea, ever since. The natives refuse to accept any modern substitute, and have used this coin for over 150 years because they prefer its pure silver and know its chief characteristics. Although these dollars are minted in London and in certain European countries at the present time, they have the same design and look exactly the same as the original. It would be impossible to estimate how many millions of these coins have been minted. Nor is this the only coin that has enjoyed so long a period of circulation. Ancient Athens minted silver coins showing the owl, the bird of Athena, Goddess of Wisdom and presiding patron of the city. These coins are among the most famous in the world, and achieved such world-wide popularity in ancient times that for nearly two centuries the owl tetradrachms were struck in the same type and style.

Then there are the odd denominations: small coins, such as Panama "pills" (small silver 2½ centesimos, dated 1904) and the very small gold chuckrum of Travencore, India; or very high denominations, such as the German billion mark of 1923 or the Roumanian 25,000 lei of 1946. The Confederate half dollar of 1861 is an unusual item and much sought after, even though only found as a much later restrike.

An out-of-the-ordinary set, small in numbers of coins, comprises the Sede Vacante coins of the Popes, issued between the death of one Pope and the election of his successor. These are a desirable acquisition and, although the main theme is always the same, a radiant dove signifying the Holy Ghost, and the arms of the Camerlengo or Papal Chamberlain, they contain few enough coins to satisfy anyone who may want a small collection without too many individual coins. A similar desirable collection is the Papal Jubilee coinage, issued every 25 years on the occasion of a Holy Year, or Jubilee, the last being held in 1950. Another interesting small series is the Maundy money of England, issued every year by the Crown and minted for distribution to the poor on Maundy Thursday. This series consists of a silver penny, twopence, threepence, and fourpence; this is the only silver coinage now issued in England since cupro-nickel was introduced to save metal after the Second World War and during the reign of George VI.

Other unusual and intriguing sets are the Swiss shooting festival talers, masonic medals for those interested in such fraternal societies, and the commemorative coins of many individual countries. The platinum money of Russia, now quite expensive, although over a million pieces were coined, between the years 1828 and 1845, for Nicholas I, was issued at a time when platinum was considered useless. Coins of unusual composition are plentiful, such as German porcelain money made at the famous Meissen Pottery Works, which proved beautiful but impractical. Then there are the communion tokens distributed at one time to members of the Scottish Presbyterian Church and others; over 7,000 varieties of these tokens are listed. Sutler's checks, in vogue at army camps during the Civil War and at other times, are collectors' items; as are Bryan's so-called silver dollars, coined to call attention to the need for increased use of that metal along with gold, and named for William Jennings Bryan; and the Lesher referendum dollars, introduced by Joseph Lesher in Colorado in 1900 and 1901.

Obsidional, or siege, coins are another historically interesting series. There are many of these, mostly of European origin, such as the Newark diamond or lozenge-shaped half crown bearing the inscription "OBS: Newark, 1646," and the other English siege coins of Carlisle, Colchester, Scarborough, and other places, issued during the rebellion of 1625-1649. Other siege coins were issued in the cities of Leyden, Osnabruck, and elsewhere in the Netherlands, and in many Italian cities. Another item of somewhat similar significance is the "gun money" which James II struck in 1689 and 1690 in Ireland from old cannon balls, bells, and other scrap metal. Many of these show the month of mintage for possible later redemption, which, of course, never came about.

Apart from the ubiquitous transportation token, familiar to all of us in at least one of many thousands of varieties, there are other tokens worthy of attention. The French *jetons,* almshouse tokens, medals or tokens of pestilence and famine, hacienda tokens of Mexico, Central, and South America, and Cuban sugar plantation tokens can be found in abundance if you know where to look. This does not mean that you are likely to find them in your small change at the supermarket. Generally they have to be pursued carefully and patiently, picked up here and there, one by one, or occasionally in twos or threes. An interesting set of coins issued by the Culion Leper Colony in the Philippine Islands consists of several denominations of silver and copper pesos and centavos which were minted at Manila between 1913 and 1927.

For those who want an offbeat collection, there are United States tokens from the Civil War and earlier, "Jackson cents," merchants' store cards, Canadian bank and other tokens, European tokens, and even prison tokens. We have mentioned just a few of the more or less unusual collections. Each of them has its own faithful following. There is even a place for the scholar or lover of literature. Writers from Horace to Shakespeare, and many later, have had something to say about money in general. For example: "Money is a handmaiden, if thou knowest how to use it; a mistress, if thou knowest not." And Shakespeare: "He that wants money, means and content, is without three good friends." Specifically, there are many references to money and coins or medals. To name one, Pepys' *Diary* mentions that in 1667 he saw the King's medal showing Mrs. Stewart's face. Mrs. Frances Stewart, Duchess of Richmond, was the model for Britannia during Charles II's reign, Britannia being the familiar seated figure which has appeared many times on English coins.

Before we go much further it would be well to become a little familiar with the ordinary language and terms applied by numismatists to the physical details of coins. As mentioned before, the two sides of a coin are called *obverse* and *reverse,* better known as "heads" and "tails." The main design on a coin is the *device,* and the *legend* or *inscription* is the wording around the coin. The *lettered edge* is self-explanatory; some coins bear inscriptions around the edges which, besides making the most of a crowded space, were originally intended to discourage clipping, a favorite occupation of greedy individuals which even the death penalty, in effect in England during the reigns of Henry V and the first Queen Elizabeth, could not stop. The rows of beads along the edges of some silver coins, such as the "pine tree shilling," were supposed to serve the same purpose. Incidentally, some of our own early coins had lettered edges. The motto is an inscription containing some guiding words such as "In God We Trust" or "E Pluribus Unum." When a head or bust is described as "Left" or "L" it means facing the viewer's left; "Right" or "R," facing the viewer's right. The *exergue* is the portion of the reverse of a coin between the device and the bottom of the edge of the coin. The *field* is the portion of a coin not used for device or inscription. These are the expressions most often found in catalogues or descriptive lists, and ones with which we become quite familiar after a short time. There are others appearing now and then, such as *jugate,* or conjoined busts, on a coin showing two rulers, occasionally more, one following the other. The only other expressions appearing as frequently as these, perhaps even more so, are those describing condition.

As to condition, coins are described as Proof, Uncirculated (Unc.), Very Fine (V.F.), Fine (F.), Very Good (V.G.), Good (G.), and Fair. Proof coins are struck by mints for the benefit of collectors, have a mirrorlike surface, and are beautiful in every way. In this country they were discontinued in 1915, but in 1936 were again issued by the United States Mint. From 1936 to and including 1942, sets of cents, nickels, dimes, quarters, and half dollars were furnished, from the Philadelphia Mint only, at $1.85 per set. Coinage of proofs was resumed in 1950, having been discontinued during the war years.* Uncirculated coins are absolutely unused and exactly as they came from the mint; very fine, slightly circulated but almost in mint condition; fine, slightly worn on the edges but sharp in all details; very good, slightly less than fine but everything clear; fair, and good, quite worn but with date discernible, although possibly a bit faint. Dealers sometimes add a few of their own descriptions, such as "almost uncirculated," "about fine," "extra good," "poor," and so on. It is well for the collector at any stage of the game to waste no time in holding coins that are not at least very fine. Coins with poor dates and outlines are practically worthless from the collecting standpoint. The only exception to this rule would be in the case of an exceptionally rare date, when a better-conditioned coin cannot be afforded and it seems advisable to purchase a poorer specimen in the hope of securing a better one when the price is advantageous. It may be that, at times, in buying a lot of a few coins at auction or when a dealer offers a certain number of miscellaneous items as one lot, some poor coins may be acquired which no self-respecting collector would care to show and which he will rid himself of promptly. Holed or mutilated coins, except those of great rarity, are worthless.

Observation will teach a new collector several ways of determining whether a particular coin is in fairly good condition. For example, Indian-head cents may be considered very fine, or otherwise, according to the comparative clearness of the word "Liberty" on the headband of the Indian; on Liberty-standing quarter dollars the knees of the figure are the first part to show signs of wear. It is the same with other coins; little details furnish a guide to a quick estimate of the condition of a coin. Observation will show that the highest points on the design of any given coin will be the first parts to show wear, since these are the portions which come first into contact with a

* Temporarily discontinued after 1964.

flat surface—counter, desk, change booth and so on. An example is the Liberty-standing quarter dollar on which the date was raised above the rest of the design, resulting in a quick obliteration and a comparative scarcity of such quarters, since a dateless coin is valueless, except to spend. Buffalo nickels are often found dateless for the same reason; the date was higher than the rest of the design. In foreign coin catalogues we may run across some words or abbreviations meaning the same in relation to condition as those in English: *Flan bruni*—Proof; *Fleur de Coin* (*F.D.C.*)—Uncirculated; *Superbe*—Extra Fine; *Très Beau*—Very Fine; *Beau*—Fine; *Très Beau Conserve* (*T.B.C.*)—Very Good; *Beau Conserve* (Good).

When buying coins by mail or mail sale (in the latter, bids are made as in an auction sale), of course, a lot depends upon the reliability of the dealer; and we hasten to add, most of them are reliable. Most hobby magazines carry advertisements of reputable coin dealers. The official magazine of the American Numismatic Association, *The Numismatist,* maintains high standards in its advertisements, as does *The Numismatic Scrapbook Magazine* and several other of the newer publications. In fact, strict attention is paid to complaints about unscrupulous advertisers. A word of caution: avoid dealers who advertise flamboyantly, particularly in the pulp magazines, offering enormous premiums for what seem to the uninitiated fairly common coins. You may be sure you will get no bargains from them. However, there are dozens of reliable dealers throughout the country, who are listed elsewhere, and coins may be purchased from such dealers by mail, with the assurance that such purchases will be satisfactory in every way, or may be returned within a reasonable time and your money refunded. There are dealers as well as collectors who have their specialties. Some are known principally as dealers in

United States coins, while a small minority specialize in, and sometimes handle exclusively, foreign or ancient coins.

To be a successful collector you must, of course, study your subject. A guide to useful and enlightening books for both the beginner and the specialist is given elsewhere. Almost every phase of numismatics is covered by some publication, book, monograph, or pamphlet. Some books which are standard for a certain series may be out of print and expensive. Standard books on any special series are almost indispensable when we are purchasing coins or paper money by auction, as it is the practice to prefix such items which are covered by standards with a number as shown therein. For example, a foreign crown might be marked "D-140," which means it is listed under that number in Davenport's *European Crowns and Talers Since 1800;* or F-100, for a paper bill listed in Friedberg's *Paper Money of the United States.* An absolute necessity for the collector of United States coins is either *A Guide Book of United States Coins,* "Red Book," or *Appraising and Selling Your Coins,* "Green Book." Both books are good. The first-named is brought up-to-date each year and is the less expensive, but one or the other is indispensable to the collector for learning numbers of coins issued, unusual characteristics of individual coins, rarity, and current market value. Dealers' prices are based largely on the retail values shown, although many dealers may advertise special offerings at "less than catalogue," and conversely, often advertise their offers to buy certain coins at so much "over catalogue." It was mentioned earlier that all one needs to make a good start is a coin board or two. This is quite true. Nevertheless, the second purchase could be the "Red" or "Green Book." With one of these, the collector of United States money is well on his way. An even less expensive book is the small *Handbook of United States Coins,* "Blue Book," which shows what dealers pay for rare coins. For our Canadian friends interested in money of that country there have lately been introduced Canadian coin boards, including some for the Provinces of Nova Scotia, New Brunswick, and Newfoundland, as well as Prince Edward Island. For the Canadian collector an indispensable book is the *Standard Catalogue of Canadian Coins, Tokens and Fractional Currency,* issued yearly. Incidentally, the Canadian, as well as the United States, coin boards are made in folder form, with holes for each date to accommodate large cents, small cents, small silver or large nickel five-cent pieces, and other Canadian denominations.

Aside from reading, one of the best ways to become quickly informed on all aspects of coin collecting is to join a coin club. There are at least a hundred such clubs in the United States. Most large cities have one, and many smaller cities as well. A list of clubs throughout the country will be found in the Appendix. Names of officers and street addresses are dependent on the incumbent secretaries and others. Since they change frequently, they are not included. If there is no such organization in your town, there are probably several in your section of the country. If none is conveniently located, there is always the possibility that you can start your own club. A half dozen fellow collectors is all you need; you can meet at members' homes, or at lodge or church meeting rooms. Many of these clubs are affiliated with the American Numismatic Association, and a list giving club names, names and addresses of officers, and meeting dates and places of meeting is published periodically in *The Numismatist,* the monthly publication of the Association. There are numerous Canadian coin clubs also, many of them affiliated with the Canadian Numismatic Association, which also publishes a monthly magazine, *The Canadian Numismatic Journal.* Club members are not always young, but almost invariably they have young ideas, and a lot of valuable information and assistance may be obtained at every meeting. Guest speakers occasionally give talks on coin subjects, papers by club members are read, and all members are expected to bring exhibits on some special series or their latest acquisitions or special "pets." Naturally, the more progressive the officers and members are in sponsoring new ideas, swap nights, auctions, and other activities, the more each will contribute and the more he will get in return. In these various ways the collector may keep informed on late issues, where to secure coins at minimum cost, and where to go for a well-informed opinion on an item that is a complete mystery to the possessor.

The new collector need have no more fear of finding himself the unwilling possessor of counterfeit United States coins than in the ordinary course of securing change from daily purchases. However, a real menace to guard against is the buying of coins with altered dates, and there are many such, particularly those altered to rare dates. For example, a very rare coin is the 1804 silver dollar, but there are many 1801 dollars on which the "1" has been changed to a "4." It is not this particular coin, however, that the collector need worry about, since there are six known specimens of the original 1804 silver dollar and the whereabouts of each is so well known that the sudden appearance of an additional specimen would create a sensation. A more common coin, the 1914-D Lincoln cent, is often altered from some other date, or the "D" added, and the 1922 plain cent may be a 1922-D from which the "D" has been removed. The 1937-D three-legged Buffalo nickel is a worthwhile coin, but often the leg is amputated from the ordinary variety by impostors. A good magnifying glass is another requisite, as even a fairly clever alteration may be detected under a powerful glass.

Some counterfeiters have gained a dubious fame through

their forgeries of rare coins. The most famous, or infamous, is Carl Becker, a resident of Offenbach, Germany, in the early nineteenth century. By trade a goldsmith, he started copying ancient Greek coins in gold. His marvelous collection became well known, but greed and vanity got the best of him. Having at one time been duped into buying coins that were spurious or clever copies, he decided to go into the business himself. His business became so profitable that he made the counterfeiting of ancient coins his life work. He made special dies for duplicating old coins exactly, and went to all sorts of trouble to give his forgeries the ancient look, even to burying them in his backyard under a manure heap. Even when Becker was exposed as a fraud, it did not disturb him too much. He catalogued all his coins and simply explained that he was a copyist of old coins for his own amusement and to supply poor collectors with cheap copies of coins they could not afford in the original. All of the Becker forgeries are well known and listed, and are offered by reputable dealers as such. The large medallions struck at Padua in Italy during the Renaissance were copies of ancient Roman coins. Called "Paduans," they were obviously copies, and were not issued to intentionally deceive. They are easily recognized by their fine workmanship and precise lettering.

In the early American series of coins and tokens there are also copies which are known as such and were executed because the originals were so scare that only one or two were known to exist. The most famous of these are the "Bolen" restrikes, or copies, which are well known and purchased as readily as the originals would be, if the latter were available at all. From all this it can be seen that it is wise to secure the advice of an informed authority before paying a high price for a supposedly scarce coin, until time brings knowledge.

Quite different from a counterfeit or forgery is a restrike, which can, of course, sometimes be used to fool the collector, but generally is sold for what it is. Aside from the Bolen restrikes and similar Robinson and Wyatt copies of American Colonial coins, the best-known example of a restrike is that of the Confederate half dollar, of which there were only four originally made in New Orleans in 1861 and several thousand restrikes made in New York in 1879. An uncirculated Confederate half dollar is listed at $5,000, but to all purposes is unobtainable. A restrike, however, may be bought for between $300 and $400.

There are other cases where portions of a coin are overstruck; for example, the 1935 Daniel Boone commemorative half dollars restruck with the 1934 date. Other coins with overstruck dates include many of the large cents: 1798 over 1797, 1799 over 1798, 1807 over 1806, and others. There is an Indian-head cent with date 1869 over 1868, and many of the early dimes had overstruck dates.

The latest dime of this kind is the 1942 which is struck over 1941. The last-mentioned dime could, at one time, occasionally be found in circulation, although this is a rarity now. A fine copy would be worth over $40 from almost any dealer, and would retail at $100.

The Spanish dollar, or eight reales, was always a favorite for overstriking. There are many varieties counterstamped with various other designs, monograms, hearts, and other symbols, and many were counterstamped with a minute head of King George III of England.

In succeeding pages attention will be given to series of coins generally collected, especial consideration being given at all times to coins that are within a moderate price range.

In concluding these general comments, it may not be amiss to mention a few well-known coin collections.

The coin room of the British Museum contains one of the

world's most famous collections. In New York the collection of the American Numismatic Society is housed in a beautiful museum containing many thousands of coins, medals, plaques, and decorations. Another well-known New York City collection is the Money Museum of the Chase Manhattan Bank. Almost every art museum in the country has one or more rooms devoted to coins; such collections, as a rule, consist of ancient Greek and Roman silver and gold coins, and in many cases tokens, medals, and other items of a purely local interest. The New National Museum (Smithsonian Institution) in Washington, D.C., has one of the most complete coin collections in the world, with over 47,000 pieces. Visitors always show great interest in these collections of coins and medals. The number of active coin collectors has risen rapidly in the last two decades. In 1938 there were an estimated 25,000 active collectors in the United States, and ten times this number in Europe. Now there are an estimated 150,000 American collectors. The number of devotees is constantly growing, and in time there will undoubtedly be as many collectors in this country as there are in Europe. Incidentally, an "active" collector is considered one who is interested enough to belong to the American Numismatic Association, or at least to a local coin club, and who is constantly adding to and improving his own collection, not merely for the sake of having a large number of items but for what he can learn from his coins, the history of the country represented, its geography, and pertinent facts about its rulers and other famous people.

Privately owned coin collections are not very well known either here or abroad, because the owners of the most extensive of such collections do not publicize them. The late William H. Woodin, Secretary of the Treasury under Franklin D. Roosevelt, owned a very famous collection. Mr. Woodin himself was one of the most widely known of numismatists for many years, and compiled a book on United States pattern coins, which has been superseded by J. Hewitt Judd's *Pattern, Experimental and Trial Pieces.*

Bibliography

There are many books in print on the general subject of numismatics that will be helpful to the coin collector. Most of the books on the general subject of coin collecting are of the same type, and any one of them will serve the purpose as well as another. As a rule, those printed in England deal particularly with aspects of collecting British Empire and ancient coins.

C. C. CHAMBERLAIN, *Collecting Coins* (London, 1957).

P. EINZIG, *Primitive Money* (London, 1949).

LEONARD S. FORRER, *The Art of Collecting Coins* (London, 1955).

HOWARD W. A. LINECAR, *Coins* (London, 1955).

MILNE, SUTHERLAND AND THOMPSON, *Coin Collecting* (London, 1950).

A. H. QUIGGIN, *A Survey of Primitive Money:* the Beginnings of Currency (London, 1949).

G. B. RAWLINGS, *Coins and How to Know Them* (London, 1935).

C. H. V. SUTHERLAND, *Art in Coinage* (London, 1955).

CHAPTER TWO

Collecting United States Money

THE NATURAL thing for anyone who begins collecting coins or paper money is to start with what is most familiar. The Englishman usually starts with England, the Canadian with Canada. The American collector will probably start with coins of the United States, unless he happens to have late and close ties with another country, or a special interest in ancient civilizations. Because of the probable affinity to familiar objects we will assume that the United States coinage will be most interesting, at least for a while. Most collectors here seem to start with our own coinage. An Englishman, Frenchman, or German may not always begin with the money of his own country, and he is more likely to take an interest in ancient coins than is the case over here. The person who collects and studies ancient Greek or Roman coins, whether here or elsewhere, is generally one whose fondness has some intellectual basis which makes him particularly susceptible to the lure of ancient coinage. He is generally a college graduate, although not necessarily so, as some of the most avid and best-informed collectors of ancient coins were grade or high school graduates only and had no family or other background that would seem to explain their interest. In other words, do not be scared away from this field of collecting for fear you are not up to it.

In order to get the proper background it is a good idea to know a little about the beginnings of our United States currency.

Colonial Days

When the first European explorers visited what is now the United States of America, the scattered inhabitants of this wild country used nothing that could even remotely be considered a metallic currency. Coins were not known to the Indians, and, when first introduced to them by the white men, were not accepted.

The tribes of the Pacific Northwest, the Algonquins, and other Indians of the Atlantic Coastal areas used shell money which is known to us as wampum. The first money used by the first settlers in New York (when it was called New Netherlands) and in New England was seawant, wampum, or peague. The more familiar word to most of us is wampum. There were two kinds of wampum (which signifies "white"), the other being suckanhock, signifying "black." The black and white beads were used in New England, and were sometimes supplemented by blue beads. The Five Nations used purple.

Since coins have been known and used in Europe, Asia, and parts of Africa for many centuries—in fact, in Asia from the seventh century B.C.—it is interesting to learn how our present-day metallic United States money came into being, and it is possible to present a picture of the development from the days when no such coinage was in use in this part of the world. Today there is no analogous condition anywhere on earth. The English settlers of New England undoubtedly brought a certain amount of English and other currencies with them. However, they could only pass it from hand to hand among their own people, or return it to England for much-needed hardware and other supplies. The native Indians would not take it and were not inclined to place any value on it, although in time they did come around. Since, for the first 150 years 90 percent of the colonists were planters and farmers, there was no great need for metal coinage. Furs of the beaver and other animals were one of the first media of exchange; in fact, the beaver was an important factor in opening up vast virgin territory from Nova Scotia to Hudson Bay and later south and west to the Mississippi, and even beyond to the Rockies. The Indians of the north were dazzled by the metal axes, hammers, and guns of the French, Dutch, and English explorers, and willingly exchanged all kinds of furs for these articles.

England refused the early Massachusetts Bay colonists the right to coin money, whereas the charter for Virginia did provide for a coinage, which never developed. In this attitude the English were more autocratic and possibly a bit less broadminded than the Spanish, whose explorers had established a mint in Mexico as early as 1535, and, in the seventeenth century, at various places such as Potosi, Lima, and Santiago, among others. The reasons for the Spanish mints may have been to use the minted silver for trading, simply to find a convenient method of transporting the silver they mined or confiscated. An idea of the number of Spanish coins minted may be obtained from the fact that well over ten million "pieces of eight" were taken by the English from the Spanish treasure ships at the battle of Vigo Bay in 1702. Most of these were melted and reminted in English money. At any rate, Spanish enterprise had a certain effect on later developments, since the Spanish "piece of eight" and other "bit" portions enjoyed a great popularity for many years in the American colonies. The piece of eight was the Spanish silver piastre, a dollar- or crown-size coin of eight reales, or "reales de a ocha," which for many years was a favorite coin in America, both North and South, and used extensively in the Orient as well. In fact, even now we come across many such coins bearing "chop" marks from their service in China. Chop marks are cuts or crosses made in silver coins to test the metal content. One reale was worth 12½ cents, or one bit, and a quarter of the Spanish dollar, or two reales, was called two bits, which is still a familiar name for our quarter dollar. Since we have never had a 12½-cent coin, we never hear the expression "one bit." In the eighteenth and early nineteenth centuries Spanish eight reales were actually cut into bits, equaling about one eighth, one quarter, or one half. The eight reales was also known as a Pillar Dollar, from the reverse design showing two globes between the Pillars of Hercules. It has a special place in any study of our metallic money, since it is the immediate ancestor of our silver dollar, which was patterned after it, more as the actual unit of currency than as a physical counterpart. In other words, the dollar was the unit of the value of the Spanish dollar, and contained two half dollars, four quarter dollars, and so on down to one hundred cents; this would apply whether the dollar was actually coined or not. Some say that the scroll around the pillar on the eight reale gave rise to our dollar sign, although there are many other stories regarding the origin of the sign. More of this later, however, as we are still studying the monetary needs of the first settlers.

Lack of a good metallic currency of a homemade variety did hamper the English colonists after the first few years, when they were able to give more thought to trade than to fighting the wilderness and the occasionally unfriendly Indians. The settlers were resourceful, though, as most people are when pressed, and various available substitutes were found. In trading with the Indians they were able to use wampum or shell money until the practice was abused through counterfeiting and other sharp practices. Such trading stopped in Massachusetts about 1660, although it continued in Rhode Island, Connecticut, and New York for some years longer.

The first real metal money not imported from Europe was the "Somer Island" currency, made for use in the Somer or Sommer Islands, later called the Bermudas. One of the islands is still called Somerset. They were named for Sir George Somers and were variously called Somer, Sommer, or Summer Islands. At one time they were called Hog Islands, since wild hogs overran some of them, descendants of hogs which had escaped from sinking Spanish ships or were left behind by Juan de Bermudez, who discovered the islands in 1510. This brass currency, also known as "Hogge Money," was issued in 1616-1624 and consisted of shilling, sixpence, threepence, and twopence. There was a hog on the obverse with Roman numerals to indicate the value, and on the reverse a ship. These coins are scarce and expensive today, although they appear from time to time at auctions and command fairly high prices when you consider that they are seldom found in better than "fine" condition. As you recall, "fine" is third in the scale for grading the condition of coins, which ranges from uncirculated to fair.

As an example of the previously mentioned enterprise of a people hard-pressed, in this instance for a suitable currency, in 1642 tobacco was established as a legal currency in Virginia and was also used in the Carolinas, being a staple crop in this area. In the Massachusetts Bay Colony it was the usual thing to pay taxes with cattle, skins, and farm products, these products being stored and sold by the tax collectors. It is interesting to note the use of cattle, because these animals have had a place in the history of money for many centuries, denoting man's dependence on the beasts since ancient times. Legally, of course, the official money was English, and bills were rendered in terms of pounds, shillings, and pence.

The first real coinage in the British colonies began in the Massachusetts Bay Colony when an act was passed establishing the first mint at Boston on June 11, 1652. John Hull, a wealthy merchant, was appointed mintmaster. The project was not well received in England and was one of the reasons why the charter of the colony was revoked in 1684. The first money struck in the new mint was called the New England shilling, sixpence, and threepence. Each of these was primitive and crude, a flat piece of silver bearing simply the initials NE for New England, and Roman numerals for the denomination—XII for one shilling or twelvepence, VI for sixpence, and III for threepence. In spite of the crude workmanship and lack of beauty, the shilling is now extremely rare and has been offered for sale in recent days for about $1,000, a price determined mainly by its historical value. The New England sixpence and threepence are even scarcer and more expensive.

It was not long before this plain and crude New England coinage was discontinued. It was not practical, the coins had no milling, beading, or other distinctive edges, and the plain edges were very readily clipped, thus detracting from their worth. It is estimated that the coinage continued from June to October, 1652, or a few weeks thereafter, when the "tree" coins were issued. Generally placed together under the one category of "Pine Tree Shillings," these actually consisted of Willow Tree, Oak Tree, and Pine Tree Shillings, sixpence, and threepence, with an exceptional twopence. The first issued were the willow tree coins, all dated 1652. These were coins of a more orthodox form, with a design and a more elaborate inscription, and with the protection of a row of beads, which showed when clipping occurred and how much. Next came the oak tree, and lastly the pine tree coins, which are the best known and which gave their name to all the Massachusetts Bay Colony coins of this period. All were still dated 1652, with one exception, the oak tree twopence, dated 1662.

These four types of coins, from the plain New England variety to the pine trees, lasted, as far as can be estimated, until 1682, but, aside from the date of the coining of the last of the New England pieces and the beginning of the willow trees, there are no definite dates for the first issues of the other "tree" coins, since all, with the one exception of the oak tree twopence, were dated 1652. The tree coins were widely accepted even outside of the Bay Colony and were of a standard of workmanship comparing favorably with contemporary European issues.

John Hull died in 1683 and left his daughter 30,000 pounds. The well-known legend says that her dowry consisted of her weight in pine tree shillings. Hull's pay for striking the New England tree coins was fifteen pence for every twenty shillings minted. Setting this against Hull's financial standing later might give an estimate of how many New England and other coins were struck, excepting for the fact that he was fairly well-to-do before the coining venture, and, together with his partner, Robert Sanderson, enjoyed a high reputation as a silversmith.

As hinted before, there was always a certain amount of clipping and counterfeiting of the New England coins at the time the coins were circulating. While these practices did not add to the difficulties of the public when the coins were circulating, they did add to the problems of later collectors. Still, there are many copies of the New England coins, including shillings and sixpence, and all of the pine tree coins, with the addition of a nonexistent penny, made by a New York counterfeiter, or copyist, Thomas Wyatt, who operated in the middle nineteenth century. He made a good many copies of these coins, for the benefit, or harassment, of collectors, of course, since they were long out of circulation. Many of the Wyatt coins, along with those of other manufacturers such as Bolen and Robinson, are sold in auctions, as such, since they are known by experienced collectors as later copies. At the present time many of them are listed in coin guides, since in many cases they are the nearest the everyday collector can come to an original issue of some of the early New England and later colonial coins. Wyatt also counterfeited a "Good Samaritan Shilling," typed after the pine shilling and dated 1652, with a design illustrating the parable of the Good Samaritan. The original is supposed to have been a trial or pattern piece and is extremely rare. There are other good and bad imitations of the early New England currency.

About 1658 the second Lord Baltimore, of Maryland, sponsored an issue of coins which were minted in England. These were the shilling, sixpence, fourpence, and penny; the first three in silver, the penny in copper. The silver coins showed the bust of Cecil Calvert on the obverse, and the reverse carried the Baltimore family coat-of-arms, value, and the legend "*Crescite et Multiplicamini*" (Increase and be multiplied). The obverse of the penny was the same, but the reverse bore a crown with pennants and was inscribed "*Denarium, Terrae-Maria*" (Penny, Maryland).

Other Colonial issues, some popular and some not, were later introduced into America from England. The St. Patrick's, or Newby, halfpence and farthing were brought over by Mark Newby and were used extensively, especially in New Jersey. The halfpence bore the legend "*Floreat Rex*" (May the King Prosper) and a figure of St. Patrick, on the obverse and reverse respectively. The farthing had the legend "*Quiescat Plebs*" (May the people be quiet). In these days, when kings are not doing so well, the two nouns would probably be reversed.

The Wood coinage, or Rosa Americana coins, were quite popular in most of the American colonies. They were specifically made for the colonies by William Wood, an Englishman, with the consent of George I, beginning about 1722 or earlier, since the first coins bore no dates. The Rosa Americana coins and the Hibernia coins, also issued by Wood at about the same time, showed the head of George I on the obverse. The Rosa Americana coins showed a rose on the reverse with the legend "*Rosa Americana Utile Dulci*" (American Rose, the useful with the pleasant). The Hibernia coins showed a figure with a harp on the reverse.

The years between the issuance of the Rosa Americana coins and others, mostly manufactured in England, until the issuance of the State coinage after the Revolution, saw the emergence of many American-made tokens which were often thought of as coins and sometimes even showed denominations, but which were privately issued and had no official standing. The latter fact did not keep them from circulating widely, however. One well-known issue is the Higley, or Granby, threepence. These copper coins were named for John Higley, who used pure copper from his mine at Granby, Connecticut. They were issued in 1737 and stated that they had "The value of threepence." This was retracted soon to "Value me as you please." Other types show an ax and the legend "I cut my way through"; still another, a wheel and "The Wheele goes round."

It will be seen that the currency of the early colonies was by no means uniform, and each colony acted on its own in the use of whatever currency it could secure or manufacture. At times exchange tables were used, and a traveler from Massachusetts to Carolina found it necessary to exchange his money on arrival at destination, as a traveler does now with his American money when visiting foreign countries. The first guide book published in New York, in the late seventeenth century, contains an elaborate and interesting exchange table of money from the different colonies. These varying exchange values were true also of foreign money. Hence, a pound sterling was worth six Spanish dollars in New England and Virginia, eight Spanish dollars in New York and North Carolina, seven and one half in the middle colonies (except New York), and four and one quarter in South Carolina and Georgia.

During the early part of the eighteenth century a great variety of foreign and local token money made up the currency of the colonies. Foreign gold and silver coins were freely used, such as the English Guinea, Portuguese Joe and Half Joe, Spanish doubloon and pistole, reale and pistoreen.

The coinage of the times immediately preceding the Revolutionary War was of a wide variety. Distances were a disadvantage, and the use of local currency was not a great inconvenience until later, when improvements in communications and transportation and an increase in trade made a national currency a necessity.

Tokens made in England were also used in these early days, as early as 1694 in the case of the Elephant tokens of Carolina and New England. These showed an elephant on the obverse and "God Preserve Carolina" and "The Lords Proprietors" and date, or "God Preserve New England" and date. Other early tokens issued abroad were the Florida token, the Pitt token, Voce Populi, and others.

For many years, in addition to the coins and tokens just mentioned, a great many foreign coins circulated in the states. They were recognized by the authorities, and, in fact, by law, since the Act of February 9, 1793 made foreign silver and gold coins legal tender at rates in accordance with their gold or silver content. Although it is often assumed that there was a gradual decline in the use of such foreign coins, it was not until the passage of the Act of February 21, 1857 that they were retired from circulation and their legal tender qualities repealed.

The following list shows many of the coins and tokens used

in the colonies before the opening of the mint at Philadelphia. Not all are listed, as a half dozen or more are exceedingly rare; some are considered, in numismatic language, "unique," which means that only one specimen is known. Others are more common, but still rare in any kind of good condition. For the sake of simplification, inscriptions and their English meanings are listed separately.

Early Coins and Tokens

New England Shillings.
Willow, Oak, and Pine Tree Shillings.
1658—Maryland silver shilling and other silver and copper denominations.
New England stiver.
1682—St. Patrick, or Newby, coppers.
1685-1688—Florida token.
1694—Carolina elephant token.
New England elephant token.
1722-1724—Wood, or Rosa Americana, and Hibernia coins.
1737-1739—Higley, or Granby, coppers.
1766—Pitt token.
1773-1774—Virginia halfpenny and shilling.
1776—Massachusetts halfpenny.
1776—Continental dollar.
1783—Chalmers Annapolis tokens.
Bar cents.
Georgius Triumpho cent.
1783-1786—Nova Constellatio patterns.
1789—Mott tokens.
1790—Kentucky cents.
1794-1795—Talbot, Allum and Lee cents.
1796—Myddleton tokens.

State Coinage

1776—New Hampshire.
1785-1788—Vermont, Connecticut.
1786—New Jersey.

1787—New York.
1787—Massachusetts.

Mottoes on Colonial Coinage

1. AUCTORI CONN.—By authority of Connecticut.
2. AUCTORI PLEBIS—By authority of the people.
3. CRESCITE ET MULTIPLICAMINI—Increase and be multiplied.
4. DENARIUM TERRAE-MARIAE—Penny, Maryland.
5. E PLURIBUS UNUM—One out of many.
6. ECCE GREX—Behold the flock.
7. EXCELSIOR—Higher.
8. ET LIB INDE—Liberty and independence.
9. ET LIB VIRT—Virtue and Liberty.
10. FLOREAT REX—May the king prosper.
11. IMMUNE or IMMUNIS COLUMBIA—Columbia safe.
12. INIMICA TYRANIS AMERICANA—America, enemy of tyrants.
13. LIBERTAS ET JUSTITIA—Liberty and justice.
14. NON VI VIRTUE VICI—I conquered by virtue and not by force.
15. NEO EBORACENSIS or NOVA EBORAC—New York.
16. NOVA CAESAREA—New Jersey.
17. NOVA CONSTELLATIO—The new constellation.
18. PLUS ULTRA—More beyond.
19. QVIESCAT PLEBS—May the people be quiet.
20. QUARTER DECIMA STELLA—The 14th star. [Vermont was the 14th State.]
21. ROSA AMERICANA UTILE DULCI—American rose, the useful with the pleasant.
22. * UTRAQUE UNUM—Make both one.
23. VERMONT AUCTORI—By authority of Vermont.
24. VERMONTIS or VERMONTENSIUM RES PUBLICA—The Republic of Vermont (Green Mountains).

* Found with PLUS ULTRA and the Pillars of Hercules on Spanish dollars or eight reales.

The Vermont cents were struck in a mint established in 1785 at Rupert, Vermont. New York, however, had a mint of its own at what is now Newburgh. This was the mint of Atlee and Machin, which also made some of the Vermont cents. It is claimed by some historians that this mint and the one at Rupert did a flourishing business in counterfeiting many of the George II and George III copper coins, as well as attending to their legitimate business of making money for the colonies. The Vermont cents of 1787 and 1788 show the insignia of Britain in the shield on the reverse, and the 1788 cent shows the head of the king and the inscription "Georgivs III Rex." Connecticut had two mints, one at Westville, later moved to New Haven, and the other at Morris Cove. The New Jersey mints were located at Morristown and Elizabethtown. The New York "Nova Eborac" cents and the "Nova Constellatio" appeared in 1787 and 1783 respectively. The "Nova Constellatio" coins were issued in silver, in dollar, 50-cent, and 25-cent denominations; and in copper, cents. The "Immune Columbia" coins of 1785 also had the legend "Nova Constellatio" on the obverse.

It will be noted that in many cases designs of state cents differed from each other only in one or two features. The reason for the relative scarcity of good specimens of certain cents, particularly the Connecticut and Vermont coppers, may be traced to the fact that the dies for each coin were used for many thousands of impressions, which in many cases left the coins defective in spots. In view of these similarities, also, it is not necessary to give a detailed description of each issue. In fact, such a procedure would require a whole volume in itself and, to all but the ardent numismatist, might prove to be rather tedious. There is a good and sufficient literature regarding early American coins. The best, S. S. Crosby's *Early Coins of America,* was issued in 1875 and covered the subject so completely that very little was left for later writers. While the early edition of Crosby is hard to obtain, a reprint was put out in 1945, which is just as good and only half as expensive. There are other very good books on various individual issues, such as Noe on the New England and "tree" coins, and others which are listed in the bibliography.

In addition to the state cents mentioned, certain copper tokens were issued in New York during this period. While the token is not always considered as money, it has often been issued by private business concerns to take the place of small change in trade. In view of this it might be well to make mention of the tokens of this period.

The first of the three earliest business tokens to be used in this country was one issued in 1789 by William and John Mott, jewelers of 240 Water Street, New York City. At that time a fashionable business section of the city, Water Street is now a row of waterfront businesses and importing houses. The Mott token, which showed a large clock on the obverse and an eagle on the reverse, did not have a very large circulation. It was made in England and is an interesting numismatic item, although not at all expensive.

The second and third tokens were issued in 1794 and 1795 by Talbot, Allum & Lee, of 241 Pearl Street, New York City. This firm was in the India trade, and the members were very wealthy for that day. Established in 1794, the concern continued in business until 1796, when Lee retired. The firm was then called Talbot & Allum until it was dissolved in 1798. These two tokens showed a ship on the obverse and "Liberty" on the reverse, and a ship obverse and "Liberty and Commerce" reverse. They were manufactured in Birmingham, England, and probably owe their origin to the English craze for tokens during this period. It is estimated that during the period from 1787 to 1797 over 600 tons of copper merchants' tokens were turned out by Boulton's mint at Birmingham.

The "Brasher Doubloon" also comes into this period. This is a large gold, privately minted coin of great rarity. It takes its name from a New York goldsmith, Ephraim Brasher, whose initials are stamped on the reverse. The device shows the sun rising from behind a range of mountains, with the sea at the foot. The legend reads "Nova Eboraca—Columbia—Excelsior." On the reverse, an eagle with 13 stars around its head and the initials "E.B." on its right wing, with the legend "E Pluribus Unum—1787."

In order of interest and rarity, rather than chronological arrangement, the "Bar Cent" is probably the leading copper of these times. It was issued about the same time as the "Nova Constellatio" coins, 1783, and is said to have been coined in Birmingham, England, by Thomas Wyon. The bar cent was first used in New York City in 1785, and got its name from the thirteen horizontal lines shown on the reverse. The obverse shows U.S.A. in the form of a monogram; there is no date or other legend. It is one of the rarest coins of this period. There are, however, copies by Bolen.

Connecticut, as we have seen, was represented as early as 1737 by the Higley, or Granby, tokens. The next development in this state came in 1785, when a bill was introduced in the General Assembly of Connecticut calling attention to the scarcity of small coins and recommending the establishment of a mint to manufacture copper coins. After some changes, the bill was presented, giving specific mention of the design to be shown, which consisted of the legend *"Avctori: Connec:"* reverse, and the emblem of Liberty with the legend *"Inde: et: Lib: 1785."* The bill was passed on October 20, 1785; and a mint was established at New Haven, where Abel Buell designed and cut the dies for the Connecticut cents and others. They were made in many different die varieties. Another mint was later established at Westville, where Abel Buell also designed and cut the dies for copper coins.

Abel Buell also designed and cut the dies at New Haven for

the "Fugio," or "Franklin," cents of 1787. These are the earliest coins issued by the authority of the United States government, and were made in accordance with the Resolution of Congress dated July 6, 1787, said to have been introduced and drafted by Benjamin Franklin, by whose name they are sometimes called. The resolution gives the design in detail: "Thirteen circles linked together, a small circle in the middle with the words 'United States' around it, and in the center the words 'We are one.' Reverse, a sun dial, a meridian sun above, on one side of which is to be the word 'Fugio' and on the other the year '1787,' and below the dial the words 'Mind your business.' " The meaning of Fugio and the sun dial hardly seems necessary to explain: "Time flies."

In New York many unsuccessful attempts were made to establish a mint. Vermont and New Jersey coppers circulated widely in this state. Ephraim Brasher, who coined the Brasher doubloons, made a petition to the Legislature in 1787 to coin coppers. For some reason his request was not acted upon. Thomas Machin, a hardware manufacturer of Newburgh, also petitioned the same year, and as a result soon began operations in that city. He was joined by James F. Atlee, who made the dies. The mint discontinued operations in 1791.

The Clinton copper cent of New York, 1787, is one of the rarest of this period. It shows the bust of Governor Clinton and his name "George Clinton"; the reverse shows the state coat of arms and "1787—Excelsior."

In 1785 Vermont, the fourteenth state, passed an act permitting Reuben Harmon, Jr., a justice of the peace of Rupert, to coin copper money. He was joined by Colonel William Cooley, a New York goldsmith, who made some of the dies, others being cut by William Buell, son of Abel Buell, who moved his machinery to Rupert from New Haven, transferring his operations to Harmon's mint. James F. Atlee, of Atlee and Machin, also cut some of the dies.

In Pennsylvania so many bogus British halfpence of George III were in circulation that the legislature passed an order in 1781 prohibiting the receiving of such coins. In 1786 Thomas Smyth, Jr., and Thomas Hardwood III, owners of copper and silver mines in Maryland, petitioned the General Assembly of Pennsylvania for the exclusive right of coinage. It appears that no action was taken on their petition and no attempt was made to establish a Pennsylvania coinage, that state continuing to struggle along with whatever makeshift currency and paper money came to hand.

New Hampshire was the first state to give consideration to a metal currency. An act was passed on March 13, 1776, providing for a committee to pass on the question of making a copper coinage. The committee recommended that such a step be taken and asked that coppers of pure metal be coined based on the Spanish milled dollar as a unit—108 cents to the Spanish dollar and equal in weight to the British halfpence. On June 28, 1776, the New Hampshire Legislature voted that the Treasurer should accept for the Treasury any quantity of copper coins with the "Pine Tree Device" on the obverse, and the wording "American Liberty" and a harp and "1776" on the reverse. There are coins with this device and legend generally credited to Massachusetts rather than New Hampshire, and it is probable that they were struck in the former state. This is further borne out by the fact that there is no record of any mint being established in New Hampshire.

Massachusetts established a mint at Boston in October, 1786, having passed an act on August 8, 1786, authorizing the issuance of copper half cents and cents. Captain Joshua Wetherle was appointed mintmaster. The dies were made by Jacob Perkins, of Newburyport, and Joseph Collender, of

Boston. Two dates appeared, 1787 and 1788, for both the cent and half cent. The design was as prescribed by the act of August 8, 1786—that is, a clothed Indian standing, with bow and arrow in right and left hand respectively, and the legend, "Commonwealth." The reverse bore the legend "Massachusetts," a spread eagle, with a shield containing six vertical bars, and "Cent" or "Half cent" on the upper part of the shield and, in exergue beneath a horizontal bar, the date.

The General Assembly of New Jersey, on May 23, 1786, read the proposal of Walter Mould, Thomas Goadsby, and Albion Cox to strike a copper coin for the state, and a committee was formed to study the subject. On June 1, 1786, an act was passed to establish a copper coinage for the state, and a mint was established at Morristown under the direction of Walter Mould, an Englishman, formerly employed at the Birmingham mint. Gilbert Rindle did the actual coining under the direction of Goadsby, Cox, and Mould. Later, another mint was established in Elizabethtown.

Kentucky, while not numbered among the thirteen original colonies, is also represented about this time by the Kentucky copper cent of 1791 and the Myddleton Token of 1796. The Kentucky copper cent of 1791, struck in England, shows a hand holding a scroll inscribed "Our Cause is Just" and the legend "Unanimity is the Strength of Society"; reverse, 15 stars enclosing rings facing a triangle, each star bearing the initial of one state in the Union, with Kentucky in the leading position, and the legend "E Pluribus Unum." On some, the edge is inscribed "Payable in Lancaster, London or Bristol"; on others, the edge is plain.

The Myddleton token shows a figure representing Hope beside an anchor, urging two children toward a female figure who is extending her hand in reception; the left hand supports a staff crowned with a liberty cap; in front of the latter figure is a staff with olive wreath and branch, to the rear a cornucopia. The legend reads "British Settlement Kentucky." Reverse, Britannia seated with downcast emblems of her power, holding an inverted spear, at her right side a bundle of fasces near the cap of liberty, upon the ground the scales of justice with broken blade. The left arm of the figure rests upon a large shield bearing the cross of Britain. Legend, "Payable by P. P. P. Myddleton."

It is not necessary to go into further detail regarding the coins of the period between the Revolution and the establishment of the United States mint under the new government. Other states do not enter into the monetary history of the times during and immediately after the Revolution, as far as metal currency is concerned. Georgia, South Carolina, North Carolina, and Maryland did not establish mints and had no metal state coinage. They contributed in some degree to the history of the currency of the times through the issuance of Continental paper money, and it is proper at this time to discuss that phase of operations during the period of the Confederation.

Continental Paper Money

To this day the expression "not worth a Continental" is used to denote disgust with the lack of value of whatever happens to be under discussion. However, there was a time when the Continental paper money was really worth its face value.

With the start of the Revolution, after the Battle of Lexington, April 19, 1775, it soon became urgently necessary to finance the war against England. Therefore, on May 10, 1775, the delegates to the Continental Congress assembled at Philadelphia, and on June 22 resolved to issue "Two millions of Spanish milled dollars in bills of credit" on the promise of the twelve colonies represented to redeem such bills. The bills were to be in denominations of from $1 to $20. On July 25 an additional $1,000,000 was ordered in bills of $30 each. It was also resolved, on July 29, that each colony should redeem the bills in four equal payments, beginning November 30, 1779, in proportion to the number of the colony's inhabitants.

Once started, however, the issues of Continental paper currency did not stop at $3,000,000; and an additional $6,000,000 was issued in 1775, four times this amount in 1776, and so on, until at the close of 1779 the amount reached a total of more than $200,000,000, in denominations ranging from one sixth of a dollar to $80.

The Continental paper money rapidly depreciated, due to the turbulent conditions, lack of trade, and to a great extent to the efforts of the Tory element to discourage the patriots in their war with the mother country. In 1776 small change and all silver money disappeared from circulation. Great effort was put forth by the Colonial Government to increase confidence in paper money. However, the prices for the bare necessities of life rose to exorbitant levels. Connecticut, in November 1776, found it necessary to pass a law regulating prices, a phase which many of us understand from our experiences with price regulation during the Second World War. It became necessary in this same year, 1776, for the Continental Congress to give Washington the power to take whatever he needed for use of the Army; if the owners would not sell for a reasonable price in Continental paper they were to be arrested for refusal to accept the currency.

Conditions steadily grew worse, due to the lack of a definite financial policy. In 1778 the Continental paper money was worth only 33⅓ percent of its face value; in November, 1779, when it was supposed to have been redeemed, it was worth but 2½ percent of face value, and in 1781 $1 in specie would bring from $200 to $500 in Continental currency. Washington remarked that "a wagonload of money will hardly purchase a wagonload of provisions." One of the best illustrations of conditions is given by Dr. Henry Bronson in his *A Historical Account of Connecticut Currency,* published in 1865, wherein he states that "a merchant of Boston sold a hogshead of rum for 20 pounds cash. The purchaser did not settle for it until after the seller applied to him for an empty hogshead, for which he was charging 30 pounds. When they came to settle, the merchant found upon examination that he had to pay a balance of 10 pounds on that particular cask, which, with the rum it contained, had been sold for 20 pounds."

In round figures, the estimated expense of the Revolution was $135,000,000; but the amount of Continental paper money issued to finance the war was over $200,000,000. In fact, the amount of such paper printed was nearer $250,000,000, but not all of it got into circulation.

It is hardly necessary to describe in detail all the issues of Continental paper currency by states. The form was similar in most cases, except that in some colonies denominations were given in dollars and cents; others, in pounds, shillings, and pence. For example, the Connecticut one shilling and sixpence note read: "The possessor of this bill shall be paid by the Colony of Connecticut One Shilling and Six Pence lawful money by the First Day of January A.D. One Thousand Seven Hundred and Eighty-two. By Order of Assembly, dated Hartford, June 19th, A.D. 1776, [Signed] John Wood [Committee]"; and showed the state seal of Connecticut, which reads *"Connecticensis Sigillum Colon,"* or "Seal of the Colony of Connecticut," and three stands of laurel with ribbon, reading *"Qui Tran. Sust."* (*Qui Transtulit Sustinet*), or "he who transplanted still sustains." The reverse read "One Shilling and Six Pence Lawful Money—New London—Printed by Timothy Green."

The one shilling and threepence note of Connecticut was

practically the same, but was signed "E. Williams [Committee]."

The Maryland notes were in dollars and cents, and the six-dollar note read: "This indented bill of Six Dollars shall entitle the bearer thereof to receive bills of exchange payable in London, or gold and silver at the rate of four shillings and six pence Sterling per dollar of the said bill, according to the directions of An Act of Assembly of Maryland, dated in Annapolis this tenth day of April Anno Domini MDCCLXXIV (1774), [Signed] H. Clapham—Wm. Eddis"; and bore the seal of Maryland—a farmer with a shovel and a fisherman with fish on either side of a shield with the motto *"Crescite et Multiplicamini,"* or "Increase and be multiplied." Compare this with the design of the Maryland commemorative half dollar of 1934, which shows the present seal with the motto, *"Fatti Maschi, Parole Femine,"* meaning, "Deeds are manly, words womanly." The reverse of this note shows a tobacco leaf and "Six Dollars —equal to 27 S Sterling—'Tis Death to Counterfeit—Printed by A. C. and F. Green."

The New Jersey fifteen-shilling bill reads: "This bill of Fifteen Shillings Proclamation is emitted by a law of the Colony of New Jersey. Passed in the Fourteenth Year of the reign of His Majesty King George the Third, dated March 25, 1776—Fifteen Shillings—[Signed] Rob. Smith, Jona Deak, John Smyth"; and shows the familiar seal of Great Britain, instead of the seal of New Jersey with its present motto, "Liberty and Independence." The reverse shows a tobacco leaf and "Fifteen shillings—To Counterfeit is Death—Burlington in New Jersey—Printed by Isaac Collins, 1776."

From the Maryland and New Jersey notes we again see the significance of the tobacco plant and its use as money, real and figuratively, in the early days of the colonies.

None of the signed names are outstanding, and it is hard to

find anything of interest recorded concerning the private or public lives of the men whose signatures are shown on these bills, all written in pen and ink and quite legible even at this distant date. The printers, too, are unknown. In all probability, they were simply local craftsmen who secured the job of printing the bills.

After the Revolutionary War and during the formation of our national government this Continental and state paper money was practically worthless. Connecticut and Maryland claim to have redeemed the greater portion of their notes, but the majority of the bills were worth no more than the paper on which they were printed. A few were redeemed at the rate of about one cent on each dollar, face value. The unfortunate experience of the government and the colonists in this instance made people very wary in pursuing any policy which favored the indiscriminate issuance of paper bills. A few small issues were circulated during the War of 1812 and later; but the first authorized large-scale issuance of paper money did not occur until the passage of the Legal Tender Act in 1862, when the first greenbacks were printed.

The Beginnings of Our National Currency

Under the Articles of Confederation, the Congress in 1785 adopted the dollar as the monetary unit of the United States. In 1786 the value of the dollar was fixed at 375.64 grains of pure silver.

The references to money and coinage and the regulation of them contained in the Constitution are as follows:

Section 1, Article 9—"No money shall be drawn from the Treasury, but in consequence of appropriations made by law, and a regular statement and account of the receipts and expenditures of all public moneys shall be published from time to time."

Section 8, Article 1—"The Congress shall have power to borrow money on the credit of the United States.

". . . to coin money, regulate the value thereof, and of foreign coin.

". . . to provide for the punishment of counterfeiting the securities and current coin of the United States."

Section 10, Article 1—"No State shall coin money."

It will be seen that the exclusive power to coin money and regulate its value is conferred upon Congress. At times, as we have seen, the coining of money was a monopoly given to one man or a small group. This could no longer be true after the framing of the Constitution. Today no man or group of men outside of Congress, and no state, county, or city could suddenly decide to issue its own currency. It is true that many localities in various parts of the country have issued "wooden nickels," "cardboard nickels," and the like; but these issues are known as token money and are generally redeemed for United States coins. As a matter of fact, most, if not all, of them are gotten out as advertising schemes for a particular section or industry.

Notwithstanding the fact that the government is the exclusive coiner of money, however, there have been any number of private coinages, all of which will be taken up in due course. These included the private gold coinages of Templeton and Reid, the Bechtlers, and the various private gold coins issued in the West, as well as the Lesher Referendum dollars of 1900 and 1901. Some of these issues did cause agitation for a correct interpretation of the coinage provisions of the Constitution. The proponents of such issues contended that they were legal so long as they did not simulate the government's issues, while their adversaries declared they were illegal and that the states themselves could not issue them, so why should private individuals be allowed to operate their own mints?

A considerable quantity of foreign silver circulated in the United States. These coins were legal tender according to the act of February 9, 1793. The final provision for the retirement of foreign coins from circulation and the repeal of their legal tender qualities was not made until the passage of the Act of February 21, 1857. Even then, in some remote rural sections of the country, foreign silver coins continued to circulate almost to the beginning of the Civil War.

After a few years of unsatisfactory results from the many issues of Continental and Colonial currency, the acute need for a uniform government currency was met when President Washington, on April 2, 1792, signed an act of Congress establishing the first United States Mint. The city of Philadelphia was selected as the site, since the Congress met in that city, which was then the capital.

David Rittenhouse was appointed by President Washington on April 14, 1792 as the first director of the mint; and on July 31, 1792, Director Rittenhouse laid the cornerstone of the first mint at Seventh and Arch Streets, Philadelphia, this being the first public building authorized by the Federal Government. The site of the mint was an old distillery which was razed. An interesting item appears in an old account book with the entry, under date of July 31, 1792, of the receipt of seven shillings and sixpence for the sale of some old machinery in the distillery, which Mr. Rittenhouse directed should be spent for "punch" in laying the foundation stone.

The first coinage of the new mint consisted of silver half dimes, or "half dismes," produced in October, 1792, supposedly out of George Washington's private plate. Around the same time, "dismes" were also struck, and it is commonly assumed that the portrait on these coins was that of Martha Washington. The first metal purchased for coinage was six pounds of old copper, and the first deposit of silver bullion was made on July 18, 1794 by the Bank of Maryland, in the amount of $80,000 in coins of France. The first deposit of gold bullion was made by Moses Brown, a Boston merchant, in 1795, in gold ingots valued at $2,276.72.

There are some interesting and illuminating sidelights on the customs and manners of our forefathers, as well as an insight into the economic conditions of the late eighteenth and early nineteenth centuries.

Henry Wm. De Saussure was appointed director of the mint in July, 1795, on the resignation of David Rittenhouse because of ill health. George S. Evans' *Illustrated History of the United States Mint,* published in Philadelphia, 1886, by the author, shows a copy of an old payroll giving names and salaries of officers, clerks, and workmen employed at the mint as of October 10, 1795. Director De Saussure received $2000 a year. Henry Voight, chief coiner, and Albion Cox, assayer, each received $1500, the next highest salary. Robert Scott, engraver, received the modest sum of $1200 per annum. The workmen were paid by the day. The chief pressman got $1.80 per day, while three ordinary pressmen (obviously nonunion) received $1.00 a day, the same as Barney Miers, cleaner, Martin Summers, doorkeeper, and Adam Seyfert, hostler. Evidently there was a horse somewhere about the establishment. At the bottom of the list stands John Bay, with the simple title "boy," at $.66 a day.

Congress passed a resolution on March 5, 1838, raising the director's salary to $3500 a year, the chief coiners' to $2000, and the engraver's to $2000. The salaries of the others mentioned in the payroll of 1795 are not included in this resolution. It is hoped that all those who held jobs at this time received a raise.

The act of April 2, 1792, also provided for denominations in gold: the eagle ($10 of 270 grains standard or 247.5 pure, which means that it contained 247.5 grains of pure gold and that the standard weight included alloys), the half eagle ($5), and the quarter eagle ($2.50). The half and quarter eagles were of proportionate weight and the same fineness. Silver dollars were to be 416 grains standard or 371.25 pure silver; the silver half dollars and quarter dollars and the dimes and half dimes were of proportionate weight and fineness. Copper cents were also provided for, of 264 grains of copper; and half cents of 132 grains. In 1793 and 1795 the copper content was reduced, and in 1837 was fixed at 168 grains of copper for the cent and 84 grains for the half cent. The act of February 21, 1857, discontinued the two copper coins, but provided for a cent weighing 72 grains and containing 88 percent copper and 12 percent nickel. A bronze cent, 95 percent copper and 5 percent tin and zinc, was authorized by the act of April 22, 1864, which at the same time discontinued the cent containing nickel. The weight of the bronze cent was fixed at 48 grains; this composition and weight were incorporated in the Coinage Act of 1873. A bronze two-cent piece of 96 grains was authorized on April 22, 1864, but discontinued by the act of 1873. Silver was to be coined in conjunction with gold at a ratio of eighteen to one. There have been several changes regulated by Congress since 1792, so that at present no gold at all is coined.

A five-cent piece, the "nickel," hardly used any more, was authorized by the act of May 16, 1866, and continued with the act of 1873. Its weight was fixed at 77.16 grains, 75 percent copper and 25 percent nickel. A three-cent piece of nickel, weighing 30 grains, authorized on March 3, 1865, was discontinued by the act of September 26, 1890. In March 1942 a change in composition of the five-cent piece took place. The new coin was composed of 35 percent silver, 56 percent copper, and 9 percent manganese, and was produced from October 1, 1942, through December 31, 1945.

Production of a new wartime one-cent coin was provided for in the act of December 18, 1942, effective to December 31, 1946, to save strategic copper and tin for war uses. Production of a zinc-coated steel one-cent piece was begun in February, 1943, and was discontinued on December 31, 1943, after the acute phase of the copper stringency had passed. On January 1, 1944, coinage of a modified copper alloy cent was begun.

The only other coins issued were the silver twenty-cent piece introduced by the act of March 3, 1875, and discontinued by the act of May 2, 1878, and the silver three-cent piece authorized by the act of March 3, 1851, and discontinued along with the silver half dime by the act of February 12, 1873.

Until recently the metal content and gross weight of coins were as follows: *

	Metal content (grains)			*Gross weight* (grains)
Silver	Silver	Copper		
Dollar	371.25	41.25		412.50
Half dollar	173.61	19.29		192.90
Quarter dollar	86.805	9.645		96.45
Dime	34.722	3.858		38.58
Minor Coins	Copper	Nickel	Tin; zinc	
Five cents	57.87	19.29		77.16
One cent	45.60		2.40	48.00

The names of many of the earlier officers of the mint and the Treasury Department, of which it is a branch, are well known to numismatists. There was Doctor Benjamin Rush, first treasurer of the mint; Henry Voight, the first chief coiner, whose name appears on the early payroll previously mentioned,

* The composition of dimes, quarters, and half dollars was changed by the act of 1965 reducing or eliminating the silver content of these coins. Dimes and quarters are called clad coins because of the copper core within an outer layer of copper-nickel (75 percent copper, 25 percent nickel). The half dollar has an outer layer of 80 percent silver, an inner core of 21 percent silver, a total content of 40 percent silver.

and who was appointed by George Washington; William E. Dubois and Jacob R. Eckfeldt, assayers, who published in 1842 *A Manual of the Gold and Silver Coins of All Nations Within the Last Century,* which is one of the most enlightening of the early works on the operations of the mint and the adoption of our money system, and even more valuable because of the fact that it was written just a half century after the establishment of the mint. Another well-known figure is Christian Gobrecht, engraver from 1840 to 1844, the only engraver in this country to sign his full name on any of our coins, although the dollars on which his name appears were patterns or trial pieces, and the name is not shown on the regular issues. James B. Longacre is another engraver whose name is a byword to collectors as the designer of the Indian-head cent, on the earlier issues of which his initial is shown on the ribbon.

While the mint, as well as the Bureau of Engraving and Printing, where paper money is made, come under the jurisdiction of the Treasury Department, the Secretary of the Treasury and the Treasurer of the United States, whose signatures appear on old bank notes, are different officials. There have been 57 Secretaries of the Treasury from Alexander Hamilton, the first, to the present Secretary. Hamilton, of course, is the most famous. In addition to those of later years, who naturally are well remembered, such as William G. McAdoo, Carter Glass, Ogden L. Mills, and William H. Woodin, there are others whose names are familiar to those who have made a study of our coins and money system. These include Robert J. Walker (1845) and Wm. M. Meredith (1849), whose pictures are shown on many fractional currency notes; John A. Dix, Salmon P. Chase, and Wm. P. Fessenden, Civil War Secretaries; Hugh McCulloch, and one or two others. The Treasurer of the United States, whose name appears on our present paper money, has of late years been a woman, the present Treasurer being Kathryn O'Hay Granahan.

During the first years of the mint, the mill and screw process of coining was used—as in all mints of the time. This method had been in use in Europe and Spanish America from the middle of the seventeenth century. The Spanish mints at Mexico City, Potosi, Lima, and other cities in Central and South America had been turning out coins by this same method for almost two centuries before the United States Mint was established.

It was not until 1836, under the direction of Doctor Robert M. Patterson, that the method of coining was revolutionized by the introduction of steam power. This momentous occasion was commemorated by a medal issued by the mint, which can still be obtained there. It is of interest to note in this connection that the use of the steam coinage system originated through the experiments of Matthew Boulton, partner of the famous James Watt, inventor of the steam engine. Matthew Boulton, who established a mint in Birmingham, England, which manufactured many of the famous merchants' tokens of that country, is called the reformer of the process of coinage. The improvements in the machinery of the mint inaugurated in 1836 were in use for over half a century.

The total coinage for the first 56 years of the existence of the mint (i.e., 1792 to 1848), including gold, silver and copper, amounted to 343,281,250 pieces, with a value of $151,017,714. Compare this with 1,932,170,240 pieces of domestic coinage (not including 2,903,152 proofs) produced for the fiscal year of 1957 alone. In addition to this, during recent years the mint has coined money for Cuba, Honduras, Venezuela, Colombia, and other South and Central American countries. During and after the Second World War, coins have been produced for The Netherlands, Philippine Islands, and many other countries, as well as gold issues for Saudi Arabia, and many coins for Indonesia. As for paper currency, the annual production at the Bureau of Engraving and Printing has at times been as high as one billion separate notes, valued at over six billion dollars! At the same time, as much as 42 billion dollars' worth of securities and from 11 to 17 billion individual postage and revenue stamps have been turned out in one year by the same bureau.

Paper money, as we know it, is of comparatively recent origin in this country. Except for the limited colonial issues mentioned, and other emergency issues connected with the War of 1812 and the panic periods around 1837 during President Andrew Jackson's administration, paper money was not issued for general circulation until 1861, during the Civil War. Congressman E. G. Spaulding, of New York, called the "Father of Greenbacks" and a close friend of Abraham Lincoln, drafted the Legal Tender Act to meet the emergencies brought on by the war. The Legal Tender Act and the National Bank Act of the same period marked the beginning of the issuing of paper money by the government. During the first few years the paper money was printed by private companies, such as the American Bank Note Company and the National Bank Note Company, of New York City and Washington, D.C., respectively; but for over eighty years all of our paper money has been produced at the government's Bureau of Engraving and Printing in Washington.

Prior to the enactment of the National Bank Act, most of the paper currency in use was issued by state banks. Practically all of these state banks have been out of business for many years, and the bank notes issued by them are very much in demand by collectors of paper money. Most collectors specialize in the notes of banks which formerly functioned in their particular states. Some exceedingly interesting examples of the engravers' art may be seen in these old bank notes.

The average cost of printing paper bills is about $.30 per 1000, regardless of denomination. Paper money is naturally less long-lived than metal coinage. It is estimated that $1 bills, which constitute more than one half of the number of bills in circulation, have an average life of about nine months. Other forms, of course, last longer, but it is estimated that at least 10 percent is lost or burned beyond recovery. To illustrate this in the case of paper money: while the small bills now in use have circulated for twenty years, there are still many millions of dollars of the old large-size bills still out.

The collector of paper money has several interesting fields to which he can devote his energies. He can bring together many varieties of ordinary paper money in general use now or in the past, or he can concentrate on the thousands of different kinds of broken bank bills, fractional currency, or state bills.

Paper money, as such, originated in China about 1400 A.D., during the Ming Dynasty, and was printed on mulberry bark paper. This kind of money is by nature more fragile than metal coins, so that there are apt to be difficulties in securing the less widely circulated varieties. The practice of many governments of destroying old and obsolete paper money, particularly in countries having many changes in administration, also enters into the problems encountered by the paper money specialist.

The denominations of United States paper money are: $1, $2, 5, $10, $20, $50, $100, $500, $1000, $5000, and $10,000. There are also $100,000 notes for bank use only. Bills are of various kinds: silver certificates with blue seal in denominations of $1, $5, and $10; United States notes with red seal in denominations of $2 and $5; gold certificates with yellow seal in denominations of $100, $1000, $10,000 and $100,000.

These last are issued only to Federal Reserve banks against certain credits established with the Treasurer of the United States, and do not appear in circulation. In addition, there are Federal Reserve notes with green seal in denominations of $5, $10, $20, $50, $100, $500, $1000, $5000, and $10,000. Of the latter, denominations of $500 and over have been discontinued, but notes of these denominations will continue to be paid out as long as existing stocks last. The portraits shown on faces of bills and the designs or embellishments on the backs of the several denominations are shown below:

Denomination	*Portrait*	*Back*
$1	Washington	Great Seal of the United States
$2	Jefferson	Monticello
$5	Lincoln	Lincoln Memorial
$10	Hamilton	United States Treasury
$20	Jackson	White House
$50	Grant	United States Capitol
$100	Franklin	Ornate denominational marking
$500	McKinley	" " "
$1,000	Cleveland	" " "
$5,000	Madison	" " "
$10,000	Chase	" " "
$100,000	Wilson	" " "

The collector of paper money looks for oddities such as a creased note, that is, one which has been folded in printing leaving a blank space through the printing or an oversize corner; a low-numbered or odd-numbered note such as 1,000,-001; four or more notes in a cut or uncut sheet of consecutive numbers; and other unique features, including inverted reverses, where the back of the note is printed upside down. Some of these oddities—which happen in printing, cutting, or packing once every several million bills—escape detection.

Other incentives to collecting present issues occur when low-numbered notes with signatures of a new Treasurer or Secretary are issued, or when a new motto is first shown, as in 1957, when "In God We Trust" first appeared on the back of our dollar bills.

For obvious reasons, the collecting of current United States paper money, regardless of an individual note's distinctive features, has its limitations and cannot be indulged in by everybody. A man of moderate means will hardly feel like putting away an album of fifty or more one-, two-, or five-dollar bills, for which he may have paid from two to eight dollars apiece. However, it is not beyond the income of many collectors to purchase an odd or interesting bill of small denomination for about double its face value. In a pinch, after all, it can still be used for groceries, and there are few collections that are as satisfying as a paper money collection, all crisp, new bills of considerable interest, neatly arranged in pockets in a paper money album, easily shown, and taking very little room in a crowded apartment or small house—not, however, without some risk of loss through burglary, if not well protected.

Much interesting information may be gleaned from a study of United States and foreign paper money. For example, our $1 small note, Series of 1935, bore for the first time both the obverse and reverse of the Great Seal of the United States. In 1776, when Thomas Jefferson and Benjamin Franklin were members of a committee to draft a suitable design for the seal, Jefferson suggested the pillar of cloud by day and the pillar of fire by night that guided the Children of Israel on their forty-year march through the wilderness to the Promised Land, because he believed that divine guidance had assisted the American colonies in their difficulties. Benjamin Franklin submitted a design showing the Children of Israel safely across the Red Sea, and he, like Jefferson, believed that the assistance given to the colonies was little short of miraculous. Both these men chose as a motto for the seal, "Rebellion to Tyrants is Obedience to God." These designs, however, were not accepted, but six years later, in 1782, the present seal was adopted substantially as it appears in the aforesaid series of dollar bills. The reverse of the seal represents a pyramid unfinished. Thirteen courses of masonry, representing the thirteen colonies, are laid, and above, in the air, is the completing capstone, with the All-Seeing Eye symbolizing Divine blessing. Above it is the motto, "Prosper our Beginnings," and beneath it, "A New Order of the Ages." The unfinished pyramid means that the country is not yet completed, and is still in the making.

The large-sized bills, replaced by the smaller notes in 1929, are a curiosity. People soon forget what was once commonplace, as witness the fact that the noncollecting public seldom knows that two- and three-cent pieces were in general use not so many years ago. In fact, many of the younger generation may have never even seen a large-sized dollar bill. Therefore, uncirculated or very fine large paper bills carry a premium at most dealers, which will continue to grow higher as the supply of these bills dwindles through destruction by the government and redemption for new notes.

In Canada also, where large-sized notes once were in general circulation, smaller-sized bills are now used exclusively, and the older bills are worth saving, provided they are in excellent condition.

Continuing with our own currency along the lines of what is acceptable and desirable for a paper collection, there are the special wartime currencies such as the Hawaiian series and the "yellow seal" notes. In July, 1942, as a step toward the economic defense of Hawaii, a special Hawaiian dollar currency was introduced. This currency consisted of United States silver certificates and Federal Reserve notes bearing the distinctive overprint "Hawaii" in bold open-faced type on each end of the face of the note and the word "Hawaii" in large open-faced type across the reverse side of the note. After August 15, 1942, no currency other than United States currency, Hawaiian series, could be held or used in Hawaii without a license from the Governor of the Territory. On the other hand, in order to effectuate the purposes of its issuance, the United States currency, Hawaiian series, was kept from circulating on the mainland of the United States by virtue of a prohibition of its export from Hawaii. On February 9, 1944, it was announced that the special Hawaiian series of currency had been taken by the armed forces of the United States into Central Pacific strongholds from which the Japanese had been driven. This step was taken to facilitate identification of the currency being used in combat areas, and to make easier the isolation of this particular currency in the event that it should fall into enemy hands.

On October 21, 1944, it was announced that the economic controls in the Hawaiian Islands, of which the issuance of the Hawaiian series currency was a part, were terminated, and while further issues of Hawaiian series notes were not made, they continued to circulate both in Hawaii and on the mainland. Needless to say, these Hawaiian notes are now scarce and make a worthwhile acquisition.

In November 1942, at the request of the War Department, the Treasury Department furnished to the War Department a special series of United States currency for use of the American military forces in North Africa. This currency consisted of silver certificates, in the usual denominations of $1, $5, and $10, but bearing a yellow seal in place of the customary blue one. One purpose of the special series of currency was to prevent the use in North Africa of United States money which the Axis might have seized in occupied areas.

During the year 1945, in Chicago, the Treasury Department issued 1,000,000 silver certificates in $1 denomination, bearing on the face the red letter "R," and an equal number of the same certificates on which were printed a large red "S." These letters represent "Regular" and "Synthetic," and were used in a test by the Treasury Department to determine the wearing qualties of the paper regularly used and of a special paper it was proposing to use. These notes appeared in circulation a short time, and then disappeared. Each of them in crisp uncirculated condition carries a premium.

In conjunction with the other Allied nations during the Second World War, a great deal of wartime currency was issued. These are small notes, used in Italy, France, and Germany, which circulated generally in those countries during the Allied occupancy. In the Pacific Area, currency was issued for Okinawa, the Ryukyu Islands, Iwo Jima, and other places, and circulated freely in those parts of the war zone. The Japanese also issued many different pieces of occupation paper money for the Philippines, Netherlands East Indies, and China. Soon after our forces arrived in Japan, arrangements were made for the use of regular Japanese bank notes.

Broken bank bills are those which have been issued by banks and business firms which have ceased functioning. None of them have any value as legal tender today. There are hundreds of issues, as, unfortunately, many banks have gone out of business, or went "broke," which accounts for the designation "broken bank bills" being applied to this form of money by collectors. There are also numerous counterfeits, which accounts for some of the defunct banking institutions. However, this is one time where in many cases the spurious bills are almost as interesting as the real. There is no way of telling whether a good many of the counterfeits are the real thing unless one is an experienced collector, or studies some of the old "Bank Note Detectors," as most of them are as good in appearance as the genuine and are so worn that they must have passed through many hands, indicating that many of our grandfathers were not as wise as our parents would lead us to believe.

The beginner will facilitate matters for himself by simply taking a certain period of time, say, a decade, and starting by cities, states, or localities. Most broken bank bills do not run into big money, although it is more difficult to secure crisp, uncirculated bills than those showing much wear and tear. A signed bank note is worth more than an unsigned one; and a sheet of four or more uncut bills, consecutively numbered, is worth a lot more than the same quantity cut and not in sequence. Here, again, a bill of low serial number is more sought after than one with a high number.

A good set of paper money for a beginner to start with is the Confederate notes, which are in denominations from $.50 to $1,000. They are interesting from an historic point of view and will in time be rarities. At present, however, the ordinary kind can be purchased for a dollar or so, and this embraces the great majority of these bills, excepting the $500 and $1,000 denominations. However, one of the great mysteries of numismatics is the fact that certain series run along for years at ridiculously low prices, and suddenly in the course of a year or so are priced at ten times their former value. The probabilities are that a few dealers begin to realize all at once that there is a scarcity of notes or coins; people are putting them away, and they do not show in the market; and no doubt many are destroyed in fires and floods. The conclusion to be drawn from this, of course, is that the novice in any field of numismatics should not be self-conscious about beginning in a small way with inexpensive material. It is the best way to learn the ins and outs of the game. After all, there are many, many things to learn, and dealers can be as wrong as the rest of us. Right here it is well to impress upon the young or inexperienced collector that there is no numismatist who can truthfully say that he has not been "stuck," not once, but a hundred times. It's part of the game—a little of the overhead, we might say. The thing to remember, though, is not to get stuck the same way twice. And at the same time, consider that at least fifty percent of the time we are fooled through our own neglect or carelessness. This can happen in a dozen ways, such as bidding too high at an auction, neglecting to notice the advertised condition of a coin or bank note, assuming that a high-priced coin is rarer than it really is, and in other ways.

Another interesting branch of paper money collecting is fractional currency, sometimes called "shinplasters" because of its use by Union soldiers during the Civil War inside their worn shoes to keep their feet warm, or so it is said. This currency was first introduced to meet the shortage of small currency due to hoarding during the same war. The first issue was in 1862 in the form of postage stamps, an act being passed by Congress permitting use of such stamps for payments of less than $5. The Treasury of the United States, under Secretary F. G. Spinner, had small notes printed in denominations of $.05, $.10, and $.50. The first issue by the government was made on August 21, 1862, and was called postage currency. Illustrations of stamps were printed on the notes—Jefferson, $.05 stamp; Washington, $.10 stamp; Jefferson, five $.05 stamps for $.25; Washington, five $.10 stamps for $.50.

The second issue of fractional currency was authorized March 3, 1863, and in place of postage currency was called fractional currency. The third general issue was printed from December 5, 1864, to August 16, 1869, when the $.03 note was first issued. This is the hardest to secure in good condition, and is worth almost as much as some of the $.25 and $.50 notes. The red-back notes of this issue are quite rare, particularly the $.50 notes with signatures of Rosecrans and Spinner. The fourth issue of fractional currency was issued from July 14, 1869 to February 16, 1875; the fifth and last issue, February 26, 1874 to February 15, 1876. This issue was of $.10, $.25, and $.50 notes, all of which may be secured at fairly low prices for crisp bills in new condition.

With some exceptions, fractional currency notes, like Confederate notes, are cheap when you consider their historic value. Their number is reduced every year by government redemption. They are often sold in lots at auction, and most such lots contain notes of decidedly inferior quality. However, while Confederate bills have no value at all except from a collector's viewpoint, these fractional notes are redeemable at face value through the Currency Redemption Division of the Treasury Department, Washington, D.C. Therefore, any of the fractional currency notes purchased blind or in lots with other good bills, which are sold as one lot, are not a total loss. There are still counterfeit fractional notes to be found now and then among good ones. Such notes, of course, are cancelled and delivered to the Secret Service Division of the Treasury Department, a receipt being sent to the remitter.

Closely associated with Confederate state notes and fractional currency, being issued during the same period of our history, are the other issues of Southern state notes, printed between 1861 and 1865. The states of Alabama, Arkansas, Florida, Georgia, Louisiana, Mississippi, North Carolina, South Carolina, Texas, and Virginia, all issued state notes in denominations from $.05 to $100, the former being confined to Alabama, Georgia, North Carolina, and South Carolina.

It should be mentioned that in a general work of this nature space will not permit more than a cursory outline of various types of the more popular forms of currency. Attention, of necessity, must be given to the type rather than to series of any particular national, state, or private issues. The student of paper money who specializes in Confederate, state, broken bank bills, fractional currency, or United States Treasury notes may avail himself of the several excellent check lists showing each separate issue by name and number with value. Such lists are given in the bibliography at the end of this chapter.

In the field of foreign paper notes, numerous specimens of interest may be gathered together at low cost. A popular and splendidly engraved series of notes are the Russian Imperial rubles, particularly those of high denomination. They have had no exchange value for many years, and are interesting only as collector's items. The same applies for Austrian and German postwar inflation notes. The latter are the best examples we can find of the evils of inflation of the national currency. A German billion-mark bill issued after World War One may be purchased for about two or three dollars, and has no value as money whatsoever. Incidentally, the German billion equals our trillion; and a billion-mark note, if redeemable at the present time, would be worth $400,000,000. The term *notgeld* is used for the German postwar emergency notes. These notes are small, like our own fractional currency, but are on plain paper. They were issued after World War One by the towns and cities of Germany, and are now becoming quite popular with collectors. There are several thousand varieties, most of which are extremely cheap. Like nearly all obsolete forms of currency issued in times of great stress, these small notes are of historic importance. Furthermore, although they are printed on cheap paper, many of the designs are noteworthy for their artistic beauty.

The collector of an inexpensive set of paper money representing all countries possible would get some interesting United States and Canadian notes; Mexican revolutionary notes, such as those of the states of Chihuahua, Sonora, Sinaloa, etc; and old German, Austrian, Russian, Cuban, and Polish notes. These could be supplemented from time to time with some colonial notes of New York, Connecticut, Massachusetts, New Jersey, and others of the original thirteen colonies. It might be thought that the colonial notes would be beyond the limits of the ordinary pocketbook. However, good one-shilling notes of Connecticut may be secured for well under two dollars, and the others very often for less. They are curious and full of historic significance.

While our paper money is seldom, if ever, considered in the nature of commemorative money, it is a source of regret that better use is not made of these notes for that purpose. The back of a one-dollar bill would surely serve as well to commemorate historical events as the commemorative postage stamps which our government, like so many other governments, issues in such profusion. The crowded condition of some of our stamps speaks volumes in favor of the idea of using paper notes for commemorative purposes. The one big objection, of course, is that the life of a paper bill does not compare with that of a metal coin, which may last for several centuries.

Nevertheless, paper money has been used, to some degree, in the United States to commemorate certain events. Many of us remember the old large bank notes bearing reverses resplendent with beautiful engravings such as "Washington Crossing the Delaware," "Signing of the Declaration of Independence," and a dozen others. One very popular note which might truly be called a commemorative bill is the dollar, series of 1896, entitled, "History Instructing Youth," bearing on its face in the center a figure representing History holding in her arm a young boy, and pointing with her left forefinger across the Potomac to the National Capitol. A book opened in the right center contains part of the Constitution. On the left, right, and top borders are wreaths enclosing the names of famous Americans, from Cooper to Emerson, and including Washington, Jefferson, Franklin, Hamilton, and many others. The reverse carries busts of Martha and George Washington.

The order of the present day, however, insofar as paper notes are concerned, seems to be plainness and severity. The old-style bank notes are a relic of a more leisurely age, the days when even such prosaic things as moving vans bore masterpieces on their sides. To the numismatist who likes his currency a trifle, shall we say, on the gaudy side, the present-day bills seem unnecessarily severe and plain.

Then, of course, it is probable that commemorative bills would be severely abused by politically minded government officials and would doubtless be issued in such profusion as practically to lose their significance in honoring any specific great event or personage.

Among the more interesting stories told about money is the one explaining how Dixie was named. The French in Louisiana made a practice of printing the word *Dix* on the $10 notes issued in New Orleans before the Civil War, together with other French lettering. Hence the South, particularly the state of Louisiana, became known as Dixieland. However, there are a half dozen other explanations for the origin of Dixie, and this one may not be authentic.

The Encyclopaedia Britannica defines the expression "paper money" in a broad sense as covering "all printed or written documents which are promises to pay money, either on demand or at a future date," and adds, "It covers not only bank notes but checks, bills of exchange, postal money orders, etc." Some collectors look for old checks of business firms dated in the early and middle nineteenth century. They are interesting, as all old documents are, as mementos of past days, also for their record of old and, in most cases, long-deceased banking firms. Such a collection would be a good supplement to one of broken bank bills. Money orders very seldom appear in the collecting scene. Other documents such as old bills of lading, express waybills, ships' manifests, etc. would hardly classify as numismatic items, although there is considerable interest in old bonds, particularly those of the Confederacy and some of the extinct railroads.

Extensive and highly valuable collections of paper money are rarely given publicity. There are undoubtedly many such, but they are seldom heard about; their owners keep them for their own private satisfaction. Only in cases of great loss by fire or theft do the newspapers print articles regarding paper note collections, while such articles are very frequently written regarding metal coins.

It might be well to add a word of warning: never, except in the case of a great rarity, purchase a bank note or piece of paper money which has been folded and therefore creased. A creased bill, even though otherwise brand new, is only fifty percent as effective in an exhibit as a crisp, unfolded, and uncirculated bill. In the case of an extremely rare note, the paper money specialist might try to iron out the creases, and if he made a good job of it would be as happy as if he had a brand new bill. However, be careful.

The Making of Paper Money

The handiwork of individual artists and steel engravers, and the most modern machinery designed especially for its work, are combined in the production of currency and other products of the Bureau of Engraving and Printing. The result is an unusually high type of work, making counterfeiting difficult of execution and easy of detection; and at strikingly low cost, considering the value of the products and the uses to which they are put. The average cost of producing a currency note, of whatever denomination, is less than one cent.

When a new note or other engraved work is to be produced, a model is prepared by an artist in the engraving division. The work of this designer is based upon discussions of officials of the various branches of the government interested in the product. The model finally must secure the approval of the Secretary of the Treasury.

The design is then reproduced in soft steel by engravers. Separate portions of the design, such as the portrait, vignette, ornaments, and lettering, are commonly executed separately by experts who specialize in individual branches of the work. Each works with a steel tool known as a graver, aided by a powerful magnifying glass. The combined work of the engravers is known as a die. The steel comprising the die is heated in cyanide of potassium and then dipped in oil or brine to harden it. The die is then placed on the bed of a transfer press, and under heavy pressure, a cylinder of soft steel, called a roll, is rolled over the die. The work of the individual engravers is thus transferred to the roll, in combined form, the soft steel of the roll being forced into the lines of the original engraving so that the lines stand out in relief on the roll. The steel of the roll is then hardened, and the design is transferred to soft steel plates, again by rolling under great pressure. The steel plates, with the design in the intaglio or cut-in impressions as on the original die, are then hardened and cleaned and are ready for the printer. The original die may be used to produce numerous rolls, and each roll is available to make additional plates, as those originally put into service become worn. An electrolytic process for duplicating plates has also been developed in the Bureau.

Ink for the printing of currency is mixed in the Bureau. Distinctive paper used in printing currency and securities, prepared under a special formula, is secured from the contractor by the Treasury Department, and is drawn by the Bureau from the Treasury Department's Bureau of Paper Custody, in packages of 1000 sheets each. The paper first goes to the Wetting Division, which first counts and then moistens the paper. Especially designed machinery has been used for wetting since 1911; before that it was done by hand.

After being seasoned for several days, the sheets are ready to be fed to a flat power-plate printing press, operated by a printer and two assistants. In 1957 the Bureau of Engraving and Printing installed new presses capable of printing a sheet of thirty-two notes in one impression as compared to the previous practice of printing eighteen notes to a sheet. The plates are inked by rubber rollers, then surplus ink is removed by a mechanism known as a wiper, and by hand work by the plate printer, so that ink is left only in the etched lines of the design. The plates are then pressed against the moistened paper, which absorbs the ink, making it an integral part of the note. The backs of thirty-two notes are then printed on each sheet. The face of the notes are printed by a similar procedure. After the sheets have been printed on both sides, they are put through a sizing operation which gives a better finish to the currency and strengthens the paper by making it more resistant to dirt, grease, and wear.

The final printing operation is the sealing and numbering of the notes. In the case of some notes the signatures of the Secretary of the Treasury and of the Treasurer of the United States are printed in facsimile in connection with the numbering and sealing; in other cases these signatures are included in the die engraved for the face of the note. The Numbering Division separates the sheets into notes and counts the notes into packages of 100. Some notes may be found in circulation with a star prefixed to the serial number rather than a letter, which is found in most cases. These "star" notes are later substitutions for previous bills of the same number which have become worn and withdrawn from circulation.

At each stage of the procedure every safeguard is used to prevent losses of partially executed or completed work, and to make impossible any unauthorized use of any portion of the government's machinery. All dies, rolls, and plates are kept in a burglarproof and fireproof vault, from which they may be removed only by requisition. From the time the paper is received from the Treasury Department by the Wetting Division, each division receiving it must account for each sheet of paper which came into its control during the day, before any of the personnel is allowed to leave the building at night. Mechanical counting appliances record accurately each operation of the presses, which are locked when scheduled work is completed. The output must be reconciled with these records. Each operating division makes reports through a central Accounting Division to provide a constant check on the whereabouts of all paper and partially prepared product. In addition, Treasury Department auditors not connected with the Bureau are constantly at work, checking the Accounting Division balances against their own counts in the several divisions.

Faces and backs of bonds, notes, and other securities are plate-printed, following a process similar to that used for currency.

More than 1000 tons of paper are used yearly in producing currency, and about 2700 tons of ink are manufactured in the Bureau from raw materials.

Finished currency is delivered by the Bureau to the Federal Reserve Banks in the case of Federal Reserve notes and Federal Reserve bank notes, and to the Treasurer of the United States in the case of other notes. The Treasurer of the United States sends notes and silver certificates to Federal Reserve Banks, which distribute them to commercial banks. As notes become worn and unfit for circulation, they are turned in by commercial banks to Federal Reserve Banks, which in turn transmit them to the Treasurer of the United States for redemption in new currency or credit. A special force of experts operates in the redemption division to identify and reclaim currency which has been damaged by fire, water, or other agents. Currency turned in as unfit is macerated to wet pulp, which is then sold or destroyed.

Currency Redemption Division

The Currency Redemption Division of the Treasury Department takes care of the redemption of obsolete paper money such as fractional currency and the like. Although fractional currency has been long out of circulation and was issued during and for a short time after the Civil War, these small paper notes of 3-, 5-, 10-, 15-, 25-, and 50-cent denominations are still received and redeemed by the Treasury Department in sizable amounts each year.

Another function of the Currency Redemption Division is the redemption of burned and mutilated paper money. It may be news to some that paper money which has been burned, torn, or damaged by water, acids, or other elements may be redeemed, provided not less than two fifths of the original proportions of the bill remain, at one half the face value of the whole note. Fragments of less than two fifths are not redeemable except when accompanied by satisfactory proof that the missing portions have been totally destroyed. This proof should be in the form of an affidavit from the owner, setting forth that he is the owner and the cause and manner of destruction. The affidavits must be subscribed and sworn to before a notary public or other officer authorized to administer oaths. Applicants must furnish their own forms of affidavits, as blank forms are not supplied by the Treasury Department. No recompense is made for currency totally destroyed.

All counterfeit notes and coins found in remittances are cancelled and delivered to the Secret Service Division of the Treasury Department, and receipt for same sent to the remitter.

There are still outstanding many old coins in denominations no longer issued, such as 2-cent bronze, 3-cent nickel, 3-cent silver, and so on. A great many such coins, of course, are held in collections of numismatists. However, coins which are in such bad condition as to be worthless from a collector's standpoint gradually find their way back to the Treasury to be remelted. Since the opening of the mint in 1792, the government has recalled only one issue of metal coins. This is the silver Trade Dollar of 420 grains, issued from 1873 to 1885 (in proof only from 1879 to 1885). The issue was not successful and the government redeemed any outstanding trade dollars turned in. However, we will discuss the trade dollar later.

The Secret Service Division

At the time of the opening of the mint in 1792 in Philadelphia the penalty for counterfeiting was death, the same as it had been in England for many centuries. This no longer applies, of course, although counterfeiting is still considered a serious crime. Appropriations for the suppression of counterfeiting were first made in 1861, and a Bureau was established in 1864. Now the chief of the Secret Service Division is appointed by the Secretary of the Treasury. In addition to the suppression of counterfeiting, the Secret Service Division has numerous other duties.

The elaborate processes of both the Bureau of the Mint and the Bureau of Engraving and Printing make it impossible for counterfeiters to produce either coin or currency that can fool the experts; but they still try it now and again.

Counterfeiting is not only a fraud upon the government; it entails heavy losses upon innocent persons who accept bogus money. For his own protection, everyone should know something about the detection of counterfeit money.

A bogus coin differs from a genuine coin of the same denomination in appearance, weight, feel, or in the "ring" given off when the coin is brought in contact with marble, glass, or other hard materials; or it may differ in all these respects.

Genuine paper currency is produced by the steel engraving process, the ink impregnating the paper. Most counterfeit currency is produced by a photoengraving process, and the ink remains upon the surface of the paper. The difference between a genuine note, produced by steel engraving, and a counterfeit note, produced by the photoengraving process, is essentially the same as that between an engraved card and a printed card. The lines of the steel engraving are much more distinct and characteristic. This difference is especially noticeable when the portrait on a doubtful bill is compared with the portrait on a genuine bill of the same denomination.

The Treasury Department has at times conducted a widespread educational program of lectures, bank and other displays, and distribution of cards and booklets entitled "Know Your Money."

Occasionally a counterfeit note is found which has been produced from a plate made by an engraver. In this case it will be impossible for the engraver of the counterfeit to copy accurately all details of the genuine bill. The expression on the face of the portrait, especially around the eyes, is almost impossible to reproduce accurately, and comparison with a genuine note, if possible with a magnifying glass, will generally result in the ready detection of a bogus bill.

Citizens can aid in the suppression of counterfeiting by notifying the Secret Service or local police officers of the discovery of any spurious coin or currency. In spite of the visions of easy money which have led many criminals into the counterfeiting field, it is an established fact that no counterfeiter has ever become wealthy. The activities of the Secret Service have led to early apprehension of most counterfeiters, and a large proportion of the spurious money is seized before it enters into circulation. The percentage of convictions in counterfeiting cases is unusually high, and the heavy penalties provided by Federal law show the detestation which the public feels for this crime.

The Making of Coins

In coining metal currency, the first step is to prepare the alloy. See page 59 for details of alloys and compositions. With gas or oil as fuel, the alloy is melted in crucibles. The molten alloy is poured into molds to form ingots. The ingots are in thin bars, varying in width and thickness according to the size of the coins for which they are to be used. The width is sufficient to allow three coins to be cut from each strip.

The ingots are next put through rolling mills to reduce the thickness to required limits. The strips are then fed into cutting presses, which cut circular blanks of the approximate dimensions of the finished coin. The blanks are run through annealing furnaces to soften them; next through tumbling barrels, which are rotating cylinders containing chemical solutions for cleaning and burnishing the metal; and finally into centrifugal drying machines. The blanks are now ready for the processes which transform the bare metal disks into coins.*

* For "clad" coins the metal strips are provided in the sandwich condition as it appears in dimes, quarters and half dollars.

They are next fed into a milling, or "upsetting," machine which produces the raised or upset rim. Next is the important operation of the stamping or coinage press. As it is struck, the blank is held firmly by a collar under heavy pressure, varying from 40 tons for one-cent pieces and dimes, to 170 tons for silver dollars. Upper and lower dies impress the design on both sides of the coin. The pressure is sufficient to produce raised surfaces level with those of the milled rim. In the case of silver coins, the collar holding the blank is grooved. The pressure forces the metal into the grooves of the collar and produces the "reeding" on the finished coin, which makes it impossible for a coin to be shaved without detection.

Silver coins, with the exception of dimes, are again separately weighed, and if found to be outside of legal limits, they are condemned and remelted. Dimes, five-cent, and one-cent pieces are not weighed separately on completion, but frequent test weights of blanks are taken. Scrap metal left over when blanks are cut from the strips is returned for remelting, with constant checking at all stages of operation to prevent loss of precious metal. An accurate record is kept of all metals handled in order that losses may be held to a minimum. The floors of the mint workrooms are swept every day, and the "sweeps" thrown into the melting pot. In fact, the word "sweeps" includes all kinds of waste material which is likely to contain the precious metal, including old crucibles, cans, ashes, aprons, and gloves, packages in which bullion is received, and everything of a like character.

The Annual Assay Commission

There are few institutions which date back in our history as far as the Annual Assay Commission, which meets each year at the United States Mint in Philadelphia on the second Wednesday in February.

The Assay Commission is appointed each year by the President. Three members are in regular attendance: The Judge of the District Court for the Eastern District of Pennsylvania, the Comptroller of the Currency, and the Chief Assayer. These three officials meet with such other persons as the President may designate, and are termed Assay Commissioners. The commission was created in 1792, and is one of the oldest government institutions. In England the "trial of the Pyx" dates back to mediaeval times. The word "pyx" is derived from the "pyx-chest," a receptacle for new English coins once kept in the chapel of the Pyx in Westminster Abbey, London.

Briefly, the duties of the commission in our country are to examine the coinage from three angles: counting, weighing, and assaying. At the United States mints at Philadelphia and Denver not less than one silver coin of every 2000 delivered from the coining room must be reserved for test by the commission to determine whether the coins conform to legal requirements as to weight and fineness. The sample coins are required to be sealed and carefully preserved in a pyx under the joint care of the Superintendent and Assayer for delivery to the commission. The coins are delivered to the Philadelphia mint and carefully guarded, awaiting trial by the commission. The commission is divided into three working committees: counting, weighing, and testing. Silver coins only are tested, and gold, of course, when issued. Copper and nickel coins and the foreign coins occasionally coined at our mints are not tested. The Counting Committee selects the pyx coin envelopes at random and checks through a counting machine the number of coins in each envelope with that marked on the package. The Weighing Committee selects coins, also at random, from the envelopes, alternating between those for individual assay and those for the "mass melt." Records are kept of such coins in both lots, and the coins are taken to the assayers at the mint, who do the actual melting in the presence of the committee and test to find the silver content. The assays on individual coins usually develop silver content from a high of 900.6 to a low of 898.4, while the mass melt runs from 900 to 898.9. The Weighing Committee in turn selects coins from the envelopes and weighs them against a set of sealed coin weights supplemented by a set of grain weights certified by the National Bureau of Standards at Washington, and coins are weighed to an accuracy of 0.01 grains. While a legal deviation in weight of 1.5 grains is allowed, the tests of coins over a period of years have developed a difference of only about 0.84 grains heavy to 0.85 grains light, with an average deviation of but 0.29 grains. There are scales at the Philadelphia mint so delicate that a human hair could be weighed, and the difference in weight between a plain sheet of paper and one on which a pencilled line two inches long would be registered. Each committee makes its report to the chairman, and after general approval by all members, the meeting is over for another year. Members are not paid, although transportation is provided for, and they receive a copy of the Annual Assay Commission medal in bronze with the individual member's name engraved on the edge. Much importance has been placed on the work performed by the commission, so much so that in 1801, when the government moved from Philadelphia to Washington and the session was overlooked, President Adams, on having his attention called to the omission, immediately ordered it to be held in April of that year. In one way, the commission's work has been lightened since the number of mints decreased to only two, Philadelphia and Denver, and there is no gold coinage to consider. The half dollar will now be the only silver coin tested.

United States Mints and Mint Marks

At the present time there are two mints in operation, at Philadelphia and Denver. Until quite recently San Francisco had a mint, which was established in 1854 and closed in 1955.* There have been other mints at various times:

Philadelphia—1792 to date. No mint mark excepting on the wartime five-cent piece 1942 to 1945.
New Orleans—1861-1909. Mint mark O.
Charlotte, North Carolina—(gold only) 1838-1861. Mint mark C.
Carson City, Nevada—1870-1893. Mint mark CC.
Dahlonega, Georgia—(gold only) 1838-1861. Mint mark D.
Denver, Colorado—1906 to date. Mint mark D.
San Francisco—1854 to 1955. Mint mark S.

The half cents, large cents, and flying eagle cents were all issued at the Philadelphia mint and have no mint marks. Indian-head cents of 1908 and 1909 have the "S" mint mark under the wreath on reverse. The two-cent bronze and three-cent nickel have no mint mark. The only three-cent silver having a mint mark is dated 1851 with New Orleans "O" on reverse. Shield nickels have no mint marks, and the only Liberty nickels with mint marks are the 1912 "S" and "D," reverse to left of "Cents." Buffalo nickels show mint marks under the words "Five Cents"; Jefferson nickels, reverse on right of building. Jefferson five-cent wartime issues 1942 to 1945 have the mint mark above dome on reverse. Incidentally, while these are commonly called mint marks, they also serve the purpose of calling attention to the different composition of the coins, somewhat similar to the placing of arrows through dates of quarter dollars and half dollars in 1853, and again in 1873, to indicate a change in weight. Half dimes show the mark on

* Partly reactivated in 1964 for quarter dollars and cents bearing no mint mark.

reverse either below or inside wreath. Positions of other mint marks are as shown below:

Lincoln cents—under date.

Dimes—older types, reverse below or within wreath; Mercury—1916 to 1945—reverse to left of fasces; Roosevelt type, left of bottom of torch on reverse.

Twenty cents—reverse under eagle.

Quarter dollars—older types, reverse under eagle; standing Liberty type, to left of date; Washington type, reverse under eagle.

Half dollars—1838 and 1839 O above date; others to 1915, on reverse under eagle; 1916, on obverse; 1917, on obverse and reverse; after 1917, on lower left reverse; Franklin type, above bell beam; Kennedy type, on reverse at left near claw and laurel.

Dollars—old types, on reverse under eagle; peace type after 1921, on reverse above eagle's tail feathers.

Trade dollars—on reverse under eagle.

Gold dollars—reverse under wreath.

Quarter eagles ($2.50)—1838 and 1839, over the date; other dates before 1907, on reverse under eagle; Indian-head type 1908-1929, on reverse lower left.

Three dollar gold—reverse under the wreath.

Half eagles ($5.00)—same as quarter eagles.

Eagles ($10)—reverse under eagle; after 1907, at left of value.

Double eagles ($20)—old types, on reverse under eagle; St. Gaudens, after 1907, above the date.

Gold was discovered in Georgia in 1830, and shortly thereafter in North Carolina, Virginia, and Alabama. As a result, in 1838 two mints were established in the South, at Dahlonega, Georgia, and Charlotte, North Carolina, and were operated until 1861. These mints coined gold only. It is of interest to note that these two Southern mints used gold from local gold mines, and at the time they were established, this Georgia and North Carolina gold was the best to be had in this country. Nevertheless, the mints ran for many years after gold was discovered in California, and it was not until the start of the Civil War that they were closed. In fact, as late as 1884

Georgia delivered $10,000 in gold bullion to the Philadelphia mint, while North Carolina delivered over $50,000 for the same year. The mint marks of gold coins minted at Dahlonega and Charlotte were D and C, respectively; these coins are becoming scarce and are much in demand by collectors. At the present time and almost for the entire period from 1792 to date, coins issued at Philadelphia show no mint marks. World War II changed the traditional picture for coins issued at Philadelphia, which had shown no mint marks from 1793 to 1942. A coin without a mint mark was therefore considered to have come from the Philadelphia mint. In 1942 the P mint mark appeared for the first time on any coin when it was shown on the five-cent piece. This was shown as a large letter above Monticello, and coins issued in San Francisco and Denver were shown with S or D in the same position. These letters are essentially mint marks, but as pointed out previously, they serve another purpose, since almost a hundred years before, in 1853, an arrow through the dates of quarters and half dollars was used to denote a change in the metallic content of the coin. The five-cent piece issued between 1942 and 1945, containing 56 percent copper, 35 percent silver, and 9 percent manganese, was restored to its regular copper-nickel composition in the last-named year, and the mint marks reverted to other positions on the coin, the larger P, S, or D being discarded. Since the San Francisco mint closed, there has been a considerable demand for coins with the S mint mark, even those of recent years, and it is expected that in time this demand will increase. The mint at Carson City, Nevada, was established in 1870, and continued in operation until 1893, with mint mark CC. This took care of a good deal of the silver coinage, particularly silver dollars, and even at this late date a good many of the latter are found to be in existence in uncirculated condition. Silver dollars of this mint, however, from the years 1870, 1871, 1872, and 1873 are exceedingly rare and, in uncirculated condition, high priced.

Composition and Designs

Our national currency, as we know it today, seems such a simple system that we seldom realize how much earnest consideration was given to its beginnings. There was no easy path to follow, and it would have been simpler for the committee in charge of working out a system to continue in the English system, using pounds, shillings, and pence. We can be everlastingly thankful to Thomas Jefferson, whose report of 1784 carried most weight in the ultimate adoption of the decimal system. His arguments were, of course, aided in some measure by the aversion of the young republic to calling its monetary unit a "crown," after such a tremendous struggle to shake off the authority of the English crown. This republican idea was responsible, in fact, for the firm resolve not to show any ruler's, or for that matter any man's, portrait on the new coins. Washington himself was strongly opposed to the movement to have his portrait appear on the first coins. The simple head of Liberty, in one form or another, was the favorite for many years, succeeded by Liberty seated, and by symbolic portraits of Liberty, such as the Indian.

The question of the metals to be used was also an important one to consider. Gold is the ideal metal for coinage. Platinum is too expensive, although it has been used at times in Russia and for special issues in other countries. Gold was not too plentiful, yet there was an adequate supply for coining purposes, and it could be minted into coins with a minimum of waste. Silver was considered second best, being about half as heavy as gold and plentiful for purposes of coining. Copper, not being a precious metal, was considered suitable for the small coins, cents and half cents. Other metals such as tin, lead, zinc, and nickel were too plentiful and too cheap to be considered. It was also thought that the use of too many metals for coins would lead to confusion. The last-mentioned metals, however, have been used as alloys, and it may surprise some people to know that the present-day "nickel" is 75 percent copper and only 25 percent nickel. In fact, our nickel will not react at all to a magnet, while the nickel coins of some countries are readily attracted. The silver coins, dollars, half dollars, quarters, and dimes are 10 percent copper. The cent is 95 percent copper and 5 percent tin and zinc.

It was prescribed at the opening of the mint that each dollar was to contain 371.25 grains of pure silver, or 416 grains of standard silver. Silver was to be coined in conjunction with gold at a ratio of eighteen to one. There have been several changes, regulated by Congress, since 1792, so that at present no gold at all is coined, and the silver dollar would contain 412.50 grains if any were minted.

Some European countries have at times used the billon system of coinage. This means that coins contain a base alloy with only one half, or as low as one quarter, silver. These billon coins are not considered honest currency by most people, as they are not of the full value. They are a depreciated currency, primarily issued to yield a profit to the government. It is a credit to our government that in all the ups and downs of our monetary history, through times of depression and panic, even through periods of political corruption, the billon system has never been used, or even considered. Of course, there have been lawful changes in the weight and fineness of our gold and silver coins.

The resolution of Congress dated April 6, 1792, establishing the mint, prescribed the devices and legends for the new coins and stated that:

Upon one side of each of the coins there shall be an impression emblematic of Liberty with an inscription of the word "Liberty" and the year of coinage; upon the reverse of each of the gold and silver coins there shall be the figure or representation of an eagle, with the inscription "United States of America"; and upon the reverse of the copper coins there shall be an inscription which shall express the denomination of the piece, namely, cent, or half cent, as the case may require.

The Goddess of Liberty was chosen as the usual representation of that symbolic figure. The head was often shown with the familiar Roman liberty cap, worn by freed Roman slaves. In connection with the showing of the Liberty head and cap, an odd design is shown on the cents of 1793, 1794, 1795, and 1796, called the "Liberty cap" cents, in which the cap is not on the head of Liberty, but to the left and barely touching the flowing hair. On the half cents of 1793 and 1794 the Liberty head faces left, and the cap, resting on a pole, is to the right of the flowing hair, while on half cents of 1795 to 1797, the Liberty head faces right, and the cap is touching the flowing hair to the left, as in the cents of 1793 to 1796.

The eagle was considered our national bird and also represented freedom. At one time the Philadelphia mint actually had a live eagle as a pet, which also served as a model for some of the early coins. Unfortunately, it was killed in the mint machinery. The eagle has been represented in many different aspects, from the spare thin eagle of the early dollars to the robust and full-winged specimens that appear later on. He was not the unanimous choice as a national bird; some people have preferred the turkey, because he is native American and more symbolic of our early traditions. However, the eagle had its defenders, and while some have derided the appearance of the thin fellow on some early coins, he has as often been defended as the ideal young fledgling, and therefore most appropriate for the coinage of a new country.

The stars shown on coins were originally meant to represent the states, and it was at first the practice and intention to add a star for each state as it was admitted into the Union. However, this was later found to be impractical because of the rapidly increasing number of states. Stars are no longer shown on cents, nickels, or dimes, and are generally shown in representation of the original states, to the number of thirteen, on quarters, half dollars, and silver dollars. On the "Standing Liberty" quarter dollars, in use from 1916 to 1930, the thirteen stars are shown on both the obverse and the reverse.

The act of September 26, 1890, provides that changes in designs of United States coins cannot be made oftener than once in every twenty-five years. There have been design changes in all denominations since then. Within a comparatively few years we have seen the Indian-head cent change to the Lincoln-head in 1909, and in January 1959 the reverse of this cent was changed from the wheat sheaves to a picture of the Lincoln Memorial at Washington, D.C. The nickel has changed from the Liberty-head to the Jefferson nickel; the dime, from the Liberty-head, or "Mercury," to Roosevelt; the quarter dollar, from standing Liberty to the Washington quarter; and the half dollar, from the Franklin to the Kennedy half dollar. Even the silver dollar has changed from the Liberty-head to the so-called "Peace" dollar of 1921, even though this denomination has not been coined in quantities for some years. The frequent change in designs has increased interest in coin collecting to a considerable degree, and there is always more or less favorable comment on a new design.

Mottoes

There have been few deviations from the wording of the mottoes appearing on our coins.

"E Pluribus Unum" was first used on the coins of 1795. It appears on the scroll held by the eagle on the Great Seal. This motto was also shown as early as 1786 on the New Jersey "Immunis Columbia" cent. "E Pluribus Unum" has not appeared on coins with any consistent regularity. Thus, it is not shown on the silver dollars from 1840 to 1873, or on the half dollars from 1836 to 1892.

"In God We Trust" first appeared on the two-cent piece of 1864, and was an outgrowth of the religious fervor created by the Civil War. Secretary of the Treasury Salmon P. Chase received so many requests from devout citizens, suggesting that some reference to the Deity be shown on our coins, that on November 30, 1861, Secretary Chase wrote the director of the mint at Philadelphia requesting that a "device be prepared without delay with a motto expressing in a few words the recognition of the trust of our people in God." The one most responsible for the motto was the Rev. M. R. Watkinson of Ridleville, Pennsylvania, who wrote the Secretary suggesting a motto on the theme of God, Liberty, Law. A bronze pattern for a ten-dollar gold piece with the motto "God Our Trust" was prepared, and a pattern of a two-cent piece dated 1863 shows the bust of Washington and the legend "God and Our Country." The motto as it now appears was finally selected, and first shown on the two-cent piece of 1864, as mentioned. This motto has not always been shown on our coins, but every time it has been omitted, since its first appearance in 1864, such a clamor has been raised for its restoration that it now appears on all minor coins. It was not until 1957 that the motto "In God We Trust" appeared on our paper money, and it is now shown on the reverse of all one-dollar bills. The first were issued October 1, 1957, and are the silver certificates designated as Series 1957. The older bills bore the designation "Series of 1935." There were other changes in the design of the bill at that time, 1957, all of them minor except the deletion of the large "One" on the right side in favor of "One Dollar," which was added above the seal of the Treasury. New machinery was used at this time, making it possible to print on dry paper.

It is significant that the portrait of a living person on our coins is not looked upon with favor, even by the recipients of this honor. There are no regular issues showing a portrait of a living man. But with commemorative coins we have not always observed this rule. The Alabama half dollar of 1921, for example, shows the portrait of the then Governor of Alabama, Thomas E. Kilby, and Senator Carter Glass, when still living, was given a place on the Lynchburg half dollar of 1936. There is no law forbidding the showing of any national figure's likeness on our coins; it is rather popular sentiment that has governed our practice in this respect. Senator Glass strongly objected to the showing of his portrait on this commemorative issue.

Almost anyone whose importance justifies the honor may have his portrait shown on commemorative coins after death. For example, Ira Allen, founder of Vermont, is shown on the Bennington half dollar of 1927; Cecil Calvert is shown on the Maryland half dollar of 1934; Joseph T. Robinson, on the Arkansas Robinson half dollar of 1936; and on other commemorative coins, Lafayette, Monroe, Adams, and Moses Cleaveland, founder of Cleveland, Ohio, are shown. All of these men are more or less nationally famous. On other coins, however, designers have gone far afield for portraits, as in the many purely symbolic likenesses of Pilgrims, Indians, Dutch settlers, and so on; while the Bridgeport, Connecticut, half dollar of 1936 is in a class by itself, showing P. T. Barnum, the famous showman, who made his home in that city for many years.

Many foreign issues in times past have shown the full name of the designer, a practice dating from ancient Greece and continued in several countries of Europe; many early crowns, including the Papal scudi, show the complete name of the designer or engraver. But the general custom has been to show simply the initial of the designer. The use of the designer's full name has its good features, but has never been popular with us. The nearest attempt to show the name of the engraver was made in 1836 with the silver dollar designed by Christian Gobrecht. However, no regular issues bear his name, and the trial or pattern pieces showing his full signature are called "Gobrecht Dollars," and command a very high price.

Designers' initials are shown on many American coins. The first such initial is found on Indian-head cents of 1864, which bear an "L" on the ribbon in honor of the designer, J. B. Longacre.

The Lincoln-head cent of 1909 showed the initials VDB, for Victor D. Brenner, the designer, on the bottom of the reverse; but the letters were discontinued in that position after 28,000,000 had been issued. They are now placed under the bust in such minute characters that they can be seen only under a magnifying glass. The reverse of the cent with the new design also shows the initials FG at the lower right side of the memorial for the designer Frank Gasparro, a sculptor and engraver at the Philadelphia mint. The half dollar of 1916 bears on the reverse the letter W for A. A. Weinman. This letter, for the same designer, also appears on the reverse of the winged-head, or Mercury, dime. The initials JS for John (R.) Sinnock, mint engraver, appear on the truncation of the neck on the Roosevelt dime. They also appear under the shoulder on the Franklin type half dollar, first issued in 1948. The obverse of the standing-Liberty type quarter dollar bears the letter M for Hermon MacNeil; the Buffalo or Indian-head nickel had the initial F under the date on the obverse for J. E. Fraser. The Washington type quarter dollar, first issued in 1932, has the designer's initials under the head, JF for John Flanagan. The earlier Liberty-head dime showed the initial B for Charles E. Barber under the head. His initial also is found under the Liberty head on the quarter dollar of that type and on the Liberty-head half dollar. The letter M appears on the Liberty-head, or Morgan type, silver dollar for George T. Morgan, the designer.

There have been many different designers of our commemorative coins. Mint engravers have executed many of these designs; in fact, engravers Charles E. Barber and G. T. Morgan designed, either alone or in collaboration, no less than fourteen commemorative coins. G. T. Morgan is also credited with the design of the "Morgan Dollar," which preceded the present "Peace Dollar" of 1921, which was designed by Anthony de Francisci, who also created the design for the Maine Centennial half dollar of 1920. Laura G. Fraser, wife of J. E. Fraser, already mentioned as the designer of the Buffalo nickel, was the designer of the Alabama, Grant, and Fort Vancouver half dollars and the Grant gold dollar; while both Mr. and Mrs. Fraser designed the Oregon Trail half dollar. The Long Island Tercentenary half dollar of 1936 was designed by Howard Kenneth Weinman, son of A. A. Weinman. Other women besides Laura G. Fraser have designed commemorative coins, including Gertrude K. Lathrop, who designed the New Rochelle and Albany half dollars; Constance Ortmayer, the Cincinnati half dollar; and Brenda Putnam, the Cleveland half dollar.*

* The obverse of the Kennedy half dollar was designed by Gilroy Roberts, former chief sculptor at the mint, and shows his initials on truncation of the

The new Jefferson nickel of 1938 was designed by Felix Schlag, of Chicago. A native of Germany, who had been only nine years in America at that time, Schlag won the open competition for this piece against 390 entries. The nickel at the time received both favorable and unfavorable comment, but the design is pleasing to most people. Incidentally, Mr. Schlag received the prize of $1000 for his design, although his initials do not appear on the coin.* The two-dollar bill is not popular in most places; therefore, it may be news to some that the design is in general the same as the Jefferson nickel—bust of Jefferson obverse, and Monticello, his home, reverse.

The fasces (a bundle of sticks tied together, with the head of an ax protruding) is a relic of ancient Rome and an emblem of power carried by the lictors at triumphal occasions. It was accepted as the emblem of the Fascists of Italy and in this connection caused some comment because of its use on our dime. However, the Mercury dime was adopted in 1916, several years before Mussolini came into power. The fasces as a symbol has been used by various countries, not so often on coins, but in other ways, as in the national seal or coat of arms of France. It also appears on the reverse of our Gettysburg half dollar of 1936.

In forming collections of large cents, half cents, and other denominations, it is well for the beginner to confine himself principally to the collecting of types, rather than to attempt to secure a complete collection of die varieties and consecutive dates. The noncollecting layman always finds it a source of wonder, and sometimes of amusement, to meet a coin collector who has, for example, a complete set of consecutive dates of Lincoln cents, Buffalo nickels, or other sets; and there undoubtedly is something to be said for the layman's viewpoint. "Your set of cents," he says, "all have the same design, even

---

bust. The reverse showing the presidential coat of arms was designed by Frank Gasparro, head engraver at the mint.

* They will appear on the 1966 and later issues.

though the dates are different. Why bother with more than one of a kind?" However, there are many young collectors who endeavor to complete a set of Lincoln cents with all dates and mint marks. There is a certain fascination in finally securing all of the hard ones and at last having a complete set, and it is certainly an innocent pastime, though not one that will add much to one's numismatic knowledge.

The Indian-head cent, which preceded the present Lincoln-head cent, is familiar to all of us. It may surprise some people to know that the Indian is not an Indian at all, but the portrait of Sarah Longacre, daughter of James B. Longacre, chief engraver of the mint from 1844 to 1869. The Indian has proved to be popular on other coins as well; no less than four commemorative half dollars bear the likeness of an Indian, as well as the familiar Buffalo, or Indian-head, nickel.

The Lincoln cent was adopted in 1909 to replace the Indian-head. That year the country celebrated the one-hundredth anniversary of the birth of Abraham Lincoln. The designer of the cent was Victor D. Brenner, who used as his model a Civil War photograph of Lincoln. Brenner, also, like the designer of the Jefferson nickel, claimed this as his adopted country, having emigrated from Russia, where he was born in 1871. It is of interest to note that both our present cent and nickel were designed by men who were not natives of this country but were born in other countries and came here as young men. Brenner was nineteen years old when he arrived in New York. Abraham Lincoln's portrait is also shown on the Illinois Lincoln commemorative half dollar of 1918. With the issuance of the Lincoln cent with new reverse, it is interesting to note that Lincoln actually appears on both the obverse and reverse, since his full-length statue is shown in the center of the Lincoln Memorial on the reverse.

There is a certain fascination for coins no longer issued,

such as the half cents, which have always been a popular collection and a series which, in some instances, is quite hard to complete. However, a collector of types who does not go in too much for dates will have no trouble. There have been many different designs of half cents, as this was undoubtedly one of the most widely used coins of our forefathers. It is rather hard in this day and age to try to think of anything that could be purchased for a half cent, but evidently the thrifty people of an earlier age had many occasions to use such a coin.

A set of bronze two-cent pieces is not hard to complete; there are only eleven varieties. These could have been acquired a few years ago in uncirculated condition at very moderate cost. However, like all other coins, they have risen in price. The 1873 proof is about the hardest to obtain, and would cost over $700. The three-cent nickel is another good series, and for these the 1877 and 1878 proofs are expensive, about $800 and $200, respectively.

Another interesting collection is the three-cent silver piece. There are not many dates to worry about, and those from 1863 to 1873 inclusive are the really expensive ones, being found in proof only. It is rather hard to get this denomination in a reasonably good condition. This is the smallest silver coin ever issued in this country; in fact, the smallest in size of any metal, and, since it is very thin, the wear and tear is considerable.

The half dimes, while not commanding the same attention as some of the other series, such as the large and small cents and commemorative coins, are popular, and some of them are hard to obtain.

The hardy five-cent nickel makes a good collector's item in proof and uncirculated coin. The famous 1883 nickel without "Cents" under the "V" is interesting to new collectors. This is not a rare coin; uncirculated specimens may be obtained for as little as $4. There are several stories regarding the omission of the word "Cents," the most popular being that it was left off in error by the engraver and that the omission caused so much comment that, after several millions were coined, the same date was reissued with the word "Cents." Incidentally, the one with the word "Cents," in uncirculated condition, sells for about $35. One writer claims that some unscrupulous people used to gold-plate the coin and pass it for a five-dollar gold piece, and that they were accepted as such too. Another well-known nickel, at least by reputation, is the 1913 Liberty-head nickel, which is used extensively by certain dealers in their advertising as a "come-on" for the sale of their coin books, at a quarter or more per book. The story is that a half dozen of these nickels were slipped out of the mint by an unscrupulous mint employee, leaving exactly that half dozen on the loose somewhere around the country. Whether this story is true is impossible to say, or, for that matter, the story that five of these nickels were originally owned by Colonel Green, son of the famous Hetty Green, were later sold by his estate, and are now held in the collections of several individuals. The writer has seen three different 1913 Liberty-head nickels.

The silver twenty-cent piece can form one of the smallest collections of all, since it was issued from 1875 to 1878, and only in 1875 and 1876 in any but proof condition. People did not take to the coin, since it was too similar in design and size to the quarter dollar, and coinage was discontinued in 1878.

There are good coin-record books on the market, as mentioned elsewhere, giving the dates of issue of all of the United States coins and numbers minted; therefore, this information is not shown here. However, a short list is given of the particularly rare dates of some of these coins, together with the dates of issue:

Half cent (1793-1857)—None issued: 1798, 1799, 1801, 1812-1824, 1827, 1830. Issued in proof only: 1836, 1840-1848. Rare dates: 1793, 1796, 1852.

Large cent (1793-1857)—None: 1815. Rare dates: 1793 wreath, 1793 chain, 1799-1804.

Flying eagle cent (1856-1858)—Rare date: 1856.

Indian-head cent: Copper-nickel (1859-1864)—Rare dates: 1859-1861.

Bronze (1864-1909)—Rare dates: 1864 with L on ribbon, 1872-1877, 1908 S, 1909 S.

Lincoln-head cent (1909 to date)—Rare dates: 1914 D, 1922 no mint mark.

Two-cent bronze (1864-1873)—Rare dates: 1864 small motto, 1872.

Three-cent nickel (1865-1889)—Rare date: 1887.

Three-cent silver (1851-1873)—Rare date: 1855. All proofs: 1863-1873.

Five-cent nickel (1866 to date)—Shield type: 1866-1883. Rare dates: 1867 with rays, 1871-1875.

Liberty-head type (1883-1912)—Rare dates: 1912 D, 1912 S.

Indian-head or buffalo type (1913-1938)—Rare dates: 1915 D, 1918 D over 7, 1924 S, 1937 D (3-legged variety).

Jefferson type (1938 to date)—Rare date: 1939 D.

Half-dime silver (1794-1873)—Rare dates: all early dates 1794-1805, 1849 O, 1853 O no arrows, 1864-1867, 1871 S.

Dime silver (1796 to date)—None issued: 1799, 1808, 1812, 1813, 1815-1819, 1826, 1922, 1933. Rare dates: Liberty-head 1796-1804, 1809.

Liberty-seated type—1837 (small and large dates), 1838 O, 1856 S, 1860 O, 1870 S, 1871 CC, 1872 CC, 1873 CC, 1874 CC, 1885 S.

Barber, or *Liberty-head type*—Rare dates: 1894 O, 1894 S, 1895-6 O, 1895-6-7 S.

Winged-head Liberty, or *Mercury type*—1916 D, 1921 D.

Twenty-cent silver (1875-1878)–Rare dates: 1876 CC, 1877, 1878.

Quarter-dollar silver (1796 to date)—None coined: 1797, 1803, 1808, 1814, 1816, 1817, 1826, 1829, 1830, 1922, 1933.

Liberty-bust type—Rare dates: 1796, 1804, 1822 (25 over 50¢), 1824-1838.

Liberty-seated type—Rare dates: 1849 O, 1856 S, 1857 S, 1858 S, 1861, 1870-1873 CC mint, 1877 S.

Barber, or *Liberty-head type*—1896 O and S, 1897 O and S, O and S mint marks through 1905, 1914 S.

Liberty-standing type—Rare dates: 1916-1918 S over 7, 1919 S, 1927 S.

Washington-head type—Rare dates: 1932 D and S, 1936 D.

Half-dollar silver (1794 to date)—None issued: 1798, 1799, 1800, 1804, 1816, 1922, 1924, 1925, 1926.

Liberty-bust type—Rare dates: all early dates to 1825, 1839 O.

Liberty-seated type—Rare dates: 1839-1842 O small date, 1846 large date, 1850, 1852 O, 1855 S, and all S mints to 1865. All CC mints 1870-1874, 1878 S and CC.

Barber, or *Liberty-head type*—1892 O and S, all O and S mint dates to 1909, 1913 S, 1914, 1915.

Liberty-walking type—1917 D and S (on obverse), 1919 S, 1920 D and S, 1921 D and S, 1923 S, 1935 S.

Dollar silver (1794-1935)—None issued: 1805-1835, 1837, 1874-1877, 1905-1920.

Liberty-head type—Rare: 1794-1804, most dates of Liberty-seated type in the 1840s and 1850s; all CC mints 1870-1873.

Liberty-head, or *Morgan type*—1893 S, 1898 O, 1903 O, 1904 O.

Peace type—1934 S is the rarest after the 1921.

The first few decades of the nineteenth century found the country gradually becoming more used to its own currency, and therefore less dependent on foreign issues. In time, of course, such foreign coins as formerly were freely passed became objects of curiosity instead of money used in daily trade. Nevertheless, money of all kinds was scarce during the early part of the century. The condition was somewhat helped in 1836 by enlarged quarters and the installation of more modern machinery in the mint, thus increasing the output of small coins. Still, the shortage continued until well into the middle of the century. Thus, Richardson Wright, in *Hawkers and Walkers in Early America*, says that "in New England barter was the only feasible method for rural sales," and "in the country actual money was even a rarity." Elsewhere he writes, "Frederic Law Olmsted in his travels in the Southern Cotton States during 1853-54 heard of men in isolated country districts who had never seen a dollar in their entire lives. For some years in some districts of the South the Spanish dollar was the only silver known. It was cut with a hammer and chisel into halves and quarters (hence our common names for such values), the quarters into 'bits,' and these again into 'picayunes.' "

The conditions prevalent during the eighteenth century, when almost all foreign currency was acceptable, left little impression on the customs and language of the people. As far as the language goes, a word here and there reminds us of the old conditions. For example, a cent is still called a penny by most people. Literally, an English penny is two cents in our money. This is a habit of speech that has never been broken, and it is small wonder, because until almost the middle of the nineteenth century even the daily newspapers showed their price opposite the date line as "One Penny." A picayune was a Spanish copper coin valued at about 6½ cents in our money. "Two bits" is a common expression which we have mentioned before.

When we say that only our own currency is acceptable at the present time, an exception must be noted in the case of Canadian money, which is readily accepted in all places within about 100 miles of the Canadian border in the upper New York State section, Vermont, and other New England states, as well as in practically all states in the Middle and Far West within a reasonable distance of Canada. In the fifties the Canadian dollar was worth more than ours. This has changed, and now a Canadian dollar is worth about 93 cents. Therefore, it would be accepted at a discount, and it would be to our advantage to change United States dollars into Canadian at a bank before spending in Canada. Also, any Canadian money brought back would be subject to a discount when exchanged here.

Mexican money does not pass in states near that country, because of the great difference in the exchange value.

Examining the list on page 101, we note that, even omitting gold coins, which are no longer minted, there are several denominations never seen in circulation today, including the half cent, two-cent bronze, three-cent nickel or silver, half-dime silver, twenty-cent silver, and trade dollar. The half cent and one cent were undoubtedly a concession to the English custom of coining halfpenny and penny. The two-cent piece was undoubtedly useful at the time it was coined, as were the three-cent nickel and silver pieces, although the three-cent silver coin was rather impractical due to its small size. The half-dime silver outlived its usefulness when the five-cent nickel appeared. It is hard to see how the twenty-cent silver served any useful purpose, except to use some of the large surplus of silver on hand at the time. Anyway, minting of it was soon stopped, since people complained that it was often mistaken for the quarter dollar. The trade dollar was a dollar intended solely for competing with other silver currency in securing an increased trade with China and the Far East.

Many other things of interest having to do with the early nineteenth century can be recorded. Paper money entered into the scene, too, when in 1812 Congress authorized an issue of $36,000,000 in Treasury notes to finance the war with England. Later, paper money was issued to an alarming extent through the medium of state banks. In 1810 there were less than a hundred state banks, but this number increased more than fivefold, so that in 1834 there were well over five hundred. Practically all of them issued their own bank notes against their own capital. Newspapers of the time show "New York Bank Note Tables" for banks in all states east of the Mississippi River and for Canada. Many collectors of paper money specialize in broken bank bills. It is interesting to note that these Bank Note Tables show quotations for bank notes in such expressions as "Par," "Uncertain," and, not rarely, "Broken." The latter expression means that the bank had stopped operations, or was "broken." In the 1830s there were many such "broken" banks, particularly in the Middle West.

During the period of President Andrew Jackson's administration, the issuance of bank notes by state banks grew to a national scandal. Every bank issued notes, often with no financial backing at all. Many notes bore the names of banks that never existed. In 1836 the Bank of the United States, chartered in 1816, closed its doors; and on May 10, 1837, the New York banks suspended specie payments, followed shortly after by banks in all the New England states.

When specie payments stopped, metal coins were hoarded, causing a shortage of all kinds of small coins, which was filled by notes of small denomination, as low as 6¼ cents, issued by business firms and individuals. These notes, or "shinplasters," were unacceptable to the public, and the need for a metal substitute became acute. The result was the so-called "hard-times" tokens, which were issued in great numbers by individuals and business houses, to the number of almost two hundred different varieties. These tokens were struck in copper or brass, and were similar to the merchants' tokens or store cards issued for many years in England. Other tokens of a political nature were also issued and are known as "Jackson cents," named after Andrew Jackson. The merchants' tokens are of particular interest, having been issued in New York, Massachusetts, Rhode Island, Connecticut, New Jersey, Ohio, and in some

Southern states. They bore advertisements of groceries, shoe stores, coal dealers, and many other business establishments.

The political tokens are historically interesting. For example, one such token reads "Special Payments Suspended—May tenth, 1837" and on the other side shows a donkey and "I follow the illustrious steps of my predecessor." Another shows an eagle carrying a safe, while still another variety shows a turtle with a safe on its back. Some read "General Andrew Jackson—the Nation's Pride," or "General Andrew Jackson—Hero of New Orleans."

Charles I. Bushnell, in his *Arrangement of Tradesmen's Cards, Political Tokens, Election Medals, Medalets, etc.*, published in New York in 1858, lists most of such tokens issued before and during this period.

The next most extensive use of tokens and merchants' store cards occurred during the Civil War. These generally showed some reference to the Union, such as "Union Forever," or a patriotic theme, "Army and Navy," "The Flag of Our Country," and so on. Some had an Indian head on the obverse and have sometimes been mistaken by the uninitiated for some sort of odd cent.

Around Jackson's time Dr. Lewis Feuchtwanger came in for a certain share of prominence by endeavoring to induce the government to use his composition of "German silver" instead of copper for minor coins. Feuchtwanger was born in Bavaria and emigrated to America, where he established the first German drugstore in New York City. He later became interested in mineralogy, and in 1839, with permission of the government, issued a quantity of one-cent pieces, since called "Feuchtwanger cents." In 1864 he also issued three-cent pieces in the same metal; these, however, did not circulate.

In connection with the Feuchtwanger cent, a letter written on January 4, 1838, by R. M. Patterson, Director of the

United States Mint, to Senator Thomas H. Benton, is of interest, as shown in Senate Document 122, Twenty-fifth Congress, Second Session, January 22, 1838. It is in regard to "opinions to be laid before the Committee on Finance of the Senate regarding Lewis Feuchtwanger who was asking to substitute his invention of German silver for copper in the coinage of the United States." Then an analysis of the metal is shown:

First, German silver argentan, or packfong, is a complicated and very variable compound, as shown by the following table of analyses:

1. Composition of the best argentan manufactured by Henninger at Berlin, in Prussia.
2. Packfong, a compound long since employed in China.
3. Another kind of packfong said to cost in China one quarter of its weight in silver.
4. A compound known in Central Germany for more than 80 years as the Luhler White Copper.
5. Argentan manufactured in England.

The reasons for recommending against the use of the metal as given by Director Patterson were that coins of this metal were easily imitated and could be debased with cheaper mixtures of tin or zinc; it looked so much like silver that there would be confusion between coins of the two metals, and there was some doubt as to whether it was more economical than copper, as copper planchets cost $.32 a pound at that time. At the present time copper is quoted at slightly over $.35 a pound.

About this time also—to be exact, in 1836—the first proposal to coin a gold dollar was broached in Congress, but the request met with such opposition that it was laid aside for many years, and it was not until 1849 that the first gold dollar was issued. Gold dollars were then issued for forty years, until discontinued by the act of September 26, 1890.

In 1845 the Chamber of Commerce and prominent citizens of New York City memorialized Congress to establish a mint in that city, pointing out how much more important New York was as a money center than Philadelphia. Congress, or some members of it, looked favorably on the request as late as 1852, but the idea was finally abandoned. During the later discussions on the proposal, it was pointed out that in 1851 the large sum of $39,809,476 in gold arrived at the Port of New York by steamer from California. This was considered an extraordinarily high amount at that time. Compared with the quantities which arrived at New York during the 1930s, however, it was quite trivial.

New York was not the only city that felt important enough to be favored with a government mint. St. Louis, Omaha, Louisville, Athens (Ga.), and Quincy (Ill.), all put in their bids in 1878, when Congress was looking for a suitable location. None of these cities was selected for the location of a mint, and the tendency thereafter was rather toward lessening the number of United States mints than increasing it. The Carson City mint closed in 1893, having operated from 1870. The New Orleans mint, suspended in 1861, reopened in 1879, finally closing completely in 1909.

During this period of our history (1830-1861) many private gold coins were struck in various sections of the United States. The first of such gold coins was issued in 1830 by Templeton Reid, an assayer at the gold mines of Lumpkin County, Georgia, the same county in which the Dahlonega mint was located. The Templeton Reid coins were issued in three denominations ($2.50, $5, and $10) at Reid's private mint. The gold was of the best quality, and later many of the coins were melted because they were worth more as bullion than the face value of the coins. Therefore, these Templeton Reid coins are scarce and, in fact, the $10 denomination is unobtainable. The pieces were inscribed "Templeton Reid—Assayer" and "Georgia Gold $5," or other denomination.

Shortly after Reid issued his first gold piece, probably early the following year (1831), Christopher Bechtler started his private mint in Rutherford, Rutherford County, North Carolina. Later he turned the mint over to his son, August Bechtler. Bechtler, Senior, turned out $1, $2.50, and $5 pieces, while the younger Bechtler issued $1 and $5 pieces from 1842 to 1852. The first coins issued at Christopher Bechtler's mint were inscribed in one of three ways: "Georgia," "Carolina Gold," or "North Carolina Gold," in the order of the quality of the gold contained in the pieces, Georgia gold being the finest. These coins are relatively scarce, although it is claimed that several million dollars' worth were issued, almost $2,-250,000 worth, according to Bechtler's books. The coins issued by August Bechtler bear his name, "A. Bechtler," and "Carolina Gold."

With the discovery of gold in California in 1848, many private mints issued gold pieces there, and in Oregon and Utah as well. These mints were in operation in California until 1855, and in some other states as late as 1861. A law was passed on June 4, 1864, forbidding the issue of such coins by private individuals. In Colorado some mints operated in 1860 and 1861, where the "Pikes Peak" gold pieces were turned out by J. Parsons & Company and J. J. Conway & Company, bankers.

In California, many millions of dollars in private gold coins were in circulation during this period, in all denominations from $5 up. They were issued also in odd denominations and shapes, as in the case of those of Moffat & Company of San Francisco, in rectangular ingots—$9.43 and $16; Augusta Humber—$50 octagonal gold piece; and the rectangular slugs of F. D. Kohler, State Assayer of California—$36.55, $40.07,

$45.34, and $54.09. Some high values have been placed on many of the California gold pieces. For example, the Dubosq & Company $10 gold piece of 1850 is valued at $3900; the Massachusetts & California Company $5 of 1849, at $7900; while the Cincinnati Mining and Trading Company $10 gold piece of 1849 sold for $3000.

We sometimes run across the fractional gold pieces of California, in denominations as low as a quarter dollar. Some of these are genuine, while a great many are of no numismatic value and are manufactured by jewelers or others as souvenir pieces. All of the authentic pieces show the denomination, which is not shown on the others.

After the discovery of gold in California, many of the miners in Georgia and North Carolina joined the gold rush. Thus we find that Templeton Reid also issued gold coins in California in 1849, including a $10 and a $25 piece. These, however, never were circulated and are the greatest of rarities among the private issues.

In Utah, the Mormons in Salt Lake City started their private mint in 1849 and began issuing gold pieces in denominations of $2.50, $5, $10 and $20. The coins show an eye and a bishop's mitre on the obverse, and on the reverse clasped hands, with the inscription "To the Lord Holiness." They were issued until 1860.

It is not necessary to give the history of all these private mints and of their operators. Edgar H. Adams, in his *Official Premium List of United States Private and Territorial Gold Coins,* published in 1909, gives a very interesting and complete account of such mints and operators; and we are indebted to this author for most of the information given here on these coins. A complete list of the private and territorial gold coin issuers is shown below:

Georgia

Templeton Reid

North Carolina

Christopher Bechtler
August Bechtler

California

Baldwin & Company
Cincinnati Mining & Trading Co.
Dubosq & Company
Dunbar & Company
Augustus Humbert
Kellogg & Company
Miner's Bank
Moffat & Company
Massachusetts & California Company
Norris Grieg & Norris
J. S. Ormsby & Company
Pacific Company
Templeton Reid
Schultz & Company
Wass, Molitor & Company

Colorado

Clark & Company
Clark, Gruber & Company
J. J. Conway & Company
John Parsons & Company

Oregon

Oregon Exchange Company

Utah

Salt Lake City Mint

also:

State Assay Office of California
United States Assay Office of Gold

While we are on the subject of gold coins, mention may be made of the United States gold $20 piece of 1849, valued at $35,000. This coin is unique and is in the U.S. Mint collection of coins. Another high-priced gold coin is the 1877 $50 pattern, sold at one time for $10,000.

Encased postage stamps are one of the most curious forms of money. They came into use during the Civil War period and were issued under J. Gault's patent, August 12, 1862. They served the same purpose as tokens and took the place of small change, owing to the disappearance of metal currency. Encased stamps consisted of postage stamps in denominations of from one to ninety cents, encased in metal holders faced with mica, and bearing on the back of the holders the advertisements of various business firms. They are now scarce, and are becoming more so with the passage of time, so that the prices of good specimens should increase. It is safe to say that, before many more years have passed, they will be out of reach of the average collector. Some of the well-known varieties are mentioned below:

Ayer's Sarsaparilla
Lord & Taylor
Sand's Ale
Aerated Bread Company
White, the Hatter
Drake's Plantation Bitters
Kilpatrick & Gault
New York Life Insurance Company

The only names we now recognize among these as firms still in business are Lord & Taylor and the New York Life Insurance Company. There are many others which are hard to get and, when offered at auctions, command high prices, often from $20 to $90 or more. Encased postage stamps were a unique form of money, and very fragile for passing from hand to hand. Since their introduction in this country, they have been used in various other countries, including Denmark, Russia, Sweden, Norway, and particularly in Germany, immediately after the First World War. In 1917, Imperial Russia used as money stamps that were not encased, but simply bore an inscription on the back. The foreign encased stamps, like the original United States issues, nearly all have advertising of private firms (patent medicines, breweries, etc.) and contain postage stamps of small denominations under isinglass. Some of these later varieties are enclosed in metal backs, while others have celluloid backs. The late European encased stamps, while interesting and having the possibilities of a good collection of different advertisements, are not expensive. The German specimens of the 1920s are most numerous and in most cases cost less than $1, while the Scandinavian issues are slightly higher.

Encased postage stamps may be placed in the same category as tokens, in that they took the place of metal coins which were scarce or hoarded by the panic-stricken public. Hoarding of money, a curious manifestation of fear of impending events, has been prevalent in all countries for thousands of years. The people of our country are not so prone to engage in this practice as are those of many European countries, such as France and the Middle European countries. The ancients, too, are noted for the numerous hoards of coins of all kinds that were buried in odd places, and in many cases have come to light only during recent times. For example, in England thousands of hoards of ancient Roman coins have turned up, many of them in recent years, even in London and its environs. These hoards give indications of the history of the times in which they were buried. If the times were hard and wars were numerous, or long-lasting, the hoards increased; coins of the emperor then in power, or his immediate predecessors, are found in profusion.

In America a hoard of old coins is found occasionally, most of them with dates shortly before the Civil War. Wars are always a good excuse to hoard coins and other things, and often the coins are left where they were buried because the owner never comes back. Present practice tends more toward storing currency away in bank vaults for safekeeping, rather than burying it in the ground. Owing to the unsettled money conditions in many European countries at this time, much of our money, particularly paper currency, is being hoarded by foreigners.

The postage stamps proved unsatisfactory because they became soiled and torn so quickly. A postage currency was therefore issued, each note bearing a facsimile of the current 5-cent and 10-cent postage stamps. Postage currency was issued in denominations of 5, 10, 25, and 50 cents; the 5-cent issue showed the bust of Jefferson; the 10-cent issue, the bust of Washington as used on the 5-cent and 10-cent postage stamps. The 25-cent note consisted of five 5-cent stamps. The faces of the notes were engraved and printed by the National Bank Note Company, while the backs were engraved and printed in some cases by the government, and in others by the American Bank Note Company. Following the postage currency, in 1863, small-sized notes were issued in values of 5, 10, 25, and 50 cents, called fractional currency. Still later, in 1864, these fractional-currency bills were also issued in 3-cent denominations, and in the fourth issue, 1869, a 15-cent note was also included. These notes continued to be issued until 1876.

While the North had its own money troubles during the Civil War, the Southern states were in even worse condition. Fiat money was the curse of the South during the war. While the Confederate paper money was issued with high hopes of future redemption, in 1865 the South knew that their cause was lost and that the paper money of the Confederacy, and the numerous issues of "shinplasters" or fractional notes of the separate states, were practically worthless.

In 1865, in Richmond, Virginia, an ordinary cotton dress sold for $150, a pair of blankets for $125, and a pair of shoes for $25. Foodstuffs, clothing, and household furniture were proportionately high.

Many of the Confederate paper notes are interesting. For example, the $50 Confederate bill of September 2, 1861, states: "Six months after the ratification of a treaty of peace between the Confederate States and the United States, the Confederate States of America will pay Fifty Dollars to bearer. Fundable in Confederate States stock bearing Eight Per Cent interest."

The $100 Confederate bill of September 23, 1862, states: "Six months after the ratification of a treaty of peace between the Confederate States and the United States, the Confederate States of America will pay One Hundred Dollars to bearer, with interest at two cents per day. Richmond, September 23, 1862." A picture of a Negress with a basket of cotton is shown, an old-fashioned train and cars, and a steamship. Interest was paid on such bills only until January 1, 1863.

One of the $10 Confederate issues shows Jefferson Davis and a picture of artillery. It is dated February 17, 1864, but the time for redemption has now advanced to "Two years after the ratification of a treaty of peace between the Confederate States and the United States of America." One of the $5 Confederate bills, also dated February 17, 1864, shows the Capitol at Richmond, and bears the two-year clause.

The fractional notes of the Southern states are also of great interest. The Alabama 25-cent note of January 1, 1863, reads: "The State of Alabama will pay to bearer in Confederate States

Treasury Notes, when presented at the State Treasury in sums of Twenty Dollars and upwards, twenty-five cents. Montgomery, January 1st, 1863."

Other states issued fractional notes and larger paper bills, such as the State of Georgia's $5 notes of April 6, 1864, issued in Milledgeville, Georgia. These were also redeemable in Confederate Treasury notes issued after the First of April, 1864, if presented within three months after maturity; otherwise not redeemable, except in payment of public dues.

Louisiana, Virginia, Mississippi, North and South Carolina, and other Southern states also had issues of fractional and dollar currency, all of which were of no more value than the Confederate notes at the end of the war.

It happened that the New Orleans mint, being in Confederate territory, created its own history during the war. Up to this time the mint had been issuing regular United States currency in silver and gold bearing the "O" mint mark. When the mint was threatened by the forces of the Confederacy, Secretary of the Treasury John A. Dix, on January 29, 1861, sent a telegram to the commanding officer at New Orleans containing the message, "If anyone attempts to haul down the American flag, shoot him on the spot." These words appear on one of the better known Civil War tokens, which is called the "Dix Token."

Nevertheless, the New Orleans mint fell into Confederate hands, and an attempt was made to operate it in coining money for the State of Louisiana and for the Confederate states, using the same mint officials and workmen who operated the mint during Federal control. However, a shortage of metal necessitated closing the mint on April 30, 1861.

The result of the Southern efforts to operate the mint at New Orleans at least accounted for some of the rarest coins in our history, the Confederate half dollars. The obverse of the regular United States issue was used with an original reverse. There were only four of these half dollars coined, and they are valued at between $2000 and $5000 each.

As we go along—not too hurriedly, it is hoped—it must be remembered that volumes can be written, and have been, on all phases of numismatics. A reader who wants information about an individual fractional or state note can consult a book or numismatic article bearing on such notes alone. The same is true of Confederate money, Civil War tokens, and store cards, as well as the regular issues of United States coins and paper money. Our intention here is not to bear too heavily on any one variety of our past or present money. Everyone cannot claim more than a curious interest in state bank notes, for example. Nearly all of us, however, do have a real interest in anything pertaining to the history of our country, and on this score it is safe to say that much of that history is reflected in our money. The designs of our coins touch upon a great many of the high spots of our national history. This is true mainly of the commemorative issues, of course, where we have an indelible record of such events as the discovery of America, the landing of the Pilgrims, and other events, down to the opening of the San Francisco Bay Bridge, if the latter can be considered a truly national event.

This accounts for the fact that two, three, or several of the more interesting examples of each form of money put out at various intervals are explained here, and others practically ignored. Some of the others which are not mentioned may be of greater rarity, and at times of more interest, from one or two points of view. But the ones explained in these pages are those most likely to be encountered by the ordinary man who takes an interest in such things.

We have mentioned the suspension of specie payments in 1861, which, by the way, was the third time in our history that such action was necessary, the first being 1814-1817, after the war of 1812, the second in 1837. These were all panic times. There were other panics, though, such as the one of 1857, when the banks suspended operations for two months. The years of 1860-1861, and 1866-1869 were also panic years, but it is sometimes hard to determine where a depression ends and a panic begins; and if the matter of time is considered, the period from 1860 to 1869 can be thought of as one continuous depression.

Suspension of specie payments, hoarding of coins, and deflation have troubled other countries before us. As an interesting illustration, we might mention: "A Letter to a Member of the Honorable House of Commons, in Answer to Three Queries: (1) Whether there is no other cause of our want of bullion and coin but the clipping of money, and the expense of the war. (2) Whether it is possible to manage the trade of the nation without a supply in specie equal to what we have lost. (3) Whether a forced credit can be an expedient under our present circumstances—with some other remarks in relation to our own and foreign manufactures. London, printed and sold by E. Whitlock, near Stationers Hall, 1697."

The letter is neither addressed nor signed, but it is of interest as an illustration of the point that money troubles are by no means new.

The country recovered quickly after the Civil War, much more quickly than if such a heavy catastrophe, in proportion to population, occurred today. By 1870 the agitation began for a resumption of specie payments, but, while many tracts and letters to the newspapers were favorable to the resumption, nothing was done until 1878.

The panic of 1873 resulted in the demonetizing of silver through a curious set of circumstances, and the placing of the country on the gold standard. In the Coinage Act of February 12, 1873, the silver dollar of 412½ grains, known as the "standard" silver dollar, was entirely left out, although it had been in use since 1837, when it replaced the 1792 silver dollar of 416 grains. In its place we find the Trade Dollar of 420 grains. Much has been written of the Coinage Act, which practically demonetized silver. Bitter debate ensued in Congress and elsewhere, for it was felt that the public had been defrauded. President Grant signed the bill and later said he did not know himself that it provided for the demonetization of silver; the joker being that one simple clause stated: "The silver coins of the United States shall be a legal tender at their nominal value for any amount not exceeding $5 in one payment."

A healthy outcry was raised in many quarters for the restoration of the old standard silver dollar of 412½ grains and the discontinuance of the trade dollar. The trade dollar itself was a makeshift coin designed to further trade with China in competition with the Spanish and Mexican dollars. However, it did not serve this purpose very well. It was a coin slightly larger than a standard silver dollar and was coined in the years 1873 to 1878, and in proof only from then to 1883. Trade dollars were redeemed in 1887 for standard silver dollars. They bore many of the characteristics of the other silver coins and in addition showed the weight (420 grains) and fineness (.900 fine), as prescribed by law.

In 1874 Germany, which had always used silver as a base, abolished its use and went on the gold standard, having received a large sum in gold from France as a war indemnity. This had a bearing on the silver market, of course, and added to the money troubles of this country. England and France were in the midst of panic and depression, and it was pointed out by the silver advocates that all former depressions involving England, France, and the United States had lasted about the same length of time, whereas France, by keeping to her silver currency, recovered much sooner from the panic of 1873 than did the others.

In this year, 1873, much gold was shipped to this country from Europe; on the other hand, much of our gold was sent to Europe; so that we have the curious spectacle of gold from here to Europe passing other gold on the high seas bound for this country.

On May 22, 1877, William Wheeler Hubbell of Philadelphia secured a patent for having invented a "new and useful metal alloy for coin, consisting of certain proportions of gold, silver, and copper." His proposal to change the metal in our coins received much attention from the Mint Director, Dr. H. R. Linderman, and the Finance Committee of the Senate. The resulting coins were called "goloids," and the goloid dollar was issued in an experimental way—containing 258 grains of silver .900 fine. The half dollar would therefore contain 129 grains, and the quarter dollar 64.59 grains.

In the correspondence between Doctor Linderman, Mr. Hubbell, and others it was pointed out that many more of these goloid dollars could be minted than of the standard or trade dollars, and in searching for enlarged or additional minting facilities, the interesting fact was brought out that the mint machinery from the old Charlotte mint was at that time stored in Philadelphia. This machinery, however, was not suitable for silver coinage.

The formula for the goloid dollar was: 36 parts gold, 864 parts silver, and 100 parts copper, resulting in a coin that looked a lot like a standard silver dollar, but much lighter. Mr. Hubbell wrote on January 18, 1878, to Alexander H. Stephens, Chairman of the Commission on Coinage, that he had received one of the new strikings of the goloid dollars, and it was "of a beautiful purple golden tint." They are referred to, however, as of somewhat different composition than the first pattern, consisting of 40 parts gold and 860 parts silver. Except for the purple tint, they looked more like silver than gold. In order to secure a yellow in the goloid dollar, it would have been necessary to increase the gold contained in it by 50 percent.

The goloid dollar was favored by some because it came near to fulfilling the requirements of the act of 1792 calling for a sixteen to one ratio between gold and silver; this would almost have been secured in one coin.

The design of the goloid dollar consisted of a Liberty head with "E Pluribus Unum" on the obverse, and on the reverse: "United States of America. Goloid 1G-24 S.9 fine 258 grs. One Dollar." These dollars are good types of pattern coins. The question of how such a dollar would be accepted, if at all, by foreign countries, seems to have determined against its use.

While the 1860s produced many things of interest to present-day numismatists in the form of tangible mementos of the period, such as tokens, coins, encased postage stamps, and paper money, greenbacks, and fractional currency, the following twenty years were notable more for the number of legislative acts having to do with money and the discussions that followed. Probably no other period since the framing of the Constitution, except the present, produced as many millions of words as were spoken and written by the advocates of silver, who favored bimetallism (the use of both silver and gold) at a fixed relative value, and the champions of gold alone, called the monometallists.

Members of Congress and private individuals made many speeches and wrote their views on all occasions, and the newspapers contained letters from all sorts of individuals who insisted that they, and they alone, had the solution to the country's financial problems.

Even the trimetallists put in their bid, evidently feeling that they also should have some attention. They were mostly copper mining interests, and manufacturers, who wanted to know why the currency should not be based on three metals—gold, silver, and copper. However, with so many other voices raised in favor of either silver or gold, or both, the trimetallists received little if any attention.

The seventies and eighties, however, were of interest in connection with our currency in many ways. The student who has time to find and read old government records and mint reports will find many enlightening, and sometimes amusing, entries. For example, the report dated June 10, 1877, on the operation of the Bureau of Engraving and Printing at Washington, D.C., investigated by a committee appointed by Secretary of the Treasury Sherman. During this time the National Bank notes were not printed in their entirety by the government. In 1875 the plates for the faces of the notes were transferred from the three private bank note companies to the Bureau of Engraving and Printing, and by 1877 all the plates for both fronts and backs were in the Bureau, with one exception—the black backs of the $5 notes which were still being printed by the National Bank Note Company, American Bank Note Company, and the Columbia Bank Note Company, all of New York City. Even with the additional work of printing all the notes, some members of Congress insisted that the Bureau was very much overmanned, an accusation which finally ended in an investigation by the committee appointed by the Secretary of the Treasury.

Many hardly believable things were brought out in the report of the investigation. Between April 1 and May 1, 1877, 589 of the employees of the Bureau were discharged, leaving 419 still on the payroll. The Bureau at that time evidently needed some investigating. The great number of employees was due to political preference, but also in large part to the laxity of rules which helped to place a great number of worthy Civil War veterans and their widows and relatives on the government payroll. The officials of the Bureau were of course in no way at fault. They were given the employees and were expected to find places for them.

The report of the committee reads:

> Our investigation shows that the force of the Bureau has for many years been in excess of the requirements of the work and that this was the case even when the work was greatest. We are informed, and believe, that the force employed at the Bureau was for a number of years twice as great as was required for the proper performance of the work, and in others three times as great as was necessary. In one of these divisions a sort of platform had been built underneath the iron roof about seven feet above the floor to accommodate the surplus counters. On this shelf, on parts of which a person of ordinary height could not stand erect—deprived of proper ventilation, and exposed in summer to the joint effects of the heated roof and the fumes of the wetted paper beneath—were placed some thirty or more women who had received appointments and for whom room must be found. It now appears that the room was of ample size without this contrivance to accommodate persons not really needed, that the surplus force stowed away aloft was entirely unnecessary, and that some of them at times for lack of occupation whiled away the time in sleep.

The same investigation also brought out that "There are on hand 40,000 yards of thin muslin used for wiping the ink from the steel plates, the quantity being sufficient at the present rate of usage to last for nearly nineteen months. The explanation given for so large a purchase of muslin was the lowness of price at the time."

A later report of Rules and Regulations for Operating the Mint, dated 1881, calls attention to the act of February 12, 1873—Sec. 5459:

Every person who fraudulently by any act, way, or means, defaces, mutilates, diminishes, falsifies, scales or lightens the gold or silver coins which have been or may hereafter be coined at mints of the United States shall be imprisoned for not more than two years and fined not more than $2000.

This is evidently the origin of the often expressed idea that it is a crime to mutilate or deface United States coins, which, of course, is true, but not in the sense that many people suppose. The common practice of making bracelets, brooches, and other pieces of jewelry and novelties from coins does not seem to be a crime. The offense against the law is in fraudulently lightening gold or silver coins by nicking, slicing, plugging, etc. There seems to be no law against a man lighting his cigar with a $10 bill if he so chooses.

The proponents of the coinage of silver and its use, along with gold, as a legal tender, finally found enough support in Congress to pass, over the President's veto, the Bland-Allison Act of February 28, 1878, which led to the resumption of specie payments on January 1, 1879, and the restoration of the standard silver dollar of 412½ grains in place of the trade dollar. The act provided for silver bullion purchases of not less than $2,000,000 and not more than $4,000,000 per month, to be coined into dollars. It also provided that any holder of gold or silver bullion to the value of $100 or more had the right to take the same to any United States mint and have it coined free of charge.

The country became a dumping ground for the world's silver. The trade dollar, which had been coined only to a limited extent in this country, that is, as legal tender for payments up to $5, ostensibly for use in China, found its way back to the melting pot in great numbers. In spite of its supposedly limited usage, great quantities were in circulation and held by banks in all parts of the country, particularly in the Northeastern states. It had not proved a great success in China and other parts of the Orient in competing with Spanish, Mexican, and other silver dollars; and now great numbers came back to the Treasury, bearing in many instances the chop-marks of the Chinese merchants, which are curious cross marks cut into the silver coins to test the silver content of the metal.

Conditions did not improve with the passage of the Bland-Allison Act, and the bitter battle between the advocates of gold and silver continued until, by the Sherman Silver Purchase Act of July 14, 1890, the amount of silver purchased was modified. This act provided for the purchase of 4,599,000 ounces per month to be paid for in Treasury notes, redeemable in gold or silver coin, thus still leaving the silver dollar a legal tender.

Finally, during the panic of 1893, at a special session of Congress called on November 1, the purchasing clause was repealed, which, as was expected, caused an outcry from the silver advocates, foremost among whom was William Jennings Bryan, who campaigned for some years on the "free Silver" issue.

The year 1883 brought out an issue which, though strictly speaking not American, is still of interest to collectors of United States coins, and is usually classed with them. These were the Hawaiian silver coins. Hawaii was then known as the Sandwich Islands, and was not under United States authority. The Islands were annexed to the United States in 1898, and became a territory on June 14, 1900. In 1883 the Hawaiian Government issued one million dollars in silver coins, which were designed by Charles Barber of the Philadelphia mint, and minted at the San Francisco mint in denominations of $1, $.50, $.25, and $.10. They bore the bust of Kalakaua I, King of Hawaii, and are considered a most interesting small set of coins. At the present time Hawaii uses United States money exclusively, as the fiftieth state of the Union.

Among the other outlying United States possessions, Puerto Rico used the coins of Spain until 1898, among which were the peso of Alphonse XIII, 50 centavos, 20 centavos, 10 centavos, and 5 centavos. Puerto Rico was also ceded to the United States on August 12, 1898, and at the present time coins of this country are used.

The Virgin Islands, formerly known as the Danish West Indies, were purchased from Denmark in 1917. While under the Danish flag, these islands used Danish coins minted in Copenhagen. They consisted of gold ten and four dalers; silver 40 cents and 50 bits (10 cents); nickel 25 bits (5 cents); and bronze 10 bits (2 cents), 5 bits (1 cent), and 2½ bits (½ cent). The Virgin Islands now use United States coins. The Danish coins formerly used there are of interest because, like the Hawaiian issue of 1883, they are part of an obsolete coinage and will not be issued again.

The Philippine Islands were ceded to the United States by Spain on December 10, 1898. Prior to that time Spanish and Mexican silver pesos were used almost exclusively. It was not until 1903, however, that conditions in the Islands quieted down, and in that year the first Philippine peso was coined in the Philadelphia and San Francisco mints. In 1907 other pesos were minted in both these mints, and also silver 50 centavos, 20 centavos, and 10 centavos; nickel 5 centavos; and bronze 1 centavos and ½ centavos. Most of the Philippine coins show a seated male figure with anvil and hammer, or a standing female figure with a sledge hammer, leaning on an anvil. A volcano appears in the background. The one centavo shows the denomination half in English and half in Spanish, "One Centavo," and all the coins show the country as "Filipinas." These coins were minted in Philadelphia and San Francisco

1. Dekadrachm—King Eukratides of Bactria (Persia), about 290 B.C.
2. Tetradrachm of Alexander the Great.
3. Denarius—Tiberius, Roman Emperor.
4. Denarius—Nero, Roman Emperor.
5. Tetradrachm of Mark Antony and Cleopatra.

1 2 3
1 2 3
4 5 6
4 5 6
7 7 8 8

1. Piacenza-Parma—Odoardo Farnese, Fifth Duke of Piacenza and Parma (1622–1646), Gold 4 Ducats.
2. France—Louis XIV Gold Louis d'Or, 1696 Lyons (D) Mint.
3. Brazil—Peter I (1823–1831) Gold 4000 Reis.
4. Brazil—Peter II (1831–1889) Gold 10,000 Reis, 1850.
5. Iraq—Ghazi I (1933–1938) Silver 50 Fils, 1938.
6. Denmark—Christian IX 2 Kroner.
7. Holland—Charles V (1515–1555) Gold Real.
8. Egypt—Fuad I (1917–1922) 5 Milliemes.

2	1	2
3	1	3
	6	4
	6	5

1. Bolivia—Charles IV Proclamation Peso 1789, La Plata.
2. Peru—Gold 20 Soles, 1863.
3. South Peru—Gold 8 Escudos, 1838.
4. Spain—Charles III (1759–1788) 8 Scudos.
5. Bolivia—Charles II (1665–1700) Cob 8 Reales, 1677 Potosi Mint.
6. Guadeloupe—Charles IV 8 Reales, with cressalated cut and crowned "G" counterstamp.

1. Irish Free State Florin.
2. Spanish Netherlands and Belgium-Brabant—Philip II (1556–1598) Double Dalder.
3. Sweden—Charles XIV 60 Skilling.
4. Sweden—Gustav III 3 Riksdaler.
5. Spanish Netherlands—Philip V Ducaton, Antwerp.

2 1
3 4
3 5
2 6

1. Scudo of Pope Pius VII.
2. Quarter Testone of Pius VII.
3. Baiocco of Pius VII, 1801.
4. Two Baiocchi of Fuligno Pius VI.
5. Scudo of Pope Leo XII, 1823.
6. Half Testone Pius VII.

1	1
2	2
3	3
4	4

Papal Coins—Innocent XII

1. Scudo Innocent XII—Portrait; Rev. St. Michael.
2. Testone—Arms; Rev. Fig. Dispensing Charity.
3. Half Scudo—Portrait; Rev. Pope Kneeling.
4. Half Scudo—Portrait; Rev. Noah's Ark.

1 2 1

3 3

2

4 5

6

4 5

6

7 7

1. Canada—Victoria 10¢ Silver.
2. England—William III Gold 5 Guineas, 1701.
3. England—George IV Gold 2 Pounds, 1823.
4. England—Edward VII Gold 5 Pounds, 1902.
5. England—George V Gold 5 Pounds, 1911.
6. Australia—George V Silver Florin or 2 Shillings, 1918.
7. New Zealand—George VI Silver Florin, 1937.

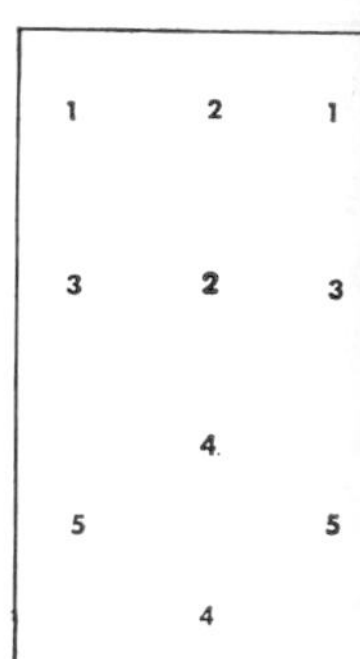

1. Spain—Philip IV (1621–1665) Gold 8 Escudos, 1635.
2. Austria—Medal from "Marriage Taler" 1479 bust of Maximilian and Mary of Burgundy.
3. Spain—Charles II (1665–1700) Gold Doubloon or 8 Escudos.
4. The Netherlands—Albert and Isabella (1598–1621) Gold Double Souverain, Antwerp Mint.
5. The Netherlands—Philip IV (1621–1658) Gold Double Souverain, 1645.

1. China—Sun Yat Sen Dollar.
2. Italy—Victor Emanuele III Gold 100 Lire, commemorating first anniversary of the Fascist March on Rome.
3. Mexico—Gold 8 Escudos, 1853.
4. Austria—Franz Joseph I Gold 100 Corona, 1908, commemorating 60th year of reign.
5. Sardinia—Charles Albert Gold 100 Lire, 1832.
6. Albania—Zog I Gold 100 Franka Ari, 1926.

1 3
2
1 3
4
5 4 5
6 6

1. Pine Tree Shilling.
2. Oak Tree Shilling.
3. Pine Tree Shilling on small planchet.
4. Hibernia or Wood's Coinage Penny.
5. Rosa Americana Penny.
6. Maryland Shilling.

1	2	3
1	2	3
4	5	6
4	5	6
7		7

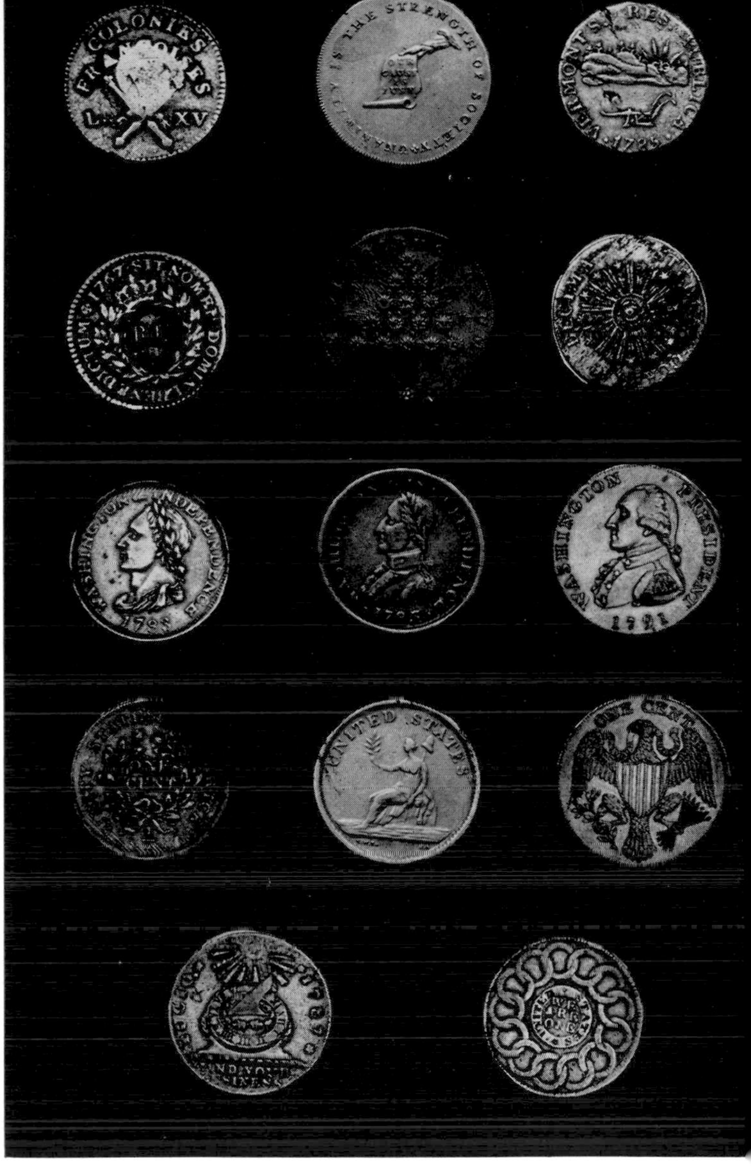

1. French Colonies Token.
2. Kentucky Cent.
3. New Jersey Cent.
4. Washington Cent, laureated bust in robe.
5. Washington Cent, laureated bust in uniform.
6. Washington Cent, uniformed bust.
7. Fugio Cent.

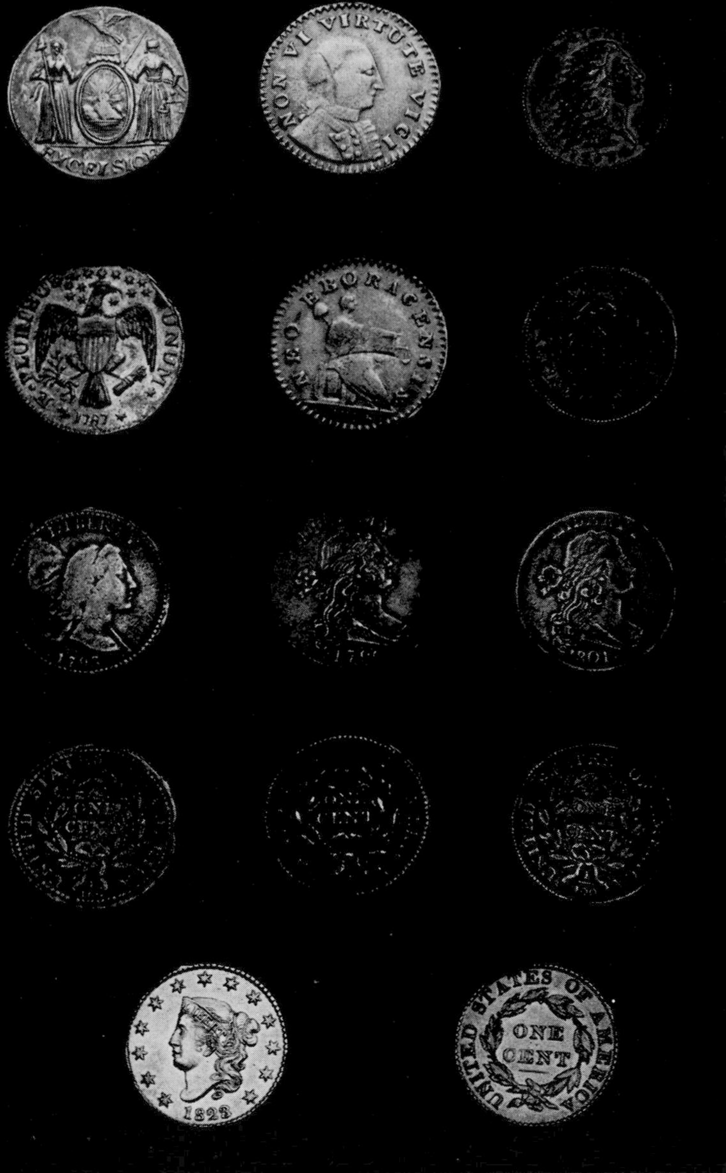

1 2 3
1 2 3
4 5 6
4 5 6
7 7

1. New York—Excelsior Cent.
2. New York—Non vi virtute vici Cent.
3. 1793 Cent, flowing hair.
4. 1793 Cent, Liberty cap with pole.
5. 1796 Cent.
6. 1801 Cent.
7. 1823 Cent.

1 2 3

1 2 3

4 5 6

4 5 6

7 7

1. Twenty-dollar Gold, 1804.
2. Silver Dollar, 1797.
3. Cent, 1807 over 6.
4. Confederate Half Dollar, restrike.
5. Half Cent, 1794.
6. Canadian Victoria 50 Cents, 1871.
7. Three-cent Silver, 1855.

1	2	1
3		3
4	2	4
6	5	7
6	5	7

1. Mormon $5 Gold.
2. United States Assay Office of Gold, San Francisco, $50.
3. Moffat & Company $16 Gold Slug.
4. Gold Dollar, 1852.
5. Bechtler $5 Gold—134 Gr., 21 C.
6. Bechtler $5 Gold—128 Gr., 22 C.
7. Bechtler $5 Gold—140 Gr., 20 C.

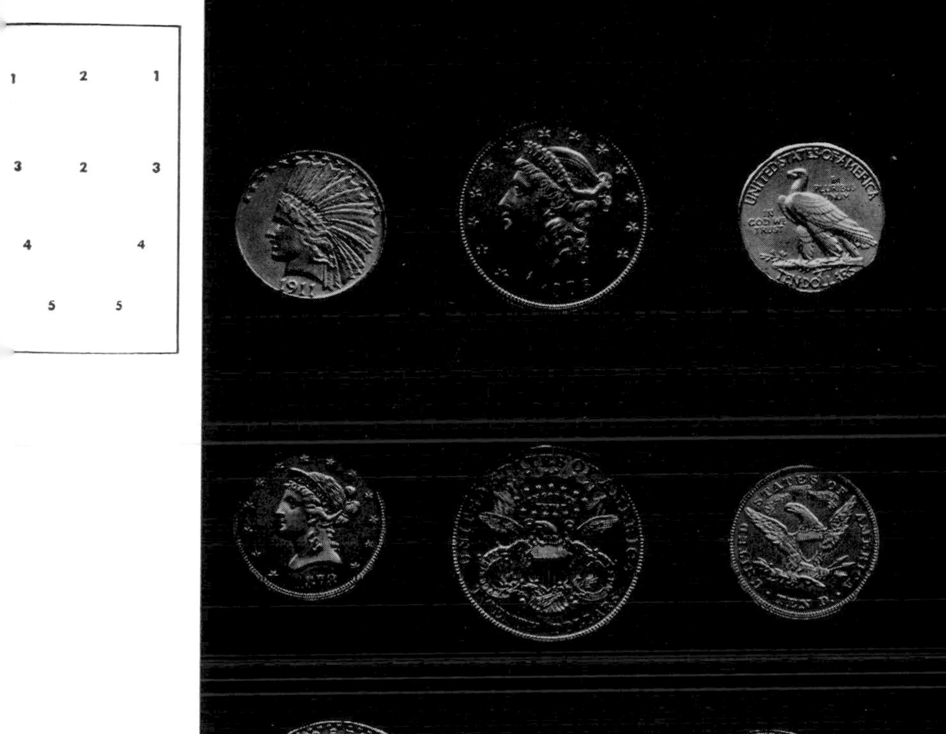

U.S. Gold

1. $10 Gold Eagle, 1911.
2. $20 Gold Double Eagle, 1906.
3. $10 Gold Eagle, 1878.
4. $20 Gold Double Eagle, 1929.
5. $2½ Gold Quarter Eagle, 1859.

1	2	3
4	5	6
7	8	9
10	11	9
12	13	14

1. Brazil—5000 Reis (Santos Dumont).
2. Brazil—2000 Reis (Duke of Caxias).
3. Reverse of Canadian George VI 50¢ Silver.
4. Brazil—1000 Reis (José de Anchieta).
5. Brazil—500 Reis (Diego Feijo).
6. Obverse of Canadian Silver Dollar.
7. Brazil—400 Reis (Doctor Oswaldo Cruz).
8. Brazil—300 Reis (Carlos Gomes).
9. Reverse of Fiji Island Penny; Obverse of Fiji Island Penny (Edward VIII).
10. Brazil—200 Reis (Viscount de Maria).
11. Brazil—100 Reis (Admiral Tamandaie).
12. Liberia—Two Cents, 1937.
13. Liberia—One Cent, 1937.
14. Mozambique (Portuguese Colony) —20 Centavos Bronze.

until after the Manila mint was opened in 1920. The Commonwealth of the Philippines was established in 1925, and from that time all the Philippine Islands coins were minted at Manila, until the Japanese invasion in 1941 when the mint was destroyed. At the close of the war, on July 4, 1946, the country became an independent nation, known as the Republic of the Philippines.

There have been some issues of Philippines commemorative coins, such as the peso of 1936 bearing the busts of Presidents Franklin D. Roosevelt and Manuel Quezon; another peso of 1936, with busts of Governor General Murphy and President Quezon; and the 50 centavos of 1936, with facing busts of Murphy and Quezon. These coins are inscribed "Commonwealth of the Philippines," and on the reverse "United States of America." In 1947 the Republic issued two silver coins commemorating General Douglas A. MacArthur and showing his portrait, one of 50 centavos and one of 1 peso denomination. These are two popular coins and are quite inexpensive.

Cuba, of course, is not a territory or possession of the United States and has its own separate coinage which consists of the silver peso as the unit, with 40 centavos, 20 centavos and 10 centavos; and nickel centavos in denominations of 5, 2, and 1. The coins of Cuba were minted for many years at Philadelphia. In 1953 Cuba issued four coins commemorative of the Marti Centennial, showing a portrait of the Cuban patriot and consisting of 1 brass centavo, and silver 25 centavos, 50 centavos, and peso. We no longer mint Cuban coins.

Panama is another country whose coins have been minted in the United States, at Philadelphia and San Francisco.

The issuance of the first United States commemorative coin, the Columbian half dollar, marks the year 1892 as worthy of note. In 1893 the same coin was issued with that date.

William Jennings Bryan has already been mentioned in

connection with his efforts to place the country on the double standard of gold and silver. His efforts interest collectors as far as the private silver coins are concerned. While the private gold coinage consisted of numerous items, it seems that private silver issues have been neglected, at least until recent years. There have been some, nevertheless; and in 1900 and 1901 the most notable appeared.

In the political contests of 1896 and 1900 an earnest advocate of the free coinage of silver at a ratio to gold of sixteen to one appeared in the person of Joseph Lesher, of Victor, Colorado. He was so firm an advocate of the free silver policy that he issued many octagonal silver pieces, sometimes called dollars, which circulated in many parts of the West. The first of the Lesher dollars were dated 1900 and contained one ounce of silver in the denomination of $1.25. The obverse was inscribed: "Jos. Lesher Referendum Souvenir—One Oz. of Coin Silver Price 1.25 M.F.G.D. Victor, Colo.—1900." The reverse reads: "A commodity—will give in exchange currency coin or merchandise at face value. No.—." They were numbered from 1 to 100, which was the number contained in the first issue.

The second Lesher dollar of 1900 is called the Bumstead type. It depicts a mountain mining town, and underneath: "Pikes Peak Silver Mine—A Commodity—will give in exchange merchandise at A. B. Bumstead No.—." Reverse: "Joseph Lesher's Referendum Souvenir—1 oz. coin silver Price 1.25 Mnf'd Victor, Colo. 1900." A. B. Bumstead conducted a general store at Victor, and the coins were numbered consecutively.

A third Lesher dollar was similar to the above, but stated: "Will give merchandise or cash at any bank." Other varieties were payable at groceries, general stores, clothing stores, and so on.

There was some question of the legality of Joseph Lesher's action in coining these "dollars," and this accounts for his having used the octagonal shape instead of using anything similar to the round silver dollar of the government. He also specifically called them "Referendum Souvenirs" instead of "Dollars." Lesher later secured a patent for the pieces, and there is no record of any attempted prosecution of the coiner for his action in putting out his private issues. The coins were evidently issued in some profusion and circulated in Colorado and other Western states quite freely, but are now comparatively rare and hard to find.

From time to time, some silver-mining states, particularly Colorado, have issued large pieces somewhat like silver dollars, for souvenir purposes, calling them "One ounce of pure silver." However, they were not intended for use as money and there is no reason to believe that they have ever been used as such.

Patterns and proofs have often been mentioned in these pages. We have given details regarding the issuance of proof coins. Patterns, as the name implies, are experimental pieces, the designs of which are sometimes accepted and at other times declined. They are in all denominations, \$.05 to \$20, and in practically all metals and shapes, even to ring-shaped coins with a hole in the center. Patterns are seldom struck nowadays. However, in former years they were issued in great numbers, sometimes two or three hundred or more for the same design, and at others only one, two, or three in number. They were also issued from the first year of operation of the Philadelphia mint, 1792, and thus are especially interesting in showing the complete history of our small coinage and the ideas behind the designs finally used. In 1792 we find patterns of the "disme" and "half disme," and there have also been early patterns of that time struck in pewter, lead, or tin.

The Gobrecht dollars previously mentioned are good examples of patterns, as are the goloid dollars. The Stella, or $4 gold piece, was another experimental piece that never got beyond the pattern stage. It was struck in gold, copper, and aluminum in 1879 and 1880.

Trial pieces are often met with, and are generally listed under patterns. They are not exactly the same, for they are mostly designs that have been accepted and are issued as trial pieces primarily to test the completed dies, usually on softer metals than silver, such as nickel or copper.

Neither patterns nor trial pieces are legal tender. The collector of United States coins will find endless gratification, however, in assembling a collection of either patterns or proofs. In collecting patterns he will come across many fine examples of engraving and workmanship. Most of them are numerous enough to be reasonably priced, but there are some extremely rare varieties.

The late William H. Woodin, Secretary of the Treasury in 1933, was an ardent collector of pattern and other United States coins. He acquired a very complete set of patterns of all varieties from the first issues. In collaboration with Edgar H. Adams, he wrote the most authoritative work on the subject, entitled *United States Trial and Experimental Pieces from 1792 to 1913,* largely superseded by Dr. Judd's book.

No pattern, trial, or experimental pieces may now be secured from the mint.

Commemorative Coins

While our coinage in general use is restricted in design to a certain more or less stereotyped pattern and is changed, at most, every twenty-five years, almost anything goes in the designs which appear on the commemorative coinage.

Commemorative coins, usually in the form of half dollars,

are issued by the government to commemorate some event that is generally of national importance. However, local organizations with enough support in Congress have at times secured approval for issues which commemorate events of little or no interest to natives of other sections. The government coins the commemorative issues, and they are given to a committee which sells them at an advance over the face value. The government receives the face value, and the local authorities spend the balance to celebrate the specific event, build a shrine, or open a museum.

As stated, much leeway is given in the designing of commemorative coins, which have for some years been limited to half-dollar denominations. From 1892 to 1954 there were a great many commemorative coins issued. For the most part, these consisted of silver half dollars; but a quarter dollar, called the Isabella quarter dollar, was coined in 1893, and a Lafayette dollar in 1900. A listing of gold commemorative coins appears on page 141.

The commemorative coins celebrate a noteworthy event in our history. Each issue is considered separately by the appropriate Senate and House committees, and is minted after Congress passes a bill authorizing such issuance.

The first of the commemorative half dollars was the Columbian Exposition half dollar of 1892, followed in 1893 by a similar half dollar. These were designed by C. E. Barber and G. T. Morgan, engravers and designers of many of the regular issues. The Isabella quarter dollar came out the same year, 1893, for the same event at the request of the Board of Lady Managers of the Columbian Exposition held in Chicago. The half dollars show the bust of Columbus, and on the reverse is his flagship, the *Santa Maria,* above two hemispheres. The quarter dollar has the head of Queen Isabella of Spain, and is the only United States coin showing the portrait of a foreign sovereign. The quarter dollar sold for $1, as did the half dollar. However, 950,000 Columbian Exposition half dollars were issued in 1892, and 4,052,105 in 1893. Of the latter number 1,550,405 were returned to the mint for remelting, while only 40,023 quarter dollars were coined; of these, 15,809 pieces remained unsold and were returned for remelting; so that, as a result, an uncirculated specimen of the quarter dollar now sells for $100, many times the price of the half dollar.

The Lafayette dollar of 1900 bears the heads of Washington and Lafayette, and on the reverse a reproduction of the statue of Lafayette erected in Paris.

The above-mentioned coins did not show the mottoes of "In God We Trust" or "E Pluribus Unum."

The general public is unfamiliar with the commemorative coinage, even though most people have encountered an occasional one in circulation. The path of the commemorative is limited generally from the mint to the selling committee, and from there to dealers and collectors. There are exceptions, of course. A large but unknown number of Columbian half dollars were placed in circulation without premium. Others found in circulation are the Stone Mountain, Monroe, Pilgrim, and, more recently, the Carver and Booker T. Washington halves. The circulated commemorative is not often sold to collectors, as the bright uncirculated specimens are more desirable and usually not hard to find. The more expensive Hawaiian ($625), Vancouver ($100), Hudson ($300), Old Spanish Trail ($275), and other high-priced coins are never found in circulated condition, although careless handling and tarnish may sometimes make such coins less acceptable and diminish their value.

Each commemorative half dollar, and, of course, the gold commemoratives, features some event bearing on the history of the United States or an anniversary of some significant event. Thus, the Panama Pacific half dollar of 1915 commemorates the opening of the Panama Canal. The Illinois Centennial half of 1918, while it shows the head of Lincoln and is sometimes called the Lincoln half dollar, celebrates the admission of Illinois into the Union. Some deviations from the principles of the commemorative idea, and the cause of some criticism, are found in the fact that some of these coins were issued in succeeding years. Thus, the Arkansas half dollar was issued in 1935, 1936, 1937, 1938, and 1939 at the three mints, Philadelphia, Denver, and San Francisco, and consists of a set of fifteen coins, the design being changed for 1936 from Indian head to Senator Joseph T. Robinson. The Booker T. Washington half dollar was first issued in 1946 at the three mints, continuing in 1947, 1948, 1949, 1950, and 1951 in all eighteen coins. The Washington-Carver half dollar was issued from 1951 to 1954, inclusive, at each of the mints.

The commemorative half dollars consist of a set of 48 types, which means that number of different designs. A complete set of such half dollars, with all mint marks and years, comes to a total of 142 coins. None have been struck since 1954.

With the possible exception of the colonial issues or the privately minted gold coins, these half dollars are the most interesting series of coins, from a historical viewpoint, ever issued by or for the American people. Most of the half dollars commemorate events that are evident in the name or design, such as the Columbian on the fourth centenary of the discovery of America; the Illinois, Maine, Missouri, Philadelphia, and other centennial coins; the Stone Mountain half dollar, which memorializes the soldiers of the Confederacy; the Oregon Trail and the Old Spanish Trail, which honor various places and episodes of history. The latter have interesting stories, often depicted in their designs.

The Oregon Trail memorial half dollar was issued in 1926, 1928, 1933, 1934, 1936, 1937, 1938, and 1939. It commemorates no particular or specific event or occasion, but the period of time covered by the early half of the nineteenth century and the movement of pioneer settlers over the Trail to the Pacific Northwest.

The Old Spanish Trail half dollar commemorates the 400th anniversary of the amazing wanderings of Alvar Nunez Cabeza de Vaca in 1535 through an untracked wilderness, swamps, bayous, plains, mountains, and deserts from Florida to what is now El Paso, Texas, and even beyond. The coin itself shows the head of a steer, for De Vaca, whose name, Cabeza de Vaca, means literally "head of a cow." The reverse is a map showing the path he took.

The New Rochelle, New York, half dollar, issued in 1938 to celebrate the 300th anniversary of the founding of the city, named after Rochelle, France, by French Huguenots, whose principal stronghold was in that city, shows a colonial figure holding a calf on a rope. The title to the land, which the founders purchased from John Pell, provided that a "fatte calf" be paid each year on June 20. This provision has generally been carried out, but since the city has changed from a rural community to a well-populated city, this has become a rather onerous bargain. Since 1956 the city fathers compromised by giving a roast beef dinner for the Pell heirs, with their consent.

Since the issuance of all commemorative coins depends on Congress, it is interesting to note the language of one or two bills authorizing their issuance, the first covering the Columbian half dollar:

Public Law–No. 203–52nd Congress

An Act to aid in carrying out the act of Congress approved April twenty-fifth, eighteen hundred and ninety, entitled "An act to provide for celebrating the four hundredth anniversary of the discovery of America by Christopher Columbus, by holding an international exposition of arts, industries, manufactures, and products of the soil, mine and sea, in the City of Chicago, in the State of Illinois," and appropriating money therefor.

Be it enacted by the Senate and House of Representatives of the United States of America in Congress assembled, that for the purpose of aiding in defraying the cost of completing in a suitable manner the work of preparation for inaugurating the World's Columbian Exposition, authorized by the act of Congress approved April twenty-fifth, anno Domini eighteen hundred and ninety, to be held at the City of Chicago, in the State of Illinois, there shall be coined at the mints of the United States silver half dollars of the legal weight and fineness, not to exceed five million pieces, to be known as the Columbian half dollar, struck in commemoration of the World's Columbian Exposition, the devices and designs upon which shall be prescribed by the Director of the Mint, with the approval of the Secretary of the Treasury; and said silver coins shall be manufactured from uncurrent subsidiary silver coins now in the Treasury, and all provisions of law relative to the coinage, legal-tender, quality, and redemption of the present subsidiary silver coins shall be applicable to the coins issued under this act, and when so recoined there is hereby appropriated from the Treasury the said five millions of souvenir half dollars, and the Secretary of the Treasury is authorized to pay the same to the World's Columbian Exposition, upon estimates and vouchers certified by the president of the World's Columbian Exposition, or in his absence or inability to act, by the vice-president, and by the director-general of the World's Columbian Commission, or in his absence or inability to act, by the president thereof, and the Secretary of the Treasury for labor done, materials furnished, and services performed in prosecuting said work of preparing said Exposition for opening as provided by said act approved April twenty-fifth, eighteen hundred and ninety; and all such estimates and vouchers shall be made in duplicate, one to be filed with the Secretary of the Treasury, the other to be retained by the World's Columbian Exposition: Provided, however, That before the Secretary of the Treasury shall pay to the World's Columbian Exposition any part of the said five million silver coins, satisfactory evidence shall be furnished him showing that the sum of at least ten million dollars has been collected and disbursed as required by said act; *And provided,* that the said World's Columbian Exposition shall furnish a satisfactory guaranty to the Secretary of the Treasury that any further sum actually necessary to complete the work of said Exposition to the opening thereof has been or will be provided by said World's Columbian Exposition; but nothing herein shall be so construed as to delay or postpone the preparation of the souvenir coins hereinbefore provided for. And there is hereby appropriated, out of any moneys in the Treasury not otherwise appropriated the sum of fifty thousand dollars, or so much thereof as may be necessary to reimburse the Treasury for loss on the recoinage herein authorized.

Section 2. That the appropriation provided in Section One of this act shall be upon condition that the said World's Columbian Exposition maintain and pay all the expenses, costs, and charges of the great departments organized for the purpose of conducting the work of the Exposition, said expenses, costs, and charges to be paid out of the funds of the said World's Columbian Exposition.

Section 3. That fifty thousand bronze medals and the necessary dies therefor with appropriate devices, emblems, and inscriptions commemorative of said Exposition celebrating the four hundredth anniversary of the discovery of America by

Christopher Columbus, shall be prepared under the supervision of the Secretary of the Treasury at a cost not to exceed sixty thousand dollars, and the Bureau of Engraving and Printing, under the supervision of the Secretary of the Treasury, shall prepare plates and make therefrom fifty thousand vellum impressions for diplomas at a cost not to exceed forty-three thousand dollars. Said medals and diplomas shall be delivered to the World's Columbian Commission, to be awarded to exhibitors in accordance with the provisions of said act of Congress approved April twenty-fifth, eighteen hundred and ninety, and there is hereby appropriated, from any moneys in the Treasury not otherwise appropriated, the sum of one hundred and three thousand dollars, or so much thereof as may be necessary, to pay the expenditures authorized by this section; and authority may be granted by the Secretary of the Treasury to the holder of a medal, properly awarded to him, to have duplicates thereof made at any of the mints of the United States from gold, silver, or bronze, at the expense of the person desiring the same.

Section 4. That it is hereby declared that all appropriations herein made for, or pertaining to, the World's Columbian Exposition are made upon the condition that the said Exposition shall not be opened to the public on the first day of the week, commonly called Sunday; and if the said appropriations be accepted by the corporation of the State of Illinois, known as the World's Columbian Exposition, upon that condition, it shall be, and it is hereby, made the duty of the World's Columbian Commission, created by the act of Congress of April twenty-fifth, eighteen hundred and ninety, to make such rules or modification of the rules of said corporation as shall require the closing of the Exposition on the first day of the week commonly called Sunday.

Section 5. That nothing contained in this act shall be con-

strued to supersede or in any manner alter or impair the force or validity of the provisions of Section 15 of the act of Congress approved anno Domini April twenty-fifth, eighteen hundred and ninety.
Approved, August 5, 1892.

By way of contrast, a much shorter act is quoted, one authorizing the coinage of the Old Spanish Trail half dollars:

Public Law–No. 97–74th Congress

H.R. 6372

AN ACT

To authorize the coinage of 50-cent pieces in connection with the Cabeza de Vaca Expedition and the opening of the Old Spanish Trail.

Be it enacted by the Senate and House of Representatives of the United States of America in Congress assembled, That to indicate the interest of the Government of the United States in commemorating the four hundredth anniversary of the Expedition of Cabeza de Vaca and the opening of the Old Spanish Trail, there shall be coined by the Director of the Mint silver 50-cent pieces to the number of not more than ten thousand, of standard weight and fineness and of a special appropriate design to be fixed by the Director of the Mint, with the approval of the Secretary of the Treasury, but the United States shall not be subject to the expense of making the models for master dies or other preparations for this coinage.

Section 2. That the coins herein authorized shall be issued at par and only upon request of the chairman of the El Paso Museum Committee.

Section 3. Such coins may be disposed of at par or at a

premium by said Committee and all proceeds shall be used in furtherance of the El Paso Museum.

Section 4. That all laws now in force relating to the subsidiary silver coins of the United States and the coining or striking of the same; regulating and guarding the process of coinage; providing for the purchase of material, and for the transportation, distribution, and redemption of the coins; for the prevention of debasement or counterfeiting; for security of the coin; or for any other purposes, whether said laws are penal or otherwise, shall, so far as applicable, apply to the coinage herein directed.

Approved, June 5, 1935.

A list of all types of United States commemorative coins follows:

SILVER	*Approximate retail price (uncirculated)*
1893—Isabella Quarter Dollar	$ 85.00
1900—Lafayette Dollar	160.00
1892—Columbian Exposition Half Dollars	6.50
1893—Columbian Exposition	4.50
1915 S—Panama-Pacific Exposition	100.00
1918—Illinois Centennial	25.00
1920—Maine Centennial	30.00
1920—Pilgrim Tercentenary	12.50
1921—Pilgrim Tercentenary	23.50
1921—Missouri Centennial (with 2x4)	175.00
1921—Missouri Centennial (without 2x4)	150.00
1921—Alabama Centennial (with 2x2)	65.00
1921—Alabama Centennial (plain)	45.00
1922—Grant Memorial (with star on obverse)	150.00
1922—Grant Memorial (without star)	25.00
1923 S—Monroe Doctrine Centennial	14.50

SILVER (*cont.*)		*Approximate retail price (uncirculated)*
1924—Huguenot-Walloon Tercentenary		$ 25.00
1925—Lexington-Concord Sesquicentennial		14.00
1925—Stone Mountain Memorial		7.50
1925 S—California Diamond Jubilee		25.00
1925—Fort Vancouver Centennial		100.00
1926—Sesquicentennial of American Independence		20.00
1926-1939—Oregon Trail Memorial	Each	25.00
1927—Vermont Sesquicentennial		50.00
1928—Hawaiian Sesquicentennial		625.00
1934—Maryland Tercentenary		36.50
1934-1938—Texas Centennial	Each	20.00
1934-1938—Daniel Boone Bicentennial	Each	18.00
1935-1939—Arkansas Centennial	Each	10.00
1935—Connecticut Tercentenary		55.00
1935—Hudson, N. Y., Sesquicentennial		300.00
1936 S & D—San Diego, California-Pacific Exposition		25.00
1935—Old Spanish Trail		275.00
1936—Rhode Island Tercentenary		20.00
1936—Cleveland, Great Lakes Exposition		25.00
1936—Wisconsin Centennial		27.50
1936—Cincinnati Musical Center		150.00
1936—Long Island Tercentenary		20.00
1936—York County, Maine, Centennial		30.00
1936—Bridgeport, Connecticut, Centennial		35.00
1936—Lynchburg, Virginia, Sesquicentennial		52.50
1936—Elgin, Illinois, Centennial		50.00
1936—Albany, New York, Charter		60.00
1936 S—San Francisco-Oakland Bay Bridge		35.00
1936—Columbia, South Carolina, Sesquicentennial		37.50
1936—Arkansas Centennial—Robinson		35.00
1936—Delaware Tercentenary		50.00

1936—Gettysburg Memorial		$ 50.00
1936—Norfolk, Virginia, Bicentennial		85.00
1937—Roanoke Island, North Carolina, 350th Anniversary		35.00
1937—Battle of Antietam, 75th Anniversary		100.00
1938—New Rochelle, New York, 300th Anniversary		85.00
1946—Iowa Centennial		25.00
1946-1951—Booker T. Washington Memorial	Each	4.50
1951-1954—Washington-Carver	Each	3.00

GOLD

1903—Louisiana Purchase Jefferson Dollar	$115.00
1903—Louisiana Purchase McKinley Dollar	115.00
1904—Lewis and Clark Expedition Dollar	400.00
1905—Lewis and Clark Expedition Dollar	400.00
1915 S—Panama Pacific Exposition Dollar	80.00
1915 S—Panama Pacific Exposition Quarter Eagle ($2.50)	385.00
1915 S—Panama Pacific $50 round	6000.00
1915 S—Panama Pacific $50 octagonal	4750.00
1916—McKinley Memorial Dollar	110.00
1917—McKinley Memorial Dollar	175.00
1922—Grant Memorial Dollar (with star)	335.00
1922—Grant Memorial Dollar (without star)	365.00
1926—Philadelphia Sesquicentennial Quarter Eagle ($2.50)	75.00

Note: The 2x4 on the Missouri Centennial half dollar indicates that Missouri was the 24th star in the flag. The 2x2 on Alabama Centennial half dollar indicates Alabama was the 22nd state. The star on the Grant half dollar and gold dollar has no significance.

Transportation and Sales Tax Tokens

We have mentioned Civil War tokens and "Jackson cents" and other items such as store cards. The collecting of transportation tokens is also worthy of a few words in itself. A good many people all over the world make a hobby of collecting railroad tickets, ferry and bus tickets, and transfers, or weekly trolley, bus, or railroad passes. This practice, however, we do not consider as coming under the heading of numismatics. It is a separate pursuit in a class by itself, similar to the practice of collecting shells, cigarette cards, etc.

Transportation tokens, however, are a different subject entirely and are as much a part of numismatics as medals, encased postage stamps, and merchants' or bankers' tokens. They are of many kinds and composition, being formed of tin, brass, lead, copper, or nickel, as well as celluloid, paper, and cardboard. Furthermore, they have been used as small change on many occasions, and, in fact, right in this country, and the consensus of opinion among the collecting fraternity seems to be that they are rightfully classed as numismatic material. To cite one example of the use of these items as money: shortly after World War I the tokens of the traction lines of the City of Buffalo, N. Y., readily passed as minor coins in the purchase of many articles. As this is being written, the Transit Authority of the City of New York is suggesting that merchants accept 20-cent subway tokens in payment of merchandise.

Transportation tokens are not a new development. Their origin is obscure, but from the great fondness of the English people for such things it is probable that that country first used them. This is borne out by the fact that a great many of the transportation tokens of England, Scotland, and Wales are similar in a general way in composition and design to many of the merchants' tokens of England issued in the early nineteenth century. Other countries also have them; for example, the Scandinavian countries. Some of these have been observed which are simply brass checks with a name or number for use on ferries; but whether they are of earlier vintage than the English it is impossible to say. Such tokens are also plentiful in South and Central America. Probably the tokens were created as a result of the inauguration of the first railroad and horse trolley cars, about the beginning of the nineteenth century. Many of the older ones are hard to find and rare, bringing as high as $5 to $10 at auction. However, there are thousands of common tokens which can be purchased for a few cents.

In this country transportation tokens have been found dating back to the 1840s. It might be well to mention that these tokens are generally of metal, although some are of celluloid or other composition. They are not at all like a railroad ticket or bus pass of paper or cardboard, but are more like a coin in construction, although it hardly seems necessary to describe them, since practically everybody has come in contact with them at one time or another. Travelers in American cities often find that the trolley or bus companies use tokens which cost in most cases ten cents to twenty-five cents each. These are the most common variety, and if one should happen to be a traveler, it is possible in time to gather quite a few of them at cost price. A really interesting collection of transportation tokens may be arranged at a cost as low as, or lower than, any other series of coins, medals, or paper money. If it is desired to have many different cities represented, alphabetically arranged, it is possible to buy lots of these tokens from dealers or at coin auctions, but the novice should be careful to bid conservatively, as the common ones can be secured for very low prices. The rare ones of obsolete companies, dated around the middle 1800s, are seldom if ever sold in lots with the current tokens, and a good stiff bid is generally necessary to acquire them at sales, as they are eagerly sought by collectors.

The collecting of transportation tokens has lately become quite a respectable section of the collection scene. There is an organization of devotees, and a list of many varieties of these tokens has been published and is constantly being revised. If one were seriously interested in this branch of numismatics it should be possible to join others of like mind, and many swapping sessions could be arranged. Quite a romantic story may be told through a good collection of transportation tokens, and it is not surprising that many people have taken up the pursuit of these items. To those who find pleasure in meditating on long-forgotten enterprises, a fine story of progress in steamboat, ferry, and railway history may be unfolded. Some of the lines which have long since died and are now forgotten are the old boat lines up the Hudson River to Albany, the old horse car lines in New York City, Brooklyn, Boston, Chicago, and other cities, and many oddly named stage and railroad lines which are no longer talked about, having merged many years ago with some of the big trunk lines such as the New York Central, the Pennsylvania Railroad, and other companies. The student of transportation history in the United States and Canada will find these tokens of great value in his research. Trolley tokens are fast becoming relics, as the old trolley lines have for some years been going out of service and are being replaced by bus lines. In a few years the old trolley lines will probably be as obsolete as the stage coach, and old tokens issued by them will then, naturally, have a great sentimental and historical value.

All in all, the collector of transportation tokens has a collection of numismatic items that will take a long time to complete. There are always new additions to search for and identify, and this hobby is becoming more popular as time goes by.

In fact, the hobby has its devotees in England and Oriental countries, as well as this country and Europe. The older and rarer tokens are a source of constant rivalry, as there are not enough of this kind to go around, and people with means generally get the best. On the other hand, the value of such tokens is not always so well known or so clearly defined in catalogues as that of coins and medals. Therefore, an alert and well-informed collector has a better chance to pick up a bargain than his colleague who collects coins.

The sales tax tokens are a late arrival, comparatively speaking, among numismatic items, but they have already taken quite a prominent place in the collecting world, in interest if not in the number of persons who collect them. The sales tax itself is nothing new, but the sales tax tokens were a development of the early 1930s. They were used in many states. If a traveler were to start in New York on a transcontinental trip, making numerous stops en route, he would have no trouble at all in making up a small but interesting collection of sales tax tokens, although current practice tends to simply charge the tax without using any token. New York has a sales tax, but no tokens are used. Tokens have been issued by the states of Ohio, which used stamps, and Illinois, which used round and now obsolete tokens, and later, square, aluminum ones reading, "Dept. of Finance 1½ State of Illinois Retailers' Occupation Token." The earlier round tokens were shown as "1½ Mills," but the word "Mills" was later omitted. Prior to the issuance of the Illinois tokens, at least two dozen towns and counties in Illinois issued sales tokens in various forms. These are all obsolete, and are scarce and becoming more so. Among these communities are Arcola, Chandlerville, Charleston, Effingham, Jackson County, Jasper County, Litchfield, Mattoon, and many others. Pickneyville and Murphysboro issued cardboard tokens; the others were of metal construction.

Such tokens were issued in Arizona, Washington, Utah, Colorado, Louisiana, New Mexico, and Missouri. The latter state issued cardboard "milk bottle cap" tokens, so-called because of their size and shape. There was a blue and white one-mill "Retailers' Sales Tax Receipt," and orange and white five-mill "Retailers' Sales Tax Receipt" with blank backs. However, in later varieties the backs were printed. All of these "milk bottle caps" are now obsolete. The later Missouri sales tax receipt is of metal, reading "Missouri Sales Tax Receipt," showing a map of Missouri with a hole in the center of the state, and the same design on obverse and reverse.

Kansas also had a cheaply made token, seemingly composed of lead, and Louisiana had a similar one. Alabama issued one-mill tokens which were called "Luxury Tax Tokens."

Colorado issued a square-holed token of one-fifth cent denomination, and, later, a round-holed token bearing the figure "2." Oklahoma also issued sales tokens of yellow metal, while the State of Utah used several different tokens, one a small-holed one-mill sales token, another a larger one, round and holed, with a star token of five mills, all bearing the words "Emergency Relief Fund." New Mexico issued very small aluminum tokens of one mill, and five-mill tokens in copper, both of them designated as "Emergency School Tax on Purchases of 5 Cents." These small tokens were much sought after by visitors, and proved so popular with tourists that the authorities found it hard to keep a supply within the state.

The State of Washington first tried thin cardboard scrip tokens, which were short-lived and gave place to metal tokens reading "Tax on Purchase 10 cents or less CH.180 Laws 1935."

It will be seen that most of these tokens were in one- to five-mill denominations and were composed of aluminum or copper, although local or city governments, and sometimes states, issued tokens or emergency scrip in cardboard, paper, and even wood. Most of the sales tax tokens are of extremely simple design. All of them, of course, have been used for small change in the past, and thus have come more or less under the same category as hard times, or emergency, money. They are interesting from the collector's point of view and have enjoyed a certain acceptance among numismatists in the past, although now they are not highly regarded. As they become scarcer, naturally, they will be more sought after. Some are already rare, such as the Illinois round tokens, and the city and merchants' association tokens of that state. Others, such as those of Kansas and Colorado, were of such cheap composition that it is hard to find any in an unworn condition. None of the early sales tax tokens, with the exception of those of New Mexico and some of the city tokens, have any artistic merit, while the chief claim to beauty of design for the New Mexico tokens is the fact that the State Seal is shown. Although tokens are generally issued in the millions, as states stop making them, or reissue them in different form, they will become curiosities and hard to find.

A curious form of money, if it can be called that, are the many issues of "wooden nickels" which have been turned out over the last twenty-five years. The first, evidently, was issued in the State of Washington and has been followed by literally hundreds of others, until now a complete collection would comprise many thousand single items. These "wooden nickels," at first in round form, are now almost always square or rectangular sheets of thin wood, printed solely for a particular occasion. They are mainly for advertising purposes, not for private individuals or firms as a rule, but for local celebrations, anniversaries and the like. Most are redeemable by local merchants, but they are picked up and held so often by collectors and souvenir hunters that there is always a good profit for the issuing committees.

Among the earlier "wooden nickels" are those of such widely separated places as Lake George, New York, Chattanooga, Tennessee, Springfield, Ohio, Astoria, Oregon, and Milford, Connecticut. Some of the nickels have elaborate designs in color and are interesting. This phase of numismatics is highly specialized and has its own following. Lists of wooden nickels issued over the years have been printed.

During the "bank holiday" of March 1933 many localities issued and used emergency scrip. Lack of banking facilities was a serious matter and led to the issuance of such scrip. The Retail Independent Merchants' Association of Evanston, Illinois, sponsored the issuance of "Prosperity Certificates" as legal tender. "Corn Scrip" was used at Clear Lake, Iowa, to buy corn for auction. Knoxville, Tennessee, and Freeport, Long Island, were among the first to issue scrip. Circulation of money rose to its highest point in our history; silver dollars and old large bills appeared in circulation almost immediately, being noted in great profusion only two days after the "holiday" started on March 5. Homestead, Pennsylvania, elected to use checks as scrip; and Atlantic City, New Jersey, and Cleveland, Ohio, issued large amounts of scrip to run the city governments. Other cities too numerous to mention put out scrip in various forms during the bank holiday, and an observation of this trying period shows the importance of a smoothly running system of currency which is not noticed in normal times, but the necessity of which becomes apparent just as soon as "something happens" to disrupt the banking facilities of the country.

Other countries have also used tokens on many occasions. Porcelain tokens originated in Siam, where they were used as gambling money by the natives. They are of unique construction, and many are beautiful in design. The use of these tokens was forbidden by the authorities of Siam and has not been legal for about seventy-five years. A later issue of porcelain tokens circulated throughout the cities and villages of Germany, a country that, during the inflationary period after the First World War, seems to have used a great variety of materials for coins, owing to the scarcity of metal. The German porcelain tokens were issued in various denominations and in many fine designs at the famous Meissen works. They are beautiful to look at, mostly clay-colored, or white, but practically worthless as money, being fragile and easily chipped. They have been reasonable in price and make an interesting collection, as few people have devoted their energies to the collecting of this series. Porcelain tokens of Siam are not rare, in the main, and can be purchased at auction for one dollar, or slightly less. Of course, a wide selection of many different designs would run into quite a few pieces, but most collectors would be satisfied with one or two specimens to keep in their "curious money" collections. Unlike the German porcelain tokens, which are thin and fragile, of dull, brittle material, the Siamese tokens are thick, small and blunt, and of strong manufacture.

Medals

While medals should not be classified simply as an adjunct of numismatics, being a very important branch of that science, they are not widely collected. As a rule, the collecting of medals is an outgrowth of a special interest in a particular personage, period of history, or human enterprise. Medals may not compare in interest with coins, which have a different kind of fascination, owing to their history or intrinsic value. But, like all general statements, this one may possibly invite criticism from those who prize medals from the viewpoints of historical interest, beauty of design and workmanship, and for their honoring of various personages, from architects to zoologists. Nearly all coin collectors do supplement their collection of coins with a few medals of special personal interest to them. In terms of quantity and variety, coins, naturally, have first place. Still, there are thousands of medals issued every year on every conceivable subject and in honor of all manner of men and women. The State of Vatican City issues medals yearly for the current Pope, and many extra medals for various ceremonies, jubilees, or special events, such as the creation of new cardinals. The medals of the earlier Popes, particularly during the Renaissance, were extraordinary examples of artistic merit and much sought after by numismatists. Other countries issue medals for all special events, such as coronation ceremonies, the launching of a new ocean liner, and many other occasions.

As an instance of the profuse issuance of medals, there are hundreds of Napoleonic medals alone. A recent list of a very few varieties of such medals from a European dealer includes such items as: "1810—The Prince Ferdinand Visits the Mint"; "1811—Birth of the King of Rome"; "1813—Maria Louisa Visits the Mint"; "Public Instruction Organized"; "Battle of Castiglione"; "Battle of Millesino"; "Attempt Against His Life"; "The Tsar in Paris (1814)"; and so on.

In the United States, however, we have either a close runner-up to Napoleon, or the real champion in Abraham Lincoln. Medals, large and small, in gold, silver, bronze, and all metals, have been issued in honor of Abraham Lincoln, and a very worthwhile collection might comprise just such medals.

Our Presidents have official medals struck on inauguration. Since his tragic death President Kennedy has been honored by medals all over the world, so numerous that a book has been written listing them.

All events of historical, and even current, importance have been commemorated by medals of some kind. The members of the Byrd Antarctic Expedition all received medals in 1937 in appreciation of their service to science, while another later issue struck by the Royal Mint of London was given as a reward to all public servants taking part in the coronation of Elizabeth II.

Of course, we can barely scratch the surface in a short outline of the study of medals. Besides those many collectors who specialize in Lincoln, Napoleonic, or Presidential medals, are others whose special interest is army, navy, and war medals; medical, or doctors' and surgeons' medals; musicians' medals; or an almost endless variety of specialties. As an illustration of the wide range of subjects, the New York Public Library contains a list, by William Blades, 1869, of *Medals, Jetons, Tokens, etc. in Connection with the Art of Printing,* and also a list, by Paul Gauvin, 1913, of *Jetons and Medals of Insurance Companies.*

Medals are a fine medium for artistic expression and, in fact, allow more latitude in this respect than coins. This is due to the restrictions of size and legal requirements on the latter. Governments often regulate inscriptions on coins, as in our country. The size is almost always the same as previous issues; a half dollar is always the same weight, thickness, and circumference, and some of our commemorative half dollars are fairly crowded with legends and designs, while, on the other hand, a medal twice the diameter of a silver dollar is not uncommon.

In addition to the great number of medals struck in honor of particular events and personages, there are some which are issued purely as examples of the current trend of art. Some of these medals or medallions date back to the days of the ancient Greeks and Romans, and are valuable for their antiquity as well as for their historical significance and artistic merit. Ancient and modern examples of these artistic medals are of value to the art student or antiquarian to an even greater degree than to the numismatist. Most of the medals issued by the Society of Medalists were not for the purpose of honoring a national character or historical event but are good examples of purely artistic merit, the outstanding exception being one issued in honor of Charles A. Lindbergh.

There has been a certain amount of propaganda for the elimination of the issuance of commemorative half dollars and the substitution therefor of some form of medal or medalet to commemorate certain important events in our history. Since commemorative coins have not been issued in the last few years, the subject is not often mentioned. However, those in favor of such an innovation claim that the substitution of medals would have eliminated much of the dissatisfaction caused by the selling out of issues to dealers and speculators. On the other hand, those opposed to the plan insist that they and many other collectors of like mind would entirely ignore such medals and give up the collecting of commemorative pieces. There is a lot to be said on both sides, and there is no doubt that issues of actual money have a certain attraction that does not attach to any other medium.

Many different varieties of medals are manufactured and sold at the Philadelphia mint. From the earliest days of the mint, medals have been issued in great numbers. There are medals for each President from Washington to Johnson. These presidential medals are often found in complete sets in museums, but any collector may have them at a nominal price plus postage or express charges, by writing the Superintendent of the Mint, United States Mint, Philadelphia, Pennsylvania, who will also supply on request a complete list of medals available, with description, size, and price. The earlier medals were called "Indian Peace Medals," from the practice of the War Department in giving them as a friendly peace offering to Indians. They are of bronze about three inches in diameter and are finely engraved; the majority of the earlier ones were designed by G. T. Morgan and C. E. Barber, Mint Engravers. Other varieties include a complete set of medals of the Secretaries of the Treasury from Alexander Hamilton to the present time. Barber and Morgan are the designers of a majority of these medals also. The Directors of the Mint are represented from David Rittenhouse, the first director, to the present time. The Army is also honored by many medals, issued under Resolutions of Congress, from the first commemorating Washington before Boston, issued by Resolution of Congress dated March 25, 1776, to Major General Grant, Resolution dated December 17, 1863, as well as other army medals for the Pennsylvania Volunteers, Major General Scott, and Colonel Armstrong (Village of Kittanning). These army medals are of bronze but of varying sizes and prices. The Navy is also honored by thirty-two bronze medals, including the first for John Paul Jones, for *Serapis*, Captain Perry for the capture of the British fleet on Lake Erie, and several shipwreck and rescue medals.

In addition to the medals mentioned, there are many issued for various celebrities and events, some small and inexpensive, such as the James A. Garfield medal, about one inch in diameter; Lincoln and Garfield; First Steam Coinage; and others honoring the Pacific Railroad, the Great Seal, the Wright Brothers, Cyrus W. Field, and Charles A. Lindbergh. George Washington is honored by ten other medals, in addition to the regular presidential medal. These bronze medals are listed, as follows, by the United States mint:

		*Size **	*Designer*
1.	Time increases his fame	16	Unknown
2.	Cabinet medal	13	Paquet
3.	Washington and Jackson	11	Unknown
4.	Commencement of coin cabinet	37	Paquet
5.	Presidency relinquished	25	Reich
6.	Allegiance	19	Paquet
7.	Washington and Lincoln	11	Unknown
8.	Washington and Grant	11	Unknown
9.	Washington Wreath	11	Paquet
10.	Washington bicentennial	36	L. G. Fraser

* The size number refers to diameter, and is based on a unit of $1/16$ inch. Thus, size 16 means one inch in diameter.

These government medals are seldom, if ever, offered by dealers, although they may be encountered occasionally in auction sales. One of the reasons for this is that a condition of sale by the mint is that they are not to be sold at a price higher than that charged by the government.

Bibliography

S. S. Crosby's *Early Coins of America* (Boston, 1875; Reprint, 1945) is the standard work on colonial coins and will probably remain the standard. The original 1875 edition is scarce and expensive, but there is a 1945 reprint which sells for about $20.00. Crosby covered the subject of colonial coins up to and including the Revolution so completely that later writers have found little to enlarge upon. However, specific details in some series have been covered by other works which are important and necessary for a complete study. These include three by Sydney P. Noe:

The New England and Willow Tree Coinage of Massachusetts (Numismatic Notes and Monographs No. 102), The American Numismatic Society, New York, 1943.

The Oak Tree Coinage of Massachusetts (NNM No. 110), New York, 1947.

The Pine Tree Coinage of Massachusetts (NNM No. 125), New York, 1952.

In addition, the interested collector should consult:

ADAMS, EDWARD H., *Official Premium List of United States Private and Territorial Gold Coins,* New York, 1909.

Appraising and Selling Your Coins, "Green Book," Coin & Currency Institute, New York, 1965.

BRADBEER, *Confederate and Southern States Currency* (Reprint), 1956.

BROWN, M. R., & DUNN, J. W., *A Guide to the Grading of United States Coins,* (4th Ed.), Racine, Wis., 1966.

BULLOWA, DAVID M., *The Commemorative Coinage of the United States* (NNM No. 83), New York, 1938.

BURNIE, R. H., *Small California and Territorial Gold Coins,* Pascagoula, Miss., 1955.

CHASE, PHILIP H., *Confederate Treasury Notes.*

CRISWELL, G. C. and C. L., *Confederate and Southern States Currency,* Pass-au-grille, Fla., 1956.

ECKFELDT, JACOB REES AND DU BOIS, W. E., *A Manual of Gold and Silver Coins of All Nations,* Philadelphia, 1842.

EVANS, GEORGE C., *Illustrated History of the United States Mint,* Philadelphia, 1886.

FRIEDBERG, ROBERT, *Paper Money of the United States* (5th Ed.), New York, 1965.

GILBERT, E., *The United States Half Cents,* New York, 1916.

LIMPERT, F. A., *United States Paper Money, Old Series, 1861-1929,* Royal Oak, Mich., 1948.

MARIS, EDWARD, *Coins of New Jersey,* Philadelphia, 1881.

MCILVAINE, ARTHUR D., *The Silver Dollars of the United States of America* (NNM No. 95), New York, 1941.

MCKAY, GEORGE L., *Early American Currency* (NNM No. 104), New York, 1944.

Medallic Portraits of John F. Kennedy, Iola, Wis., 1966.

NEWMAN, ERIC P., *Coinage for Colonial Virginia* (NNM No. 135), New York, 1956.

RAYMOND, WAYTE, *Standard Paper Money Catalog* (Part I: Colonial and Continental Currency. Part II: Large and Small Notes and Fractional Currency), New York, 1954-1955.

SHELDON, WM. H., *Early American Cents, 1793-1814,* New York, 1949.

SLABAUGH, A. R., *Confederate States Paper Money,* Racine, Wis., 1958.

VALENTINE, D. W., *The United States Half Dimes* (NNM No. 48), New York, 1931.

WHITMAN, *Handbook of United States Coins,* Racine, Wis., 1967.

YEOMAN, RICHARD S., *Guide Book of United States Coins,* Racine, Wis., 1967.

CHAPTER THREE

Foreign Coins

It is the opinion of some numismatic authorities who are in a position to know the likes and dislikes of the collecting public, that numismatists in this country do not pay enough attention to the possibilities of a good foreign collection. Compared with our short history, European countries have been minting money for centuries, and naturally many things of interest have been developed. Numismatics itself is an old story in continental Europe; there are many more people interested in the science there than there are in the United States, even though the number of active collectors over here has increased by many thousands in the last few years.

With many countries to choose from, and with new issues coming out all the time, a foreign collection of copper, nickel, or silver coins can keep one fairly busy, to say nothing of the many later issues of baser metals such as iron, stainless steel, and aluminum. These minor coins are of almost infinite variety, and practically everyone at one time or other comes into contact with some of them. Naturally, it is always well to get the best, and the collector will take more pride in uncirculated or very fine coins, purchased separately and not in lots, although many very good coins are occasionally secured in lots at auction or otherwise. Some even recommend buying in as big lots as possible, where there is always the possibility of securing some overlooked rarity. Furthermore, there is a certain amount of education and fun to be had from sorting over a large quantity of miscellaneous coins of many countries.

It is rather hard to keep informed on the latest issues of foreign countries, but a good guide is to be found in the dealers' advertisements in coin publications, such as *The Numismatist, The Numismatic Scrapbook Magazine,* and house organs published by the larger coin establishments. The magazines mentioned also have departments devoted to "new issues." A good and inexpensive guide to foreign coins is *A Catalog of Modern World Coins* by R. S. Yeoman, which any dealer can supply; also Wayte Raymond's *19th Century Coins of the World* and the same author's *20th Century Coins of the World,* both of which, unfortunately, at this writing are out of print. For those who find a special attachment for the larger dollar-sized coins, or crowns, the books by Dr. John S. Davenport are invaluable, in fact, indispensable. These are: *European Crowns and Talers Since 1800* (which does not include Germany), *European Crowns Since 1800, German Talers 1700-1800,* and for the collector who has a special interest in the earlier crowns, *Oversize Multiple Talers of the Brunswick Duchies and Saxe-Lauenburg*. These are all in print and are considered standard works, that is, the coins are listed and illustrated by numbers which are used by cataloguers in describing any particular specimen.

For study and accumulation, foreign coins might be classified under three general headings: medieval, modern or current, and commemorative. Large volumes could be written about any one of these classifications. In fact, many volumes have been written regarding subdivisions of every one of the above sections, such as money of the Orient, Chinese coins, coins of England, Scotland, South Africa, and many others, while many large volumes have been written on the Italian coinage. Therefore, the collector as a rule will progress from a general collection indiscriminately embracing money of all countries to one which is made up entirely of the issues of a certain country or period of history. Then, as time goes on and he feels he has gone as far as he cares to with that particular subject, he may start an entirely different series.

The numismatist who is starting from scratch should never worry if for the first few months he seems to be moving in circles and has accumulated a little bit of everything. As he advances in knowledge and love of the game, he will either be considered a "general" collector, or a "specialist" in one particular type or country or era. Therefore, the information given here on any of the foreign classifications mentioned previously must be general in scope and cannot obviously take in all issues and types from early times; nor can everything be described in minute detail.

It is surprising how many people desire to have just one or two coin specimens from each country. Most of them are easy to acquire. It is not difficult to get the common coins of England and the continental European countries, such as France, Germany, Poland, Italy, Switzerland, Imperial Russia, Austria, and others. Uncirculated or very fine pieces are referred to in this regard. In this country some of the other European coins are slightly more difficult to obtain at particular times. For example, there is always a demand for money of Korea, Soviet Russia, Soviet China, Bulgaria, Latvia, and other countries now known as Russian satellites. Other foreign coins which the general foreign collector may look for are the aurars of Iceland, funs of Mongolia, and coins of the Indian States, Hong Kong, Straits Settlements, and the East Indian countries. Some countries, like Soviet Russia, prohibit the exporting of their currency; this makes it hard to buy their uncirculated coins.

Since the beginner will probably start with the money of his own country and then explore that of other countries, it will be simpler to leave the issues of the Middle Ages for a little later on, and make a study of what may be called the modern or current foreign coins. By "modern" coins is meant those issued in Europe, Asia, Africa, or South and Central America from the seventeenth century to the nineteenth; "current" coins, of course, are those in use at the present time.

Many fairly cheap coins may be assembled from countries or colonies which have ceased to function under their old names. Armenia is one example; Latvia, Esthonia, and Lithuania are others. No money is issued at this time under these names; Russian rubles circulate to a certain extent. The one-, two-, ten-, and fifty-bit pieces of the Danish West Indies, now the Virgin Islands, under United States protection, are examples of coins which will never again be minted. On the other hand, in the course of a decade or so, new countries are added which have not previously had any individual currency—Israel, Pakistan, and Ghana, for example. French Somaliland, Libya, Somalia, Saarland, French Oceania, are still unfamiliar names to most of us, and, still older are the various states of India, Muscat and Oman, and the islands of St. Pierre and Miquelon, all of which have a distinctive coinage, as have other new countries—Mali, Tanzania, Nigeria, etc.

The Irish Free State had an interesting coinage depicting animals, pigs, pigeons, horses, dogs, and other animals, which appeals to the searcher for the unusual in money. Today, as the Republic of Ireland, animal coins are still issued, but with the inscription "Eire" instead of "Saorstat eireann." As a matter of fact, animal coins are a favorite of collectors, and there are many besides the Irish issues. The animal, loosely taken to include birds and fishes, is represented by the kangaroos and sheep of Australia, the horse and the eagle (single or double-headed), the elephants of the Belgian Congo and France, the wren of England, the llama of Bolivia, the turtle of the Fiji Islands, the quetzal of Guatemala, and the cow of Guernsey (coins of the island of Jersey, however, have three lions on a shield, in such odd denominations as 1/52, 1/24, and 1/12 shillings). The puffin of Lundy Island comes in denominations of one puffin and one-half puffin (a puffin is a sea bird). There are also the water buffalo of Madagascar, the ox of South Africa, the panther of Uruguay, and the dove of Vatican City, to say nothing of the figurative dragons of China and Korea. While United States money in its regular issues features only the eagle, there is a good representation of the animal kingdom in the commemorative issues. A horse appears on the Lafayette dollar and the Stone Mountain Memorial half dollar. The grizzly bear is shown twice, both times on California issues—the California Diamond Jubilee half dollar of 1925, and the San Francisco-Oakland Bay Bridge of 1936. Then there is the catamount on the Vermont Sesquicentennial half dollar of 1927; oxen on the various Oregon Trail Memorial halves; the head of a cow on the Old Spanish Trail half dollar of 1935; the badger on the Wisconsin half dollar, 1936; the beaver on the Albany (N.Y.) half dollar, 1936; the calf on the New Rochelle (N.Y.) half dollar of 1938; and the owl on the Panama-Pacific $50 gold piece of 1915, with a hippocampus on the Panama-Pacific $2.50 gold piece. A hippocampus, by the way, is a mythical sea creature with the head of a horse and the tail of a dolphin.

The searcher for the unique in money may also look for the largest and smallest money ever issued. The largest is probably the stone money of the Island of Yap, one of the Caroline Islands which was much discussed during the Second World War. These are large stones over a hundred pounds in weight and three feet in diameter. Even larger stones, some more than twelve feet in diameter, are placed in front of a native's dwelling to demonstrate his potential wealth, serving much the same function as the large and handsome automobile in front of our neighbor's door. Obviously, you won't have this kind of money in your coin cabinet.

The smallest gold coin is the gold lola of Travancore, a state of India. One of these is displayed in the exhibits of the American Numismatic Society in New York City. The smallest copper coin is the chuckrum, which is like a fair-sized seed, but with a simple design, also from Travancore, worth less than 1/12 cent in our money. A very small silver coin is the 2½ centesimo of Panama, commonly called a "Panama Pill," being of the same shape and about the size of an ordinary pill. This coin, for all its smallness, carries a very beautiful design. However, there are many small and thin coins to be found among the foreign lots. Wayte Raymond, of New York City, in his *Coin Topics* (September, 1936), describes and offers for sale what he calls the smallest denomination ever issued, his authority being H. C. Millies' *Les Monnaies des Indigenes de L'archipel Indien et de la Peninsula Malaie, 1871*. These are small lead coins known as pitis, used in Sumatra and Java about 150 years ago. As thin as paper, it took 1,500 pitis to equal one cent. Incidentally, the Malay Archipelago, being rich in tin, issued coins of that metal which were very small and holed and were attached as branches to a "tree," to be broken off and used as small change.

Among the largest coins which can be handled are the Swedish plate money, large copper plates sometimes a foot or more square, stamped in several places, which were issued to encourage the use of copper. Other large copper coins are the English "cartwheel" twopence of George III and the copper five-kopeck coin of Catherine II of Russia, each weighing about two ounces and more suitable as paperweights than as coins. The brass tempo coins of Japan are quite large and not uncommon, and the silver pack-saddle coins of Siam, named because they are in the shape of a saddle, are also rather large.

As an example of the quantity of new foreign coins issued in the past several years, the following list gives only some of the more important or unusual ones:

Saarland (1954)—The only coins of this country which was returned to France after World War II: 10, 20, and 50 franken aluminum-bronze; (1955)—100 franken copper-nickel.
Spain (1959)—50 pesetas nickel.
Somalia (1950)—1, 5, and 10 centesimi bronze; 50 centesimi and 1 somalo silver.
Japan (1955)—1 yen aluminum and 50 yen copper-nickel.
Italy (Republic, 1956)—50 and 100 lire steel.
Guernsey (1956)—4 and 8 doubles and 3-pence bronze.
Israel (1958)—commemorative 1 and 5 prutah silver.
Vatican City (1963)—500 lire silver, *sede vacante,* issued in the interregnum after the death of Pope John XXIII and before the election of Paul VI.
Egypt (1955)—100 piastres gold.
Switzerland (1955)—5 franc silver (bust of William Tell).

The new issues mentioned, of course, do not embrace the entire list, nor do they include the fairly numerous commemorative sets which will be mentioned later. It will be seen from the foregoing list, however, that the collector of even minor copper and nickel foreign coins will have a task to keep up with the new currency. None of these issues is too expensive; the Israel commemoratives and the *sede vacante* coin of Vatican City are about the dearest. However, the price of most late copper and bronze coins is well under two dollars.

The young collector may find it a good idea to start with a series embracing the English colonial or commonwealth coins. There are so many dominions, protectorates, and states covered by this classification that many people make a specialty of assembling these colonial coins. There are frequently new and quite often unusual issues, although many of the countries have used the regular coinage of Great Britain. The budding numismatist may well thank his stars for British enterprise when he realizes the extremely large portion of the globe that is covered by an English colonial series. The list of countries, some of which are about ready to become entirely independent of Britain, is as follows:

British Caribbean Territories (Eastern Group)—the combined territories of Barbados, British Guiana, Leeward Islands, Tobago, Trinidad, and Windward Islands. In 1955 a new coinage was issued to replace the regular British coins formerly used. The new issue consists of bronze ½ cent, 1 cent, and 2 cents; nickel-brass 5 cents; copper-nickel 10 cents, 25 cents, and 50 cents. All bear the head of Queen Elizabeth II.

British Guiana—distinctive issues of Queen Victoria, Edward VII, George V, and George VI.

British Honduras—coins showing same monarchs as British Guiana, with the addition of 1954 issues of Elizabeth II.

British North Borneo

British West Africa—consisting of the Gold Coast State, Gold Coast, Ashanti, and Togoland.

Australia Fiji, New Zealand, Samoa, Tasmania

Canada

Straits Settlements

The currency of the Island of Guernsey is included in the British colonial series, and is much in demand among collectors. The same applies to the Island of Jersey.

The coinage of England, Scotland, Wales, and Northern Ireland consists of the farthing, halfpenny, penny, threepence, sixpence, shilling, two shillings, half crown, and crown.

There have been several efforts in the past to convert the English coinage system to the decimal system that is used in both the United States and Canada. It will be effective, however, in 1971. We all are familiar with English pounds, and it may come as a surprise to some that Britain does issue some coins in cents and dollar denominations. Coins issued for Hong Kong, for example, while bearing the portraits of kings and queens, are issued in denominations from 1 cent to 1 dollar, although the only coin so far issued under Queen Elizabeth II is the 10-cent nickel-bronze of 1955. Other British colonial coins issued in cents and dollars are those of the Straits Settlements up to the time of George V.

Before leaving England and its colonial possessions and former possessions, it is of interest to note that the only coins issued under King Edward VIII, now the Duke of Windsor, were of small denomination issued in New Guinea, British West Africa, Fiji, and British East Africa. No coins with his portrait, however, were issued, those mentioned being simply inscribed Edward VIII, etc. On the accession of a new King of England a whole new coinage must be prepared, and the new monarch's portrait shown facing the opposite way to that of his predecessor. It was understood that Edward had already posed for his portraits to appear on the new money, but on his renunciation of the throne the dies were destroyed.

A good series, and one to which more attention should be paid, is a collection of English coins, or silver pennies, which can be obtained from as far back as King Ethelred II (979-1016), the later dates being supplemented with the copper pennies. For the student of English history, and, for that matter, American history, such a series is invaluable. Even further back than Ethelred we can find one or two silver pennies or halfpennies, beginning with Edwig (955 to 959). For your convenience, the following listing shows the English rulers who have issued coins:

Edwig (955-959)
Edgar (959-975)
Edward the Martyr (975-979)

Ethelred II (979-1016)
Edmund Ironside (1016)
Cnut (1016-1035)
Harold I (Harold Harefoot) (1035-1040)
Harthacnut (1040-1042)
Edward the Confessor (1042-1066)
Harold II (1066)
Edgar Ethling (1066)
William I (1066-1087)
William II (1087-1100)
Henry I (1100-1135)
Stephen (1135-1154)
Henry II (1154-1189)
Richard I (1189-1199)
John (1199-1216)
Henry III (1216-1272)
Edward I (1272-1307)
Edward II (1307-1327)
Edward III (1327-1377)
Richard II (1377-1399)
Henry IV (1399-1413)
Henry V (1413-1422)
Henry VI (1422-1461 and 1470-1471)
Edward IV (1461-1470 and 1471-1483)
Edward V (1483)
Richard III (1483-1485)
Henry VII (1485-1509)
Henry VIII (1509-1547)
Edward VI (1547-1553)
Mary (1553-1554)
Philip and Mary (1554-1558)
Elizabeth I (1558-1603)
James I (1603-1625)
Charles I (1625-1649)
Commonwealth (1649-1660)
Oliver Cromwell (1653-1658)
Charles II (1660-1685)
James II (1685-1688)
William and Mary (1689-1694)

William III (1694-1702)
Anne (1702-1714)
George I (1714-1727)
George II (1727-1760)
George III (1760-1820)
George IV (1820-1830)
William IV (1830-1837)
Victoria (1837-1901)
Edward VII (1901-1910)
George V (1910-1936)
George VI (1936-1952)
Elizabeth II (1952-)

While the earlier pennies do have portraits, they are by no means authentic pictures of the early monarchs. They are crude heads with a crown, which are taken to represent the king. The older pieces are crudely struck and often scratched or marred, but the inscriptions as a rule are fairly well shown, and any collector would take much pride in having an unbroken series of English monarchs in his cabinet. Furthermore, even most of the earlier issues are by no means expensive, which makes it all the more surprising that so few collectors in this country take an interest in such coins. Many old familiar names from our early schooldays appear, and some names we had begun to regard as mere legends are revived, such as Richard the Lionhearted, Edward the Confessor, William and Mary (for whom a college was named in our own country), Queen Anne, and even old Henry VIII. The earlier English silver was minted not long after the Roman era, and those crude times naturally produced crude money. Nevertheless, they are about the best the Middle Ages have to offer us, and, if for no other reason, are historically important. Some of the early English pennies are hard to read, and the practice adopted near the end of the tenth century of adding the name of the mint town to the coins may increase the difficulty, since some of the towns are abbreviated, some are written in Latin (for example, Eboracum for York, and so on), but a bit of research and study will soon pay off.

While we are discussing English money, another coinage of interest is the gun money of Ireland, coined by James II from old cannon, bells, and other scrap. Also among unusual coins encountered from time to time are the English copper "cartwheel" twopence pieces of George III, 1797. As previously mentioned, these weigh two ounces and were called "cartwheels" because of their clumsy size, although they are beautifully designed. In the past they have been popular for use as paperweights, and many have even been converted into ashtrays. George III coins are not rare or costly and he reigned a long time. They are of particular historical interest to Americans, because they display the portrait of the monarch who was responsible for the events leading to the Revolutionary War.

Among other money having unique appeal may be included the platinum money of Russia, an unusually expensive and rare coinage, wire money of Russia and Mexico, porcelain coins and tokens, leather money of postwar Germany, and old cardboard money of Japan.

Canada issues mint sets that are the next best thing to proof sets, and compare in workmanship and beauty with many specimen or proof sets. These may be ordered direct from the Bank of Canada in Ottawa.

Looking for the unique in units of currency, we find that many countries have created a unit, corresponding to our dollar unit, commemorating the names of national heroes. Thus, the balboa of Panama, bearing the name of the discoverer of that country, the colon of Costa Rica, for Christopher Columbus, and the bolivar of Venezuela, named in honor of the great South American hero and liberator, Simon Bolivar. The capital of Bolivia is named for Antonio Jose de Sucre, while the sucre is the unit of currency of Ecuador. Guatemala, on the other hand, thought so much of their national bird, the quetzal, that they adopted its name for their unit of currency, and coins have been minted showing this bird in all its splendid plumage.

In what we might call "current" foreign money, as opposed to "modern," many fine coins will be encountered. The mint-masters of Europe, particularly Germany and the Scandinavian countries, have been busy for centuries in issuing fine coins and may well be proud of their handiwork. Numismatics is widely followed in most European countries, especially in Sweden, Denmark, and Norway, and this interest is displayed in the many regular issues and commemorative pieces. In fact, the American collector often finds such a demand for foreign commemorative coins that he is sometimes unable to obtain them when he orders them. They are bought up rapidly, and in a surprisingly short time have advanced greatly in price.

Fashions, customs, and procedures change in the collectors' world, as we have seen. They also change, often through necessity, in the making of coins and in the metals used. Gold is an ideal metal, silver next best, mainly because of the quantities available. But in recent years many baser metals have been employed, such as iron, zinc, and especially aluminum. Unalloyed iron and zinc are unattractive to the collector. Aluminum is not attractive either, but the sheer force of numbers makes it sometimes necessary for the collector to consider aluminum coins, since many countries have issued almost entire series in this metal. If uncirculated and given care, the aluminum coins are not altogether unworthy of a foreign collection.

There has been a tendency in recent years to issue sets, mostly proofs, or specimen sets, but sometimes plain mint sets, in beautiful cases. The English Festival set of 1951 may be mentioned, with the coronation sets of Queen Elizabeth II.

Israel, beginning in 1949, has at times issued sets of specimens, from the 500 prutah through the lower denominations. Other late sets in such boxes or containers are those of Ceylon, which is of great beauty, and Bermuda. The South African mint at Pretoria issues yearly specimen sets in a special case and includes two gold coins. These are all nice acquisitions and worthy of attention. They are a good supplement to United States proof sets and Canadian mint sets, and all of them are quite reasonable in price if purchased at the source during the year of issue.

The collector of commemorative coins has a large field in the foreign issues. Even apart from the proof sets specially boxed, there are complete issues of mint sets or single commemorative coins. To mention just a few from the recent past, Belgium issued a 50-franc silver coin for the Brussels World's Fair of 1958—as usual for this country, in separate coins in the French and Flemish languages. Mexico continually issues commemoratives, such as the 1957 set of 1, 5, and 10 pesos in silver commemorating the centenary of the Constitution. Austria from 1955 to 1958 has issued various 25-schilling silver pieces commemorating the reopening of the National Theatre in 1955; the bicentennial of the death of Mozart, 1956; the 800th anniversary of Maria-Zell Cathedral, 1957; and the centennial of the death of scientist Carl Auer von Welsbach, 1958. Cuba, Colombia, Israel, Morocco, Panama, and Portugal are only a few of the countries which have issued commemoratives in the last few years. For a collector who wants to go further back there are numerous examples. In the 1920s and 1930s Austria issued commemoratives for composers, musicians, and other public figures. In the 1930s also, Brazil issued a whole series of copper and nickel coins which can be called commemoratives, since they honored with portraits Santos Dumont, The Duke of Caxias, Jose de Anchieto,

Diego Feijo, Dr. Oswald Cruz, and others who had helped to shape the destinies of that country. They were dated 1936, but later became the regular coinage of Brazil.

In 1936, Italy issued an entire set of commemorative coins showing Victor Emanuel III as King and Emperor, to celebrate the victory in Ethiopia. They were issued in limited quantities in 1936 as commemorative coins, while the regular issue was dated 1937. These all showed Victor Emanuel III on the obverse and bore the inscription "Victor Emanuel III King and Emperor" in Latin, while the reverse contained various designs, such as a chariot with four horses on the twenty lire, and eagles and other designs on the smaller denominations.

Commemorative money of foreign countries compares very favorably in workmanship and design with our own commemorative half dollars. Some individual pieces simply bear the portrait of the monarch or notable, or a replica of the edifice they are supposed to honor, but others—for example, the 1937 Austrian two-schilling silver piece commemorating the 200th anniversary of the establishment of St. Charles Church, and the Belgian 50-franc piece previously mentioned—are very striking in appearance and beautifully engraved. There are any number of foreign commemoratives honoring people whose achievements are unfamiliar to many citizens of the United States. World-famous figures are not always selected. We may be sure, however, that they were very famous in their own country, and it will always be found worthwhile to study the lives of these men and women.

Many times, unless orders are placed well in advance and foreign dealers kept informed of required issues, it is quite impossible for American collectors to secure desired commemorative pieces. They are bought up by European collectors, and cannot be found in the market. When this happens, it is necessary to exercise patience and await the appearance of such an item in sales and auction lists of foreign numismatic concerns, which may take quite a little time. It is well to get on the mailing list of some of the foreign dealers advertising in the numismatic publications of this country, and, further, to specifically request that you be notified as soon as announcements of new commemorative or regular issues are made. Most of the larger American numismatic firms have foreign correspondents and can take care of such new issues, as well as the commemoratives of other countries, at possibly slightly higher prices.

It is not known whether collectors in other countries are confronted with the problems that beset the activities of the American commemorative specialist, as far as speculation in these coins is concerned. It is probable that some European dealers may get possession of a large stock of some popular commemorative item and hold it for high prices, but if such is the case, their price lists do not show any such condition. When an issue is sold out, none is listed for sale in large quantities, as too often happens with our own commemorative half dollars. It is an unfortunate fact that many issues of United States commemorative coins are assumed to be completely sold by the committee in charge of distribution, and bona fide private collectors time and again have had their money returned, even though their remittance may have been in the hands of the distributors months in advance, only to find large quantities of the same coins advertised for sale later on at greatly increased prices.

At any rate, people specializing in the collecting of foreign commemorative coins do not have to contend with the mintmark feature, which causes so much dissatisfaction in connection with commemorative half dollars in the United States. Foreign coins are all from the one mint in the country concerned, which eliminates anything like the practice previously in effect here of issuing coins from Philadelphia with no mint mark, and the identical design from the Denver and San Francisco mints bearing mint marks "D" and "S" respectively, which has caused so much trouble to the collector who desires to have a complete set of such coins. (This difficulty has been reduced by a third since the San Francisco mint closed.) And, of course, the practice of issuing commemorative coins for three or more years with the same design but different dates is not prevalent abroad.

Many collectors specialize in coins of the same size and shape, regardless of denomination—that is, one coin from each country, in silver, of the same size as our dime, or quarter, or half dollar, or dollar. Silver dollars, or crowns, are not always the same size as our silver dollar, but near enough to satisfy. In late years, however, some coins that once corresponded in size no longer do so—for example, 5 pesetas of Spain, 2 kronor of Denmark, etc. It is, however, possible to secure a fairly complete set of dime-, quarter-, or half-dollar-sized coins of foreign countries. Canadian and Mexican quarters and half dollars are of about the same size as similar denominations in this country, and the English shilling, German mark, and French franc can fit easily into a quarter-dollar collection. Most countries issue a silver coin the size of our dime, and little difficulty would be encountered in completing any series of the three smaller denominations, with certain exceptions. This kind of collection has an attraction for many older people no less than for young persons. It would be nice to be able to say, "I have a quarter for every country in the world," but this would not be even approximately correct. Still, for the young collector especially, such a collection would be instructive in developing a knowledge of the denominations of foreign small coins and their value in our own money. Many South American countries issue silver in 20-cent and 50-cent sizes, the 20-cent size being smaller than our quarter dollar, and the 10-cent piece is often of nickel and not silver. Both of these conditions obtain in the case of Bolivia. Brazil had a 20-cent size called a 20 reis, but in nickel. Chile has both 10-cent and 20-cent coins, but no 25-cent size. However, those forming a collection such as this, of necessity have to be satisfied with the nearest in size and material they can get.

Under the heading of medieval coins we consider all the crude issues of the Byzantine Empire and the Crusaders, as well as those of the Italian cities, and early coins of the Slovak countries. Here also we will find coins of the early English kings, as far back as the eighth and ninth centuries. Medieval coinage followed closely the coinage of the Roman Empire, and such coins are generally found in gold, silver, and copper, with gold and copper predominating. Material and designs gradually declined. Denominations and dates were not shown, making it difficult to keep an accurate historical record down through the years. Later coins, from the tenth century A.D. onward, contained mainly religious designs, representing Christ and, later, the Virgin Mary, the saints, and angels. This religious depiction began about the fifth century A.D. with portraits of Christ, later the Virgin Mary, and finally the saints. Such coinage often bore religious aspirations or prayers, and in some cases, the name of the reigning sovereign. Well before the fourteenth century, coins of various Italian cities appeared. Thus we have the gold ducat of Venice and the gold florin of Florence. Both of these coins had a tremendous influence on the coinage of the rest of Europe. The florin, first issued in 1252, was used everywhere and accepted readily. It was also widely imitated, particularly in Germany.

The Popes began to issue money under Adrian I (772-95 A.D.). This coinage continued until the reign of Pope Leo IX (1049 A.D.), when there was a hiatus until the reign of Urban V (1362 A.D.). In 1878 the papal coinage was discontinued entirely under Pope Pius IX, until 1929, when the Vatican State again began to issue its own currency, being one of the few countries issuing gold coins at this time. The *sede vacante* coins, issued between the death of one Pope and the coronation of the next, are always interesting, showing a radiant dove and the arms of the papal camerlengo, or chamberlain. The last of these issued was the 500 lire on the death of Pope John XXIII in 1963.

It may be difficult for the novice to associate some acquisitions with their particular country and period, although a good way to begin is with portrait coins. Even these, however, may prove a bit troublesome to the uninitiated when, as on old English coins, "William" appears as "Gvilemvs," "James" as "Jacobus" or simply "Jac." "Henri" is obviously "Henry," and "Maria" is easily recognized as "Mary."

A good background of history helps, and an accomplished linguist has a distinct advantage. Latin predominates on coins of all Western countries and is found frequently even on recent issues, including our own. Some inscriptions appear the same on money of many countries, and it takes little knowledge of Latin to know that the inscription on the reverse of English, Spanish, and other coins "Rex Dei Gratia" or "D.G." means "King by the Grace of God." Other inscriptions, particularly when in abbreviated Latin, are not quite as simple, while coins of the Oriental and Near Eastern countries require a special study, as they appear in Chinese, Japanese, Arabic, Turkish, and other languages. The best advice that can be given to the serious student who has a yearning to know about the lettering on his coins is to study them and inquire, possibly through the natives of the countries concerned, such as consular officials, etc., just what the inscriptions mean. Thus, the lettering on Russian, Serbian, Turkish, and other coins may be deciphered after a little research and inquiry. Some coins, from Moslem countries, may bear a date confusing to the numismatist. For example, a coin dated 1332 may surprise you at first, since coins were not dated until one hundred years later. This date, however, is according to the Mohammedan calendar and corresponds to our 1914 A.D. Mohammed made his pilgrimage to Mecca on July 16, 622 A.D. Most Mohammedan years were based on months of 30 days, which further confuses the issue. The formula for transcribing from Moslem to Christian eras is this: 1332 A.H. (Anno Hegira) is the Mohammedan date; three percent of this is 39.96, or the nearest whole number, 40; which is subtracted from 1332, leaving 1292; to which is added 622, giving the date 1914 A.D.

Never be discouraged over temporary inability to learn what a coin represents, or what the inscription means. Some dealers who have spent years in handling all kinds of money do not know the meaning of a great many inscriptions, or even the identity or country of origin of certain coins which fall into their hands. They soon find out, however. To decipher foreign money, particularly commemorative pieces, requires a great deal of patience and study, but the numismatist who is a serious student finds pleasure in reading and noting obscure lettering. It may be that aside from reading what appears on some specimens, the collector may obtain some items, of which he cannot readily ascertain the country of origin. To facilitate matters in such cases, we have shown a dictionary containing the denominations of coins. Therefore, if we come across a coin which bears a portrait, lettering, and the denomination 50 lepta, it can be easily ascertained that lepta is applied to Greek current coins. The same procedure applies to the lei, a coin of Roumania; penni, Finland; kopeck, Russia; ore, Denmark, Norway, or Sweden, etc. Then again, some countries do not appear with the appellations commonly given them. Thus, a coin of Switzerland is shown with the country called "Helvetia," which is the old name for that land. Iceland is shown simply as "Island," and Sweden is "Sverige." However, in handling such money these features become familiar in a surprisingly short time. The coins soon can be identified immediately, and, if not known by plain English lettering, are identified by other distinguishing features, and the collector is equally at home in Gaelic or Spanish or Russian.

Other pieces of money bearing Arabic, Persian, or what appears to be Chinese or Japanese, will eventually reveal their stories by vigilant study and observation on the part of the collector, by looking through exhibits in museums, art galleries, and numismatic collections; and by inquiry among other numismatists and dealers. There is hardly a coin that will not show up somewhere, sooner or later, with the name, country of origin, denomination, and all pertinent information catalogued.

The foreign money collector will always find new worlds to conquer. The map of the world is continually changing. The present situations in China, Europe, the Near East, and Africa, all affect the development of the world's coinage, as so many changes in the past twenty years have acquired immense numismatic importance.

Bibliography

ATKINS, JAMES, *Coins and Tokens of Possessions and Colonies of the British Empire,* London, 1889.

CHARLTON, J. E., *Standard Catalogue of Canadian and Newfoundland Coins, Tokens and Fractional Currency,* 7th ed., 1959.

CRAIG, ALAN D., *The Coins of Korea.*

CRAIG, WILLIAM, *Coins of the World 1750–1850,* Racine, Wis., 1965.

DAVENPORT, DR. JOHN S., *European Crowns and Talers Since 1800.*

DAVENPORT, DR. JOHN S., *German Talers 1700–1800.*

DAVENPORT, DR. JOHN S., *European Crowns 1700–1800.*

FRIEDBERG, ROBERT, *Gold Coins of the World (from 600 A.D.)*, 2d ed., New York, 1965.

GRUEBER, H. A., *Handbook of the Coins of Great Britain,* etc., London, 1899.

KANN, EDWARD, *Illustrated Catalogue of Chinese Coins, 1954.*

KAPLAN, DR. ALEC, *Catalogue of the Coins of South Africa.*

RAYMOND, WAYTE, *Coins of the World: 19th Century Issues,* New York.

RAYMOND, WAYTE, *Coins of the World: 20th Century Issues,* New York.

SEABY, H. A., *Notes on English Silver Coins* (Vol. I: 1066-1648, Vol. II: 1649-1949).

SEABY, H. A., and P. J., *Standard Catalogue of the Coins of Great Britain and Ireland,* London, 1958.

SEVERIN, H. M., *Gold and Platinium Coinage of Imperial Russia (1701-1911).*

YEOMAN, RICHARD S., *A Catalog of Modern World Coins,* 6th ed., Racine, Wis., 1964.

CHAPTER FOUR

Ancient Coins

THERE is a certain charm connected with the study and collecting of ancient coins which is not found in any other branch of numismatics. Ancient coins have had a great influence on later coinages, just as Greek and Roman culture and customs have had a great and lasting bearing on many phases of our civilization. In art, literature, and law many of the basic rules and ideas are inherited from the early Greeks and Romans. Numismatics also owes many things to the ancients. Our own coins as well as those of Great Britain and many other European countries still use Latin as the language for mottoes and legends; during the Middle Ages Latin was used almost exclusively. Some coins of the Papal States issued by various Popes have used inscriptions borrowed from the Romans. One of these is the Pope's Latin title, "Pontifex Maximus," meaning "high priest." It is always used on papal coins, and appears on many Roman coins, mostly in abbreviated form. Also "Pater Patriae," Father of His Country, and others.

A collector should not be afraid to venture into the ancient field because of a lack of background. Many collectors without any particular classical education have found great satisfaction in studying the ancient coinages. A list of emperors and others appearing on the Roman coins is all-important, and an essential feature of an interest in such coinage is the fact that so much intriguing and helpful information can be obtained from more or less contemporary sources. Seutonius, Livy, and Julius Caesar have all contributed lively anecdotes and written many things about the times during which they lived; even numismatics comes in for its share of attention in these recountings. Similarly, a good thing for the beginning collector of Greek coins would be a popular book on the history of Ancient Greece, not necessarily anything more than an outline sufficient to obtain a knowledge of the period covered. A list of books for suggested reading, not only numismatic books, but also several bearing on ancient times, is shown at the end of this chapter. We have seen from foregoing chapters the lasting influence which Rome exerts through the many common words and expressions in our daily lives which had their origin in early Latin. In law and in many customs the Romans left a legacy to later civilization without which life as we know it would be a lot different.

The widespread might and influence of Rome is shown in a startling way when we consider that hoards of Roman coins are continually being unearthed even now from England to India —in France, Germany, and the Middle East, in all sorts of conditions and in large and small quantities, often in the original containers in which they were buried. They show in a graphic way the extent of the influence wielded by ancient Rome.

Since the study of Greek and Roman coinage is a special pursuit which follows many paths, we can only give a bare general outline of the essentials here. One who decides to explore this area of numismatics will find much useful and interesting data in books on the subject, both numismatic and historical.

The Egyptians did not have any stamped coinage, although they were rulers of that part of the world for many centuries and coins were in use in other parts of the East for a great many years. It was only in 323 B.C., on the death of Alexander the Great, who conquered Egypt, that his general, Ptolemy, established the dynasty of the Ptolemies, and coins were issued in Egypt. The first silver tetradrachm showed the portrait of Ptolemy and was the first coin ever made with the portrait of a living man.

It is generally accepted as a fact that the first stamped coins were issued by the merchants of Lydia, a seaport province in Asia Minor, about 700 B.C. There were no coins issued in Ancient Egypt, Babylon, Assyria, or other Eastern countries prior to that date. As early as 2000 B.C. copper ring money was used in Egypt showing that the Egyptians did have an idea that some form of money was needed in trading, which happened to be a monopoly of the ruling pharaohs. In early times sacks of corn were used, and later, copper utensils, pitchers, bowls, and other like objects.

With ancient Greek coins the denominations may be hard to follow, since the weight and size differ in various parts of the country. In general, the main denomination was the stater, which, however, could be either gold or silver, depending on the region in which it was found. However, the gold stater was of varying weight and subdivided into sixths, twelfths, and twenty-fourths. The silver stater of Athens, also called a tetradrachm, consisted of 4 drachms, 8 hemidrachms (half) or triobols, 12 diobols, and 24 obols; whereas the silver stater in Corinth contained 3 drachms instead of 4. In addition, while the Athens stater weighed 264 grains, the Corinth stater was only 132 grains.

About 650 B.C. the silver coins of Aegina appeared. These silver coins, similar to all such early issues, had only an obverse design, which in this case consisted of a turtle, the reverse being simply a crisscross pattern caused by the punch marks, since the coins were punched out, one by one, by hand. It was not until about 600 B.C. that designs were shown on both the obverse and reverse sides. The early Aegina coins, called staters, were of electrum, a natural mixture of gold and silver. Credit for the introduction of pure gold and silver coins goes to Lydia. The earliest known gold coin was the stater of Croesus (561-546 B.C.).

The early Aegina coins became familiarly known as the "turtles" of Aegina, from the design. Later there was the tetradrachm or stater of Athens with the owl. The "turtle" and "owl" coins were joined by the stater of Corinth, which showed Pegasus, the winged horse; these coins became famous as the "colts" of Corinth. Thus we have turtles, owls, and colts, and it would seem that we could go on to a full menagerie. Other coins bear characteristic features, such as the barley sheaves on staters of Metapontum, dolphin on those of Tarentum, and so on, each city using some distinguishing mark such as the goddess of the city. In this way coins of one city or ruler could be readily identified by traders and were accepted without question, since by their designs and origin they were acceptable as to their known value and weight in accordance with the standards of the city from which they came.

Since Greece was divided into cities which were more or less independent states, it was natural for some of these cities to assume the leadership. In this way Athens became the most famous of the Grecian cities, and since Greece had colonies all along the Mediterranean coast, it was natural that the money of Athens should eventually take the lead.

The art of coinage was brought to a high degree of excellence by the ancient Greeks, and to this day the fine art displayed on their coins has not been equalled. This beauty of design and workmanship reached its peak during the fifth and fourth centuries B.C., when almost all cities, large and small, issued their own coins showing each city's distinctive features. Athens continued to strike the owl coins for almost three centuries, because the Athenians thought that since the whole Eastern world knew them and accepted them they should not be changed in either design or weight.

During the period mentioned (500-400 B.C.) many cities began to issue bronze coins as well as silver. These bronzes are much less expensive than the silver tetradrachms, to say nothing of the gold coins. During this period also the artistic excellence of Greek coins reached its peak. This is particularly true of the cities of Sicily, where the most beautiful coins were issued. The large silver dekadrachm of Syracuse, issued about 400 B.C., is a most beautiful coin showing the head of Persephone, and on the reverse a man driving a quadriga, or four-horse chariot. This is considered a commemorative coin, celebrating the victories over Carthage and Athens. It is not the first commemorative coin, however, as Athens itself issued a similar coin about 80 years before to commemorate the victory over the Persians at Marathon.

There is a great demand among collectors for these early Grecian coins, and a collector of the ancient series is often proud to be the possessor of even one or two of the masterpieces showing the head of Athena, or Athene, as she is sometimes called, Apollo, or Zeus, the ruler of the gods.

The silver tetradrachms of Alexander the Great of Macedon, showing the head of Heracles (Hercules) wearing a lion's skin, and on the reverse Zeus with thunderbolts, are well known and plentiful and therefore not at all expensive. Some say that the head of Heracles was actually a portrait of Alexander himself, although Ptolemy I, his general, is credited with being the first living man to be shown on coins. At any rate, whether

Alexander or Heracles, the coin has always been identified with the great soldier. Since Alexander had conquered the then known world, these coins were introduced into all parts of Asia Minor and Persia and were used extensively, which accounts for their plentiful supply.

A book by Florence Aiken Banks, *Coins of Bible Days,* printed in 1955, has done a great deal to bring the many coins mentioned in the Bible to the attention of collectors. These also include the interesting Jewish coins, or shekels of Judea, bearing the amphora (a two-handled jar) and the pomegranate or the ethrog (a citrus fruit), since the Jews showed no portraits on their coins. Many coins are mentioned or referred to in the Bible, not always by familiar names. We have all heard of the "widow's mite," which is commonly thought to be the small Greek copper coin known as a lepton. There is also the "tribute penny," or denarius, of Tiberius. The collector of Biblical coins has a wide range, since the coins of many of the Roman emperors and, before or contemporaneously with them, the Greeks, Syrians, Macedonians, and Persians were referred to frequently in the Bible.

The coins of the Sassanians, a Persian tribe, are also of considerable interest in the light of the history of this people. The Sassanians were great warriors, who conquered Parthia and sometimes defeated the Romans. The Sassanian dynasty was founded in 226 A.D. by Artaxerxes, son of Sasson, who ruled until 240 A.D., instituting a great period of prosperity and national glory. Sapor I (240-273 A.D.) defeated the Roman Emperor Valerian. Sapor II (310-381 A.D.) conquered the Armenians, and defeated the Romans in eight different battles, putting to death Emperor Julian II (The Apostate) in 363 A.D. Chosroes I (The Great) ruled from 531 to 579 A.D. The Sassanian dynasty ended in 651 A.D., when the country was overrun by the Arabs.

The silver coins of the Sassanians are broad, thin, and flat, about the circumference of our half dollar. The obverse bears the effigy of the king, or a near likeness; and good specimens of these coins, with the heads, supposedly, of Sapor I, Sapor II, Chosroes I, or Chosroes II may be obtained cheaply. The reverse shows the fire altar with attendants. These coins are often called "Coins of the fire worshippers."

The first Roman coinage was cast and based mainly on a unit of weight rather than as a unit of value, such as we would use today. This money is called *aes rude* from the fact that it consisted of crude, ungainly pieces of metal, bearing no design. The term *aes rude* literally means "rude bronze," *aes* being the Latin term for bronze. Generally shapeless masses of metal, this money is sometimes found in rectangular, square, and various other shapes. Like the Jewish shekel, it can be assumed that this coinage gradually evolved from the asssigning of a certain definite value to crude metal of a certain weight. The *aes rude* dates from about the sixth century B.C., and about one hundred years after this it graduated into *aes signatum,* or "bronze seal." These large bronze pieces bore a design, usually birds, shields, cattle, etc., but there was still no uniformity of shape or size. Around 300 B.C. the *aes signatum* developed into what is called *aes grave,* "heavy bronze" or "heavy brass."

The as bore the head of the god Janus on the obverse (or rather the two heads of Janus faced right and left, as this was a two-headed god), and the prow of a ship on the reverse. The *aes grave* was divided into several denominations besides the as, which are called semis, triens, quadrans, sextans, and uncia (or ounce). All showed a reverse bearing the prow of a ship—why is not known—and since no denomination was shown, they were known by their designs; the as always had the heads of Janus, who was known as a sort of doorkeeper, and whose name gave us our word "janitor." These coins are sought after by collectors, although they are crude and heavy. The semis showed Jupiter, the Greek god Zeus; the triens, Minerva, called by the Greeks Athena; the quadrans, Hercules, whom the Greeks knew as Heracles; the sextans, Mercury, messenger of the gods, the Greek god Hermes; and the uncia, Roma.

The as was gradually reduced in weight, and later the silver denarius was equal to ten asses. The later denominations included the drachma, borrowed from Greece, and still later, about 150 B.C., the coins assumed denominations with which we are all more familiar, the denarius, sestertius, and the quinarius. These early Roman coins showed Roma and the dioscuri, better known as Castor and Pollux, the twin sons of Jupiter.

The denarius, a small silver coin, was the commonest and the standard silver coin for a very long time. It was really the ancestor of the English penny, which was originally made in silver. Later, other designs appeared on the Roman coins which had a bearing on contemporary life and celebrated honorable deeds of the Roman past. Bronze coins were gradually reduced in size and became less common toward the end of the Republic and the beginning of the Empire.

The coins of the Empire, while not comparing favorably with the Greek coins as far as artistic merit is concerned, were, in the early days, of good silver content. However, the silver content gradually declined until a denomination called the "antoninianus" was introduced by Emperor Caracalla (211-217 A.D.) The antoninianii were a very much debased coinage, and, in fact, were issued of copper with such a thin wash of silver that the outer coating of silver is in most cases entirely worn off; later on, little or no silver was used. This debasement of the silver currency reached its height about the time of the reign of the Emperor Gallienus (260-268 A.D.), and in the following years silver coins practically disappeared, and the small and extremely common bronze coins were in general use. The antoninianus is recognized by the rays surrounding the head of the emperor, this style being known to the numismatist as "radiate head." A later denomination was the follis, or double denarius.

It became customary during the last years of the Republic for the various aspirants to the title of emperor to have their portraits stamped on coins; thus, we have the series showing heads of Caesar, Brutus, and Mark Antony, as well as the first actual emperor, Octavian, known later as Augustus. All the Roman emperors after Augustus followed this custom, and the heads of the emperors began to appear as a regular thing. Their acts were also recorded on the coinage, especially when the Roman armies were victorious.

Despite the scarcity of silver denarii in the later days of the Republic, there are still a few gold coins showing these later emperors. The aureus was the standard Roman gold coin until about 300 A.D., when it was displaced by the solidus. There was also a gold quinarius, which is half an aureus. There are gold coins of Licinius I (307-324 A.D.) and Licinius II (326 A.D.), and several aureii and at least one solidus of Constantine the Great (306-337 A.D.).

In the time of the late Roman Empire, or from about 330 A.D., the siliqua replaced the denarius. The siliqua, of course, was of silver, but smaller than the denarius.

The collector of ancient coins can follow the same procedure as for a collection of United States coins of a certain series. That is, begin with the inexpensive, common varieties, and fill in as time goes on with the rarer issues. The collector of Roman Imperial coins has a fairly clear road. It is a simple matter to obtain a list of all the emperors; for that matter, several good publications list all the issues. Besides the coins of the emperors themselves, these lists also include the coins of the wives, daughters, and sons wherever issues were put out showing the portraits of the Imperial families.

The list of Roman portrait coins is so extensive that it might be well to begin with a limited period—say, Valerian (254-260 A.D.) to Diocletian (284-305 A.D.). Some issues between these dates are rare, such as the antoninianii of Julian (284 A.D.), Laelian (265 A.D.), and others. However, they can be left out, if necessary. There are some exceptionally rare coins for nearly all of the periods, and, of course, in such cases the only thing the collector can do is either bide his time or simply ignore the piece he lacks. The most important emperors all had fairly large coinages; and they are, after all, the ones we are after. Portraits of such famous emperors as Valerian, Septimus Severus, Marcus Aurelius, Hadrian, Vespasian, Nero, and many others of the better-known rulers are not difficult to come by; therefore, although nothing would be finer than to have a complete roll, the lesser rulers will not be greatly missed.

The Roman Republican coins, prior to 14 A.D., are of great interest and, as a general rule, less expensive than the Empire coins. Among these issues are found the portraits of some of the most illustrious of the Romans, names which are known by everyone—for example, Julius Caesar, Brutus, Pompey the Great, Mark Antony, Octavius, and Cleopatra, who appears on one side of a denarius with the head of Mark Antony on the reverse. Among the early Imperial coins are several of Tiberius (14-37 A.D.), during whose reign Christ lived and died. One denarius of Tiberius is known as the "Tribute Penny of the Bible."

Unfortunately, there are only a few coin dealers in this country who are well versed in the study of ancient coins.

Therefore, it is necessary for the beginner in this branch of numismatics to be careful in buying such pieces. There are many counterfeits and spurious ancient coins. It is well, therefore, to study the subject thoroughly before going too deeply into a collection. This is one reason why starting in a very modest way is the wisest course. By starting with the later bronze coins of less value, and gradually accumulating the more expensive issues of denarii, the collector will save himself a great deal of money.

However, when all is said, a good set of ancient coins is a source of great satisfaction to the numismatist. The field is large and varied, and there is no other series which offers such outstanding opportunities for study and research.

Bibliography

BANKS, FLORENCE AIKEN, *Coins of Bible Days,* New York, 1955.

COHEN, HENRY, *Roman Coins and Medals* (8 vols. in French), Paris, 1880-1892.

DURANT, WILL, *The Life of Greece,* New York, 1939.

GAVORSE, JOSEPH, *Seutonius—The Lives of the Twelve Caesars,* New York, 1931.

HEAD, BARCLAY V., *Historia Numorum* (Greek coins), London, 1911.

KLAWANS, ZANDER H., *Reading and Dating Roman Imperial Coins,* Racine, Wis., 1953.

KLAWANS, ZANDER H., *An Outline of Ancient Greek Coins,* Racine Wis., 1959.

LISSNER, IVAR, *The Caesars—Might and Madness,* New York, 1958.

MADDEN, FREDERIC W., *History of Jewish Coinage,* London, 1864.

MATTINGLY, H., *Guide to the Exhibition of Roman Coins in the British Museum,* London, 1927.

PINK, KARL, *The Triumviri Monetales and the Structure of the Coinage of the Roman Republic,* New York, 1952.

RAWLINGS, GERTRUDE B., *Coins and How to Know Them,* New York.

ROGERS, E. A., *A Handy Guide to Jewish Coins,* London, 1914.

ROMANOFF, PAUL, *Jewish Symbols on Ancient Jewish Coins,* Philadelphia, 1944.

SEABY, H. A., *Roman Silver Coins of the Republic,* London, 1952.

SELTMAN, CHARLES, *Greek Coins,* London, 1955.

SYDENHAM, E. A., *The Coinage of the Roman Republic,* London, 1952.

WARD, JOHN, *Greek Coins and Their Parent Cities,* London, 1902.

WIRGIN & MANDEL, *History of the Coins and Symbols of Ancient Israel,* New York, 1958.

CHAPTER FIVE

Making a Profit from Coin Collecting

IT HAS been truthfully said that all collectors of coins are dealers to a greater or less degree. This inevitably happens because, whether we wish it or not, duplicates will accumulate. This is perhaps more true of coin collecting than it is of any other collecting hobby. An antique collector seldom, if ever, gets two articles exactly alike; clocks and timepieces are nearly always unique, while the stamp collector will probably make but one or two major changes—say, from United States to foreign, or vice versa. However, the coin collector deals largely in dates, and the greater the rarity of such dates the more likely he is to acquire a half dozen of the same date, ranging in condition from just good to very fine or uncirculated. A man with a fine but slightly worn Indian-head 1864 L cent will find an opportunity to buy a very fine specimen, and, perhaps later on, an uncirculated 1864 L cent. This is likely to happen with almost all dates and denominations, until the collector finds himself with a fairly large supply of coins he would like to exchange for others, or which he would like to sell to buy other dates. An active member of a coin club will easily find opportunities to make such exchanges.

The man who does not belong to a coin club and has a

limited acquaintance with other collectors will either have to advertise in one of the numismatic journals or send his surplus items to an auction dealer. Naturally, the more active the collector, the quicker he will accumulate such surpluses. Results from advertising in hobby magazines and numismatic publications are always fairly good, and fellow collectors are quick to take advantage of the opportunity to get a variety they may be looking for. Contrary to what you might expect, a dealer will sometimes give better prices than the collectors themselves. A good many collectors never sell anything but keep on and on, occasionally exchanging or giving away, but never selling until possibly illness or old age finally decides.

As we have seen, the value of a coin is determined by its scarcity. While it is assumed that coin collectors are attracted to this pleasing pastime by an inherent love of the subject, it is also well to consider the game in the light of ready disposal of coins without monetary loss, and, if possible, with profit. With this in mind, it is easily seen why it is foolish to retain worn or too common specimens. Uncirculated and very fine coins can always be readily sold, and generally at a profit. Many a stamp collector has listened to a dealer's urgings to buy because "it's a good investment," and later found to his sorrow that in time of financial stress he has realized little or nothing when disposing of his stamps. So, too, many numismatists have learned with regret that what was thought to be a good investment has had to be sold at a distinct loss. It is well, therefore, to buy only from reliable dealers who guarantee the genuineness of all ancient and obscure coins. There are some dealers entirely unversed in reading ancient or medieval coins. Their guesses as to emperors and periods are often far from accurate. However, if ancient coins are purchased with clear descriptions of their denominations, rulers, and other points, we can be reasonably sure that they are correct.

A collector's ideas are always changing. A completed series of large cents, half dimes, or quarter dollars may start an urge to dispose of them and start another series of, let us say, United States commemorative half dollars, or foreign commemoratives, or ancients, as the case may be. The collector who has patiently accumulated very fine or uncirculated coins or proofs at fair prices may very easily dispose of them through advertising in the numismatic publications or through a reliable dealer either outright or at auction. Most coin auctioneers require a commission of from ten to twenty percent for disposing of coins, and it is possible to set a minimum price on more desirable items, so that the seller may know about what to expect in return.

A reader may ask, "What current coins should I set aside, hoping for a good profit in a few years?" This is a fair question, but a difficult one to answer, because it would be like knowing what horse will win a race or what stocks will advance. And if anybody knew, he would keep the secret to himself. As price is determined by scarcity, anyone who studies the mint records of United States coins can get a good idea as to future rarities. The *Guidebook of United States Coins* and the *Appraising and Selling Your Coins,* mentioned earlier, show these mint records, so that it is not necessary to secure the yearly reports put out by the Treasury Department. Without going back many years for an example, the 1931 S cent is rapidly becoming an expensive coin. Of these, 866,000 were minted, a comparatively small number compared to the millions of other dates. In 1935 or 1936 they could be purchased uncirculated for about $.30 or $.40 each. In 1937 they sold for between $.75 to $1.50. In 1959 an uncirculated 1931 S cent brings $45. This may seem a startling advance in price, but it is by no means amazing compared to the appreciation in price shown by the proof sets of earlier years, 1936 to 1942, for instance, or by some of the commemorative coins. To illustrate this we have prepared a comparison of prices of various coins at some not too widely separated dates, which will be shown presently. Incidentally, since the San Francisco mint was closed in 1955 and coinages from that mint prior to that time were not in the large quantities put out by the other mints, it does not need great foresight to predict that in coming years coins bearing the letter "S" will be scarce in uncirculated condition, and accordingly higher in price.

It is a good idea to see for ourselves whether coins advance in price enough to warrant the labor and expense of keeping them. Taking three years for samples, 1938 (before World War II), 1949 (after the war), and 1966, we can give a few examples of the appreciation of the value of a few representative coins, both regular issues and specials such as commemoratives and proofs. The latter two classifications are possibly not as typical as the regular issues, since past commemoratives and proofs from past years are closed issues. In other words, the mintages are completed and no more will be issued. While the same applies in a sense to the regular issues, that is, the dates of issue are past, numbers available are more elastic than the special issues, since the greater part of the regular issues may be assumed to have gone into circulation, which is not true of proof coins or, except to a limited degree, of commemorative silver half dollars.

This little study will be a composite of prices charged by dealers at various times. While it is not a strictly accurate guide, it is good enough for our purposes. No completely exact guide could be set up, for the reason that there is now, and was in the earlier years, a certain spread between the high and low prices charged by different dealers. Thus, one dealer might price a coin at $5, another at $7.50, still another at $6, and so on. This is the result of competition; one dealer may have enough of the same items to be able to offer them for less, or he may even be tired of carrying them and want quick cash, or he may, on the other hand, be satisfied, as a matter of policy, with less profit on all his goods. Whatever the reason, there has always been a deviation of a dollar or so between various dealers' prices for the same article, although it is the tendency of late to adhere somewhat closely to "catalogue" prices. Since, as we know, prices of coins of the same denomination, date, and mint mark will vary considerably in price according to condition (uncirculated, very fine, fine, etc.), all the prices shown, excepting for proofs, are for uncirculated specimens unless shown otherwise. The years we have used can be taken as good examples, perhaps better than others, because in 1938 the war had not had too much effect on prices, 1949 had seen the end of conflict and was still too early for inflation to make its full impact on the economy, and 1958 is the year in which inflation reached its peak.

Commemorative Gold

	1938	*1949*	*1966*
1903 Louisiana Purchase—Jefferson Dollar	$ 5.50	$ 13.50	$ 115.00
1903 Louisiana Purchase—McKinley Dollar	5.50	13.50	115.00
1904 Lewis & Clark Exposition Dollar	18.00	50.00	400.00
1905 Lewis & Clark Exposition Dollar	18.00	50.00	400.00
1915 S Panama Pacific Exposition Dollar	4.25	10.00	80.00
1915 S Panama Pacific Exposition $2.50	18.00	45.00	385.00
1915 S Panama Pacific Exposition $50 (round)	Pair 615.00	600.00	6000.00
1915 S Panama Pacific Exposition $50 (octagonal)		500.00	4750.00

Commemorative Gold (cont.)

	1938	*1949*	*1966*
1916 McKinley Memorial Dollar	$ 4.75	$ 10.00	$ 110.00
1917 McKinley Memorial Dollar	6.75	13.50	175.00
1922 Grant Memorial Dollar (with star)	7.50	25.00	335.00
1922 Grant Memorial Dollar (without star)	15.00	16.50	365.00
1926 Philadelphia Sesquicentennial $2.50	5.50	10.00	75.00

Commemorative Half Dollars

1892 Columbian Exposition	$ 1.00	$ 1.50	$ 25.00
1893 Columbian Exposition	.75	1.00	14.50
1915 Panama Pacific	14.50	17.00	25.00
1918 Illinois Centennial—Lincoln	.85	3.00	14.00
1920 Maine Centennial	3.75	6.00	7.50
1920 Pilgrim Tercentenary	1.45	2.25	25.00
1921 Pilgrim Tercentenary	7.50	7.50	100.00
1921 Missouri Centennial	16.00	25.00	20.00
1921 Missouri Centennial (2x4)	25.00	35.00	25.00
1921 Alabama Centennial	5.00	7.00	50.00
1921 Alabama Centennial (2x2)	14.50	18.00	625.00
1922 Grant Memorial	2.00	3.00	36.50
1922 Grant Memorial (with star)	25.00	65.00	20.00
1923 Monroe Doctrine Centennial	1.50	3.00	18.00
1924 Huguenot-Walloon Tercentenary	2.60	4.00	10.00
1925 Lexington-Concord Sesquicentennial	1.50	3.00	6.50
1925 Stone Mountain Memorial	.85	1.00	4.50
1925 California Diamond Jubilee	2.45	5.00	100.00
1925 Fort Vancouver Centennial	7.50	15.00	25.00
1926 Sesquicentennial of American Independence	1.50	2.50	30.00
1926 Oregon Trail Memorial	1.50	2.50	12.50
1927 Bennington-Vermont Sesquicentennial	2.75	4.50	23.50
1928 Hawaiian Sesquicentennial	12.00	25.00	175.00
1934 Maryland Tercentenary	1.50	2.50	150.00

Commemorative Half Dollars (cont.)

	1938	*1949*	*1966*
1934 Daniel Boone Bicentennial	$ 2.50	$ 3.00	$ 65.00
1935 Connecticut Tercentenary	3.25	5.00	45.00
1935 Arkansas Centennial	1.50	2.50	150.00

Proof coins are specially minted coins struck on polished dies at a much slower rate of speed than ordinary coins. They are made for collectors, and all details are clear and pronounced. The coins are on polished planchets and are not touched by hands, so that they bear a mirrorlike surface which makes for a beautiful coin. In England, South Africa, and some other countries, proof coins are referred to as specimen sets.

We can take a different basis for proof sets of the years 1936-42 and 1950-66 inclusive. In 1936 coinage of proofs in this country was resumed at Philadelphia only, after a lapse of twenty years. They were discontinued during the war years, after 1942, and resumed again in 1950. Since the first group (1936-42) all began at the same base mint price of $1.81, and the second group (1950-66) all started at the mint price of $2.10 a set, with these prices as a means, we have the following values as of early 1966:

1936—	$1000.00	1951—	$110.00
1937—	450.00	1952—	50.00
1938—	225.00	1953—	43.50
1939—	200.00	1954—	30.00
1940—	130.00	1955—	40.00
1941—	120.00	1956—	16.00
1942—	130.00	1957—	9.00
1950—	175.00	1958—	20.00

The only other comparison we will make is for a few of the older coins of various denominations, from half cent to dollar, which have steadily risen in price:

Half Cents (1793-1857)

	1938	*1949*	*1966*
1796—plain edge, pole to cap	$100.	$200.	$3200.
1796—no pole to cap	150.	300.	4250.
1808 over 7	15.	20.	155.
1811	30.	50.	600.

Large Cents (1793-1857)
(Fine Condition)

1799	50.	100.	975.
1804	20.	75.	425.

Flying Eagle Cents (1856-58)
(Uncirculated)

1856	75.	150.	2600.
1857	8.	18.	100.

Indian-head Cents—
Copper-nickel (1859-64); Bronze (1864-1909)
(Uncirculated)

1864 L on ribbon	8.	50.	300.
1871	10.	15.	220.
1877	12.	25.	950.
1909 S	4.	20.	400.

Lincoln-head Cents (1909-)
(Uncirculated)

1909 S VDB	2.	15.	300.
1914 D	1.	10.	700.
1923 S	1.	9.	265.

Two Cents (1864-73)
(Uncirculated)

1864 small motto	15.	40.	300.

	1938	1949	1966
Three Cents Nickel (1865-89)			
1877 proof	$20.	$75.	$800.
1877 uncirculated	2.	8.	37.50
Five Cents Nickel (1866-)			
1866	3.	12.	112.50
1867 with rays	3.	16.	150.
1871	5.	40.	200.
Liberty-head:			
1885	5.	25.	300.
1912 D	2.	25.	240.
Half Dimes Silver (1794-1873)			
1794	15.	35.	1500.
1846	10.	40.	285.
1849-O	10.	20.	100.
1853-O No arrows	25.	125.	450.
Dimes Silver (1796-)			
1822	7.50	35.	575.
1841—no drapery from elbow	45.	150.	300.
1856-S	10.	75.	275.
Twenty Cents Silver (1875-1878)			
1875-CC	5.	12.	150.
Twenty-five Cents Silver (1796-)			
1796	25.	65.	5900.
1804	10.	30.	650.
1822—25¢ over 50¢	75.	250.	1600.
Half dollar Silver (1794-)			
1805 over 4	5.	75.	500.
1806 over 9	10.	75.	600.
1842-O—small date	12.	60.	300.

As far as the commemoratives go this is a startling comparison, and the gold commemoratives have been priced beyond the consideration of the average collector. The commemorative half dollars are not quite in the same class, but have in some cases almost attained this questionable distinction. The outlook for the half dollars is not altogether bleak because there has been a remarkable lessening of demand, and a consequent tendency of late for prices to retreat here and there. It may be that in time a set of these desirable and historically interesting coins will be within reach of the collector with a small allowance for such acquisitions. The commemorative prices shown are for bright uncirculated specimens. It is possible to secure certain of these half dollars in circulated condition, but there is a limit here too. The Columbian, Stone Mountain, Pilgrim, Lincoln, or Illinois Centennial, and two or three others can be obtained in very fine or fine condition. Most of the others, with the exception of the late Carvers, are seldom if ever found in anything but uncirculated or almost uncirculated condition, the latter applying when the coin has been subjected to careless handling, resulting in scratching or tarnishing. There has been an appreciable rise in prices over the years for commemoratives. If there could be any guarantee that prices would continue upward at the same rate, an investment in the commemorative half dollars would be well worth while even now. In the meantime, there are a few of the half dollars which can be acquired at not too great a cost. Furthermore, it is not necessary to acquire every date and mint mark; for instance, all the Texas, Boone, Arkansas, Oregon, Booker T. Washington, and Washington-Carver sets are not necessary when one of each will do for what is called a type set, consisting of 48 pieces, as against 142 total pieces. At that, a type set is priced at the not inconsiderable amount of about $2,000.

Looking at the listing of proof sets, the reason for the extreme advance in price of the 1936 set is that there were only about 3,000 full sets minted in that year, that is, the complete set of cents, dimes, quarters, and half dollars, although some individual coins were minted to the amount of over 5,000 cents and 4,000 nickels. When 3,000 sets are divided by many times that number of collectors, this can only mean that many collectors will have to do without this set. The 1950 set is higher than the average for late sets, for the reason that there is a considerable demand and a comparatively short supply. Many new collectors started their proof sets with this issue, and have continued them each year.

Of course, the foregoing study of prices does not necessarily mean that a similar rate of appreciation of values will hold for succeeding years covering the same length of time. Compared with the low coinage of 1936 proof sets, or even the 1950s (about 51,000 sets), over 1,000,000 sets were issued in 1958, and 2,903,152 sets in 1957! In 1959 prices for a few single dates are already lower than the peak. In a few cases commemorative coins have even taken a drop, as compared with two years earlier. The drops, however, have been practically all in prices of the normally lower-priced half dollars, such as the 1921 Pilgrim, Lexington-Concord, and Philadelphia Sesquicentennial. The Vancouver, Hudson, and other higher-priced halves continue to advance. Proof sets have not maintained their former rate of increased value and some of the regular minor issues are not too much in demand. Some of the slackening off of demand and consequent decline in some prices is due to economic conditions; some is due to the fact that fashions change in collecting as much as they do in clothing and customs. What is immensely popular one year is unnoticed the next. At one time the United States commemorative coinage was in great demand and prices rose rapidly. Some say they have been priced too high for the average collector. If so, it is too bad, because this is one of the most fascinating series of American coins and of great historical interest. Prices of proofs have now stopped their rapid advance and are again popular. And, since a new set is issued yearly, a beginner can always start with the current year, or two or three years previous, and either secure the current set at the minimum government price or purchase one or two back years at a slight advance over this price. Sometimes there is a sudden unexplainable liking for a certain denomination. Cents are always well thought of, but sometimes there may be a great demand for dimes, sometimes for quarter dollars, or halves, or silver dollars. Occasionally there are sudden urges to collect foreign crowns, foreign gold, or paper money. Some believe these fads happen because one popular dealer advertises a certain series or denomination in a big way, is followed by others, and the collectors fall into line. Or a new book on a formerly neglected series may awaken interest in a particular field.

It is not our intention to emphasize the profit angle, or the excessive prices of some coins, or the increase in values over a comparatively short period, but rather to illustrate the enjoyment one may get from a most fascinating hobby, involving research, incidental reading, and so on. Unfortunately, most of us have to concern ourselves with prices, because there is always the possibility of having to sell part of one's collection. In such an event, it is comforting to know that, unlike some hobbies or pastimes in which collecting objects is involved, the coin collector may, and often does, realize more for his pets than he paid for them, depending on what he paid in the beginning and how long he has held them, and more important, whether he has shown discrimination in only holding on to worthwhile specimens in uncirculated condition, even at a higher original cost. Too many collectors are apt to be too thrifty and end up with many specimens of what can only be classified as "junk." This type of common foreign coins and only fair or poor United States coins will not even find a market, or, at best, can only be disposed of in bulk at a loss. Therefore, it is much better to spend a bit more for one desirable coin than to put the same amount of money into thirty or more ordinary pieces.

While it is all too true that a lot of recently issued coins have been priced beyond the reach of the collector of moderate income, the American colonial coins have remained fairly constant and moderate in price for a good many years. This series is a most interesting one, not so much for any great beauty of design or marvelous display of imagination on the engravers' part. In fact, the best that can be said for most of them is that they look "colonial." However, they are the early coins of our country and extremely interesting historically. While a fine Lincoln cent 1914 D may be had for $60 to $70, many New York, Connecticut, or Vermont cents of 1786, 1787, or 1788 can be had for less than $10. There are, of course, some notable exceptions here, too, as there are some New York cents of rare varieties coming as high as $100 or more, which means that they are practically unattainable. The general run on the whole is not costly, though for some unknown reason they are not as popular as late issues of Lincoln cents and Mercury dimes. We are talking here for the benefit of those who insist on collecting United States coins exclusively. If one is not so particular, there are always other branches which can be explored, such as the ancients or late foreign issues, which can be picked up at very moderate prices, and of which there is no scarcity of items.

Current and common foreign coins can seldom be sold at much more than exchange value by anyone but a dealer. They are well worth saving by a person who wants to have a representative collection of the world's money, but the collector who is not a dealer will undoubtedly have to dispose of them through a foreign exchange dealer or in lots through an auction dealer. The average person's lack of knowledge of the value of foreign coins is amusing to the coin dealer. Many extremely common pieces are offered to dealers, who would have a hard time disposing of them at any price. This lack of knowledge is not confined to foreign coins either. Hundreds of people are carrying around some old United States coin which they are sure is "worth a lot of money." They have a large cent, badly worn, of 1857 which they are anxious to dispose of for a large sum of money. The longer they carry it around with loose change the more worn it becomes, and how disappointed they are when a dealer offers them five cents for their prize!

Foreign commemorative coins, crowns, series of large Canadian cents, English silver pennies, and the rarer ancient coins may well be disposed of at a profit in the same manner as United States coins. There is almost as much competition among American collectors, particularly as regards Canadian coins of late years, to obtain certain of these series as there is in connection with United States minor coins, gold, or commemoratives.

In the selling phase of the collecting game several common-sense rules should prevail: (1) Be patient in buying coins and wait for good values. (2) Tolerate no "junk." (3) Concentrate on items for which there is a constant demand from collectors. A few months' experience in inquiring and buying will bring this knowledge. (4) Be patient in disposing of coins at your own price, within reason.

Often we may doubt the wisdom of putting a large amount of money into a collection. "Practical" people may scoff at a collector who puts away perfectly good American coins or bills for months or even years. "It's all very pretty," they will say, after examining a collection, "but you would be better off if you had your money in the bank." Fortunately, the true collector is not easily deterred by "wet blankets." He can always ease his conscience with the thought: "While I am losing a little bank interest now by tying up this money, in a year or so I will sell the collection at a profit."

As for "practical" people, there are no more practical or sharp-witted folk than numismatists attending a coin club meeting or a national convention, and it takes a good man to put anything over on the majority of them, who have all the shrewd business acumen of an old-time horse trader.

It requires a little courage to put aside a book of a hundred or more one-dollar bills of unique design, for which double or three times face value has been paid; but there is the consolation that, except in times of war or in periods of drastic inflation, the money has a definite value. The optimistic collector can always dream about, and often realize, a good profit on almost every item when he decides to explore new fields of numismatics and break up the collection, provided, of course, that good common sense has been exercised in forming the collection and no opportunities have been wasted to secure real bargains.

It is a fact which is strange but true that a great many dealers are just as anxious to buy numismatic material as they are to sell it. The dealers have as much trouble, if not more, in locating suitable items as they have in disposing of them after they are purchased. There is always a ready market for rare and scarce dates, and a good average profit may be obtained from collectors, who are always on the lookout for coins to fill in their collections. Numismatic books are always in demand, particularly the standard works, owing to the fact that a good many of them were issued years ago and are now out of print. The information they contain is still valuable, but except for a reprint of some important work now and then, these volumes are hard to find and often bring as much as $25 a copy.

In disposing of coins by mail to dealers, the collector should always advise the dealer by letter and secure his approval before sending the coins. It is hardly necessary to mention that packages or letters containing such coins should be sent by insured parcel post or express, or registered mail. Collectors should never simply mail a postal card to dealers and quote a list of coins, asking for an "offer." Such requests are naturally ignored, because all dealers receive hundreds of such communications in the course of a year, and they are considered nothing more than time wasters. However, if the collector will write a letter and explain what he has to dispose of, enclosing return postage at all times, most dealers are glad to give such requests proper and prompt attention.

It may not be out of place at this time to drop a few suggestions relating to the buying of specimens for a collection. It is not always possible to attend sales or to purchase articles personally from the numismatic dealers. People living in small cities and towns find it necessary very often to purchase their collection by mail, piece by piece. Even collectors in big cities will do a large percentage of business by mail, owing to the fact that something they need will be offered by a dealer far away from their home. While there are a great many dealers in all parts of the country and the number is growing all the time, there are many towns and fairly large cities which have no dealers at all. We have appended a list of dealers covering almost all sections of the country as well as Canada.

There are a few unsatisfactory features connected with the necessity of doing business entirely by mail. At the same time, there are a great many reliable dealers, in fact, ninety-nine percent of the total number, who will always give the customer the benefit of any doubt, and the collector's money is always safe in their hands. There have been dealers who, when the article requested is sold out, will hold on to the would-be purchaser's cash for months on end, and many letters are sometimes necessary before the money is returned or the transaction completed. Fortunately, such unreliable dealers are very few, since to advertise and stay in business any length of time it is necessary to be honest, which is a strict requirement of the numismatic publications.

While coin auctioneers do not add a commission to the buyer's price, at least in this country, a good many of them have a "handling" or "mailing" charge of a few cents, in addition to postage. In these cases it hardly pays to bid on less than $10 worth of goods. There have been cases where a person has bid $.40 on an ordinary half cent, and received a statement for the $.40 plus $.10 handling charge, plus $.30 registered mail charge, or a total of $.80, and therefore no bargain at all.

There is one undesirable feature sometimes encountered in purchasing coins by mail, namely, that all dealers are not exactly conservative in their descriptions of the condition of their merchandise. A badly worn coin can hardly be shown as in "uncirculated" condition, but coins below that classification are often very much overrated. A coin advertised as "very fine" may turn out to be less than "fine"; one advertised as "fine," less than "good." The classifying of coins as to condition is left to the individual dealer's good judgment and honesty, and no two dealers are likely to think exactly alike on this subject. Fortunately, most coin dealers are fairly conservative in their advertising of the condition of their stock, and, in fact, incline more in favor of the buyer, with the result that their "very fine" coins are almost uncirculated, and the "fine" ones in the very best condition.

Reliable dealers will readily take back any coin which is not satisfactory to the buyer and refund the price paid, provided that the piece is returned within a reasonable length of time. Most dealers restrict the time within which unsatisfactory goods may be returned to from five to ten days after receipt. Since the majority of dealers are honest and reliable, numismatic publications and hobby magazines often require the best of references from advertisers, and give prompt attention to complaints from readers who have been given unsatisfactory treatment. On the other hand, some complaints are not justified. The collector should never expect too much for his money. Rare and scarce coins have a certain rightful value, and the collector should be prepared to give a fair price for specimens. Dealers, of course, also have a few things to say about the bad habits of some collectors. Some of their complaints are justified. We have mentioned the practice of requesting prices and "offers" on postal cards or in letters without enclosing return postage. Another practice which some collectors overdo is that of looking too closely for "bargains." Desirable dates and varieties must not be expected for little or nothing. To illustrate, some auction dealers find it necessary to insert a paragraph in their catalogues: "Bids of $.55 for half dollars and like ridiculous bids are consigned to the waste basket." Don't be too exacting. Naturally, we should expect to get what is rightfully coming to us, but if we get "stuck" here and there through our own foolish mistakes, we must learn to take it with a grin.

Never bid at auction on anything you are not sure to be able to pay for. If you agree to have goods sent on approval, do not hold the material too long if you do not want to purchase it, and if you do wish to buy, remit promptly. If you are displeased in any way with the outcome of a deal, let the seller know rather than bear a grudge which will preclude future dealings.

Some dealers make a practice of sending lots of coins on

approval to known collectors. This is a practice which is not pleasing to some of the recipients, who may be short of cash and too busy to go to the trouble of returning the package. Others, however, are glad to be so trusted and will always take some of the approvals. Of course, the fact that such approval packages are received does not place the collector under any obligation to purchase any of the coins.

Most dealers are glad to receive the collector's "want lists," or lists of dates and denominations he is on the watch for. When the particular date or dates are received by the dealer, he will notify the collector. This practice is of great assistance to the busy man who does not get around much, or who does not find enough leisure to read carefully the numismatic advertisements. Apropros the busy man, it might be well to point out that the man without a certain amount of leisure may have a difficult time getting together a worthwhile collection. The science of numismatics requires a good deal of reading and studying; attending club meetings, and, now and then, a convention; contacting other collectors; and even a fair amount of walking around town, visiting coin dealers and coin exhibits. Nearly everyone, however, can find enough leisure time, at least during certain periods of the year; and at such times he can devote himself to his collection and study with that much greater zeal.

There are also other difficulties which the collector may have to put up with. Well-meaning friends and relatives will often, and, unfortunately, much too often, deride the collector for "wasting your time with that junk" or "cluttering up the house," adding many other sour reflections which will discourage all but the most stouthearted. All collectors encounter such derision at some time, but the satisfaction obtained from their possessions and the hearty approval of a host of other similarly benighted souls more than make up for an occasional sneer.

Of late years there has emerged the investing coin collector or dealer who deals almost exclusively in mint sets or rolls of minor uncirculated coins. On the face of it, it would seem to be a long-drawn-out process to secure rolls of current uncirculated cents, dimes, or other denominations and keep them for a profit. The fact is, however, that rolls of uncirculated coins—say for example, dimes of 1946—have sufficiently advanced in price over the few years up to the present time to warrant the effort and expense of keeping them. Without going into the details too exhaustively, we find a roll dealer advertising at the present time a roll of 1946 dimes for $8.50. A roll contains 50 dimes, with a face value of $5. Other dates have shown more sensational results, like the 1949 S dimes, which sell for $80 a roll, with the same face value of $5. Quarter dollars in rolls of 40, face value $10, do not show so startling an increase: 1949 selling for $12.75, 1950 for $15, and so on. Rolls of 1948 half dollars, 20 to a roll with face value of $10, however, are selling for $32.50.

As for mint sets, which are uncirculated sets consisting of cents, nickels, dimes, quarters, and half dollars of each mint for any particular year, these too have advanced year by year, possibly not enough for some years to be worth the trouble; but for some other scarce years, enough to amply reward the hoarder. Mint sets are sold by the Treasurer of the United States, Washington 25, D. C. At this writing, the price for sets of the two mints, Philadelphia and Denver, including postage and handling, is $4.43. Total face value of the coins is $3.64. In previous years the prices were about the same, and prices now asked for dates as far back as 1948 by those who deal in mint sets are not out of line, such as $5.25 for a set of five pieces for that year, face value $.91. However, in 1958, $19.50

was asked for a set of five pieces dated 1939 S, $27.50 for a set of 1938 D coins, and earlier years were correspondingly high. Coins by roll are not sold by the government to individuals. These must be secured from a bank.

My own personal opinion is that a dealer or collector of rolls, even when supplemented with large numbers of mint sets or proof sets, is purely a speculator and can hardly be considered a real collector and surely not a numismatist. In a lengthy article in the *Wall Street Journal* recently, the writer advocated coin collecting on a large scale as a hedge against inflation and discussed some of the advantages of this type of accumulation. It is impossible to say how many business men took up collecting as a result of this and other similar articles. The hoarding of gold coinage has always been a part of the inflation picture. This was even truer when gold coinages were common. Today there are few countries issuing gold coins, and even those that do issue in this metal confine such coinages to commemoratives or special strikings of some kind, with one or two exceptions. Vatican City has issued a gold 100-lire piece several times since 1929; Mexico frequently issues gold in 50-peso and smaller denominations; South Africa has had several issues of gold specimen coins, and Israel has issued gold. At this writing there are many large gold "coins of doubtful origin," as they are called, honoring odd personages from Queen Nefertete to Henry Hudson, which are manufactured in Europe purely for speculation. They cannot be considered numismatic items in the strict sense, because none of them ever saw circulation nor were they intended to.

It is hoped that no prospective collector will be scared off by all the talk of high prices and out-of-reach coins. We all have to start somewhere, and since there is no hurry, the collector can always start with what is available, even though it is a shiny new cent or dime, quarter, or half dollar, and go on from there. In numismatics more than in any other field, what at first seems commonplace, on further study turns out to be quite interesting. Take the ordinary Lincoln cent. Does it have a mint mark? When was it first issued? What years are common, what rare, and why? The initials V.D.B. appear in minute letters under the bust. Whose are they? Were they always in the same position? The answer is that they belong to a talented man who had quite a wonderful history, if you should be curious enough to find out. Whose initials, F.G., appear on the new reverse of the same Lincoln cent? When you have exhausted the possibilities and answered all the questions, there are other denominations to go after. In the case of a foreign land there are even more opportunities for research, such as whose head or coat of arms appears, the meaning of inscriptions, Latin or otherwise, mint marks and other small details, and a host of other questions that will arise. All of which is just by way of saying that, for a real collector or budding numismatist, prices are secondary and we can always make the best of what is available.

In closing these remarks on the profit angle, it seems appropriate to mention a few sources of supply through which the coin buyer may obtain coins direct from the origin. We have explained how mint sets are obtained. Proof sets of United States coins for current years may be obtained through money order, or certified check to Superintendent, Philadelphia Mint, 16th and Spring Garden Streets, Philadelphia, Pa.

Mint sets of Canada may be obtained through the Bank of Canada, Ottawa, Ontario, Canada, at a small premium.

When issued, specimen sets of English money may be obtained from the London Mint, London, England, at set prices. South African specimen sets or single crowns may be obtained through the Director of the South African Mint, Pretoria, South Africa.

In addition, many collectors join together and take turns in writing various agencies, mints, etc. of foreign countries, requesting information on new issues, prices, and postage charges. A word of advice may be added to this: Sometimes it may be just as well to wait for the dealers to offer new issues and buy from them. For one thing, the prices are not out of proportion if purchased soon after issue. In this way the dealer handles all the difficulties that might arise in getting coins from the source and through customs. In other words, the time, trouble, and expense involved in dealing with some foreign mints may not be worth the few extra cents saved by ordering that way instead of from a dealer.

CHAPTER SIX

The Care and Cleaning of Coins

THE numismatist always has a keen desire to keep his possessions in the best containers possible for readily displaying them and, at the same time, keep them in the best of condition. This is plain common sense, because it would hardly pay to spend good money for proof or uncirculated coins or sets, then throw them in a desk or table drawer where they would become scratched, tarnished, and corroded, any more than it makes sense to carry them in a pocket with loose change, keys, etc. Even if left alone in a desk drawer, it is surprising in how short a time they become soiled and tarnished; easily losing half their value in no time at all.

A man of wealth may have a separate money room lined with specially built cabinets similar to a museum. Unfortunately, we are not all wealthy enough to afford either the private room or the cabinets, or even enough coins to fill them if we had them. Therefore, we must look around to find the best holders possible for our individual requirements, and best suited to our financial means and the space available.

For paper money there are small, compact albums sold very reasonably in sizes for both large-sized bills and fractional currency. These contain fifty or more pockets of cellophane, closed on the long side by being folded over into the binding, and open at each end for inserting the bill. These pockets display the bill on both sides, and are separated by a heavy sheet of white paper on which a description of the paper currency following is entered.

For commemorative half dollars there are albums of heavy construction containing a hole for each issue, with the name of the issue printed underneath each hole. New leaves are supplied for every five or six new issues of the commemorative half dollars. The same principle is carried out in individual boards with holes for four commemorative or ordinary half dollars, kept in place by a celluloid slide. These separate boards take up very little room and show the coins on both sides. Such boards are also sold with holes for cents, nickels, dimes, quarters, and half dollars. They may also be obtained with one hole for each of these denominations, and are handy for such series as the United States proof and mint sets or the Canadian mint sets.

We have already mentioned the "penny" boards, sold in nearly all department stores, stationery stores, and hobby shops, which have tremendously increased the interest of young people in coin collecting. These may be obtained for all denominations in a folding arrangement that makes it easy to store them in a bookcase or cabinet. They have the added advantage of being printed to show at a glance all dates and mint marks, so that missing items may be added later. They are furnished separately for Indian-head and Lincoln-head cents, bust-type dimes, or Liberty-head, the late Mercury, or winged-head, dimes, and all types of quarters, halves, and dollars.

For the man who can afford them, plush-lined boxes, such as those used by jewelers, may be desirable, as they permit of attractive and easy display. Many series of special issues, such as the English Festival sets, Coronation sets, South African specimen sets, and others such as the Ceylon, Ghana, Bermuda, and Israel proofs, come in elaborate cases which protect the coins and make them easy to display. Formerly, Vatican City yearly issues came in plush-lined cases with the papal coat-of-arms. Now they generally come in attractive cardboard holders. These cases, of course, afford no great amount of protection against contact with air, dust, and moisture, but additional protection can be provided by the use of lucite plates fitted across the top of the coins, which does not harm them and does protect them from fingerprints, dust, and atmosphere. Lucite holders have recently had a great vogue among collectors. They come in all colors of clear lucite and can be ordered for any odd-sized coin or medal. Two screws at each end of the holder make it easy to remove the coins or medals. These lucite holders are also manufactured for various sets of coins, such as mint sets, proofs, a set of minor coins, or gold coins, from any country. Printing may be shown on the face with a description of the contents, and the various colors obtainable make it possible to display the coins of Ireland, for example, in a green holder, those of the Vatican in a red holder, etc.

Containers that will protect the surfaces of coins and at the same time permit them to be exhibited when desired are a most important consideration. All collectors are interested in the subject, and much has been written about it in the various numismatic publications. Many suggestions have been advanced, and most of them are good. The old way, in use by dealers both here and abroad, is to keep coins in a cabinet on trays which contain a depression for each coin and hold a space for the insertion of a ticket showing complete description of the coin. The cabinet contains rollers, so that each tray rolls in and out with ease, and can be locked when all the trays are put away for the night. Of course, in a private apartment or dwelling this takes more room than cardboard holders without providing additional security against burglary. In any case, such cabinets should not be of cedar, pine, or other woods that contain oils which are harmful to silver surfaces. This also means cedar chests or closets, cigar boxes, and most other wooden boxes.

For the beginner who does not desire penny boards or collects odd sizes of foreign coins, coin envelopes are sold by all dealers, in various sizes of brown manila paper, or plain white paper. Each coin can be kept in a separate envelope, with a description of country, denomination, inscription, mint mark, and price paid typed on the outside. To hold the envelopes, long narrow boxes either of tin or cardboard may also be obtained from any coin dealer. Each box holds from one hundred to two hundred envelopes, depending on the thickness of the coins. Coin envelopes also come in various sizes of cellophane, which may be used to cover the coins before placing them in the ordinary paper envelopes of a slightly larger size. This method keeps the coins from receiving more handling than is necessary, as they can be readily examined through the cellophane envelope. For coins which are not taken out often, the same or better protection is provided by wrapping each separate piece in a "no tarnish" tissue, which may also be obtained from a dealer in numismatic supplies. Of course, steel boxes are better than the cardboard variety, but cost more, and sometimes are hard to find in the proper size. Coins should be kept as airtight as possible to reduce the tendency to tarnish. Never allow loose coins to come in contact with rubber bands. This applies to copper and nickel as well as silver coins, as even a short contact will ruin the coin.

While the collector is cautioned time and again not to clean old coins, as such cleaning is likely to reduce their value, this advice may be modified to some extent. (If care is taken when coins are bought to secure only bright uncirculated or at least very fine specimens, there will, of course, be no cleaning problems.) It must be remembered that any unnecessary rubbing will increase wear, and there is always the possibility of scratching the surface. If a coin has to be cleaned now and then, one thing to remember is to rub it with absorbent cotton or a very soft brush. Gold coins may be brightened with a little lemon juice, and silver with soapy water or bicarbonate of soda. It will never hurt a copper coin to rub it very lightly with olive oil, using a small piece of cotton, to bring out whatever outline of date and features may be there. Of course, if a coin is badly worn, no amount of cleaning will bring back the design.

Experiment with a few coins of no particular value. Use soap and water, oil, or bicarbonate of soda. Soaps containing lye, ammonia, grit, or acids should not be used. Although they may remove the dirt, they will also destroy the luster. Copper coins will acquire a sickly green color, and silver coins will be practically ruined. The ordinary liquid or paste silver polishes should not be used. Continued use of such preparations will leave minute scratches, which will increase with continued cleaning to such an extent as to ruin the surface. And don't forget that when you have to sell a coin, if it must be described as "cleaned" it detracts a lot from its value.

An uncirculated or proof coin is much less valuable if marred by even the slightest scratch. An uncirculated coin is one that is considered to be in "mint state," that is, in the same condition as when it came from the mint. If carried in the pocket for a week, or even a day, it becomes a "very fine" coin and no longer "uncirculated." Many coins are in actual fact uncirculated, but cannot be sold as such because they have been handled to such an extent that they have become dull and slightly scratched. This is often caused by customers' and dealers' handling. Such coins are called "cabinet-worn" and are usually sold at a reduced price. To save such wear and tear on the surfaces of uncirculated coins, special care should be taken in handling them. The best way to do this is to grasp the coin on its edges, between the thumb and index finger. A coin should not be shown by holding it flat in the palm of the hand. This is especially true of proof coins, which have a shiny mirrorlike surface that is easily damaged by exposure to moisture and dirt, as happens when the coin is grasped carelessly. This is an important point to remember. An old-timer will believe himself justified in committing murder if the beginner grasps his prized specimens in a careless manner.

APPENDIX

Coin Exhibitions

PRACTICALLY all art museums in the larger cities contain displays of coins, some of them more extensive than others, but all of them interesting. Some of the outstanding collections are:

American Numismatic Society Museum. 156th Street and Broadway, New York City. One of the largest collections of coins and medals in the world.

National Museum—Smithsonian Institution. Washington, D.C. Over 48,000 varieties of coins and paper money.

Money Museum of the Chase Manhattan Bank. 1254 Ave. of the Americas, New York City.

Newark Museum. Newark, N.J. A collection of ancient gold coins.

Metropolitan Museum of Art. New York City. An extensive collection of ancient and modern coins, particularly the former.

Brooklyn Museum. Brooklyn, N.Y. A collection of medals of all Presidents of the United States.

Buffalo Museum of Science. Buffalo, N.Y. The famous Knox Collection of Moneys of the World—from the earliest times to the present day.

Coin Dealers—American

THE following list is representative rather than inclusive. All sections of the country, however, are covered, so that the reader will undoubtedly find the name of a dealer in his approximate vicinity. Some areas, of course, are oversupplied with dealers, as on the West and East coasts, but there are many others throughout the United States. This does not mean that, if you live in the East, a dealer in California will not welcome your trade, and vice versa. Most dealers in our country handle United States coins to about eighty percent of their total business, although most of them have a selection in all series. However, a few specialize in ancient and medieval coins. These are marked with an asterisk (*).

CALIFORNIA
S. J. Kabcalo, 2214 East Colorado Street, Pasadena 91107
Samuel M. Koeppel, 307 West 8th Street, Los Angeles 90014
A. Kosoff, P.O. Box 456, Encino 91317
Abner Kreisberg, 228 North Beverly Drive, Beverly Hills 90210
Kenneth W. Lee, 422 Security Building, Glendale 91203
*Numismatic Fine Arts, 10 Rock Lane, Berkeley 94708

COLORADO
Dan Brown's Coin Shop, Inc., 1532 Broadway, Denver 80202
Al Overton, P.O. Box 967, Colorado Springs 80901

District of Columbia

Frank J. Katen, P.O. Box 4271, Takoma Park Station, Washington 20012

Woodward & Lathrop, Rare Coin Department, 10th and F Streets, N.W., Washington 20013

Florida

French's, P.O. Box 256, Jensen Beach 33457

Sidney W. Smith, 2512 Biscayne Boulevard, Miami 33137

Georgia

Rich's Department Store, Coin Department, 45 Broad Street, S.W., Atlanta 30303

Illinois

Marshall Field & Company, Rare Coin Department, 111 North State Street, Chicago 60690

Iowa

Lauren Benson, 512A Putnam Building, Davenport 52801

Hollinbeck Kagin Coin Co., Suite 400-03, Royal Union Building, Des Moines 52809

Kansas

Sunflower Coins, 537 Marceline Terrace, Wichita 67218

Kentucky

James, Inc., 105 West Main Street, Louisville 40202

Lee's Coin Shop, P.O. Box 58, Hardin 42048

Louisiana

Orleans Coin Shop, 517 Baronne Street, New Orleans 70112

Maine

Toivo Johnson, P.O. Box 247, Brewer 04412

MARYLAND
Alfred Hutter, P.O. Box 122, Cumberland 21502
Mason-Dixon Coin Exchange, 208 West Saratoga Street, Baltimore 21210

MASSACHUSETTS
Ambrose J. Brown, 63 Pond Street, Marblehead 01945
Copley Coin Company, 581 Boylston Street, Boston 02116
Court Coin Company, 40 Court Street, Boston 02108
Mayflower Coin Auctions, Inc., 40 Bromfield Street, Boston 02108

MICHIGAN
Detroit Coin Company, 818 Lawrence Avenue, Detroit 48202
J. L. Hudson Company, Rare Coin Department, 1206 Woodward Street, Detroit 48226
Earl Schill, 1434 Farmer Street, Detroit 48226

MISSOURI
Hansan's Coin Shop, 18 West 13 Street, Kansas City 54105

NEBRASKA
Bebee's, 4514 North 30th Street, Omaha 68111

NEW JERSEY
Henry Christensen, Hudson County National Bank Building, 95 River Street, Hoboken 07030

NEW YORK
Coin & Currency Institute, 393 Seventh Avenue, New York 10001
William P. Donlon, P.O. Box 144, Utica 13503
Gimbel's, Rare Coin Department, 33d Street and Broadway, New York 10001
Max Hirschborn, 34-08 Northern Boulevard, Long Island City 11101
M. L. Kaplan, 550 Fifth Avenue, New York 10036

*Frederick S. Knobloch, P.O. Box 104, Williamsbridge Station, Bronx 10067

New Netherlands Coin Company, Inc., 1 West 47 Street, New York 10036

Hans M. F. Schulman, 545 Fifth Avenue, New York 10017

Stack's, 123 West 57 Street, New York 10019

Syracuse Stamp & Coin Company, 217 East Fayette Street, Syracuse 13202

Louis S. Werner, 1270 Broadway, New York 10001

OHIO

Federal Brand Enterprises, Inc., 4263 Pearl Road, Cleveland 44109

Sol Kaplan, 1103 Transit Building, Cincinnati 45202

Lu Riggs, 617 Vine Street, Cincinnati 45202

PENNSYLVANIA

C. E. Bullowa, 1616 Walnut Street, Philadelphia 19103

Gimbel's, Rare Coin Department, Pittsburgh 15222

*Hesperia Art, 2219 St. James Place, Philadelphia 19103

Kaufmann's, Rare Coin Department, Pittsburgh 15222

Pittsburgh Coin Exchange, 212 Park Building, Pittsburgh 15222

UTAH

Norman Schultz, P.O. Box 746, Salt Lake City 84110

VIRGINIA

Randolph Zander, P.O. Box 3013, Alexandria 22302

Coin Dealers—Foreign

Canada

Alberta
Marles & Co., P.O. Box 833, Calgary

Manitoba
International Coin Co., 157 Rupert Street, Winnipeg 2

Ontario
Canada Coin Exchange, 80 Richmond Street, E., Toronto 1
Carmichael's Stamp & Coin Co., 31 Bloor East, Toronto
International Coin Co., 227 Victoria Street, Toronto
Ottawa Stamp Shop, 86 Sparks Street, Ottawa

Quebec
Spier's, 1817 St. Catherine Street, West Montreal 25

Brazil
Santos Leitão & Cia, Rio de Janeiro

England
Raven Coin Co., Ltd., 10 New Street, Chelmsford, Essex
Spink & Son, Ltd., 5-7 King Street, St. James, London, S.W.1
B. A. Seaby, Ltd., 65 Great Portland Street, London W.1

HOLLAND
Jacques Schulman, Keizersgracht 448, Amsterdam-C

ITALY
Dott. Cesare Gamerini, Casella Postale N. 440, Bologna
P.&P. Santamaria, Piazza di Spagna, 35, Rome

JAPAN
Kugahara Stamp & Coin Company, No. 204, Wakabayashi-Cho, Setagaya-Ku, Tokyo

LUXEMBURG
Charles Winandy, 13, Rue The Eberhard

SPAIN
Juan Llorente, San Jose No. 42-44, Murcia
X.&F. Calico, Plaza del Angel 2, via Layetana 25, Barcelona

SWITZERLAND
Munzen und Medaillen, A.G., Malzgasse, 25, Basel

Glossary

Dictionary of terms commonly used by collectors and dealers in numismatic material, with names of denominations of some of the more common United States and foreign coins.

A

Abassi	—Persia. Silver ⅕ Kran.
Aes Gravo	—Regular Roman coinage of uniform size and weight.
Aes Rude	—Early Roman coinage of rough and unwieldy formation.
Albert	—Flemish (Belgium) gold coin.
Alloy	—A mixture of more than one metal.
Amphora	—Two-handled jar for wine or oil, found on Jewish shekels.
Angel	—English gold coin introduced by Edward IV.
Angelet	—English. Half angel.
Antoninianus	—Roman. Double denarius bearing radiate bust of the Emperor.
As	—Roman copper coin. Unit of weight.
Aur	—Iceland. Nickel coin equivalent to 1 cent.
Aureus	—Standard Roman gold coin to fourth century A.D.

B

Balboa —Panama. Silver dollar. 100 centavos.

Bani —Roumania. Nickel. 1/100 leu.

Belga —Belgium. Silver. 5 francs.

Bezant —Byzantine gold coin.

Bilingual —In two languages. Example: Canadian paper notes series of 1937, in French and English.

Billon —Mixture of silver and copper.

Bit —Nickel coin of Danish West Indies (now Virgin Islands of U.S.). Cut piece from Spanish milled dollar or "piece of eight." A "bit" from this dollar was worth 12½ cents; therefore, the slang expression "two bits" or 25 cents.

Bolivar —Bolivia. Silver dollar. 100 centavos.

Brilliant —Bright, uncirculated condition.

Bracteates —Medieval European coins of thin silver with the obverse design in incuse.

Brokage —A coin mis-struck, showing the obverse type on the reverse.

Bronze —Alloy of copper, zinc, and tin.

C

Carolus —Old Spanish dollars with head of King Charles II.

Cartwheel —English twopenny piece of copper with head of George III.

Cash —China. Usually brass. Coins with hole for stringing. 1/10 candareen.

Cent —Small copper coin of many countries. Generally 1/100 of the standard unit (dollar: United States, Canada and others; peso: Cuba; guilder: Netherlands). Also called centavo: Mexico and most Central and South American countries; centesimo: Italy; centime: France and Switzerland; centimo: Spain and Venezuela.

Chalcus —Greek copper coin.
Chon —Korea. Copper coin.
Chuckrum —Travancore, India. Smallest copper coin, worth about 1/12 cent in United States money.
Cob Money —Rough silver Spanish-American coins.
Colon —Costa Rica. Silver dollar named after Christopher Columbus. 100 centimos.
Condor —Chile. 20 pesos.
Cordova —Nicaragua. Silver dollar.
Countermark —A stamp placed on a coin when reissued for another state or for revaluation.
Crown —Dollar-sized silver coin of Great Britain (5 shillings); also, Swedish krona, Austrian krone, etc.

D

Daler —Netherlands. Dollar.
Daric —Ancient Persia. Gold coin named for Darius I.
Decadrachm *or* Dekadrachm —Greece. 10 drachmas.
Decimo —Chile: 10 centavos. Spain and Colombia: 1/10 peso.
Denarius —Standard Roman silver coin.
Denier —European silver coin (France: 1/12 sou) derived from denarius.
Device —Main design on a coin.
Didrachm —2 drachmas.
Die —Piece of metal containing the impression of the design, from which coins are struck.
Dilepton —Greek. Copper. 2 lepta.
Dinar —Yugoslavia: 100 paras. Also Persian coin.
Dirhem —Morocco. Silver coin.
Disme —United States pattern dime and half dime—1792.
Dollar —Standard unit. 100 cents of various countries, including the United States.

Double —Island of Guernsey. Copper coin worth about 1/4 cent United States money.

Double Denarius —Follis. Roman bronze of late third century A.D.

Double Eagle —United States. $20 gold.

Doubloon —Spanish and Spanish-American gold coin, equaling 4 pistoles or $16.

Drachma *or* Drachm —Greek coin and monetary unit.

Ducat —Gold coin of several European countries. Originated about the middle of the twelfth century in Italy. Also silver ducat, about one-half gold ducat.

Ducatoon —The Netherlands. Dollar-sized coin.

Dupondius —Roman. Value 2 asses. Second bronze.

E

Eagle —United States. $10 gold.

Ecu —Originally a French gold coin. Later dollar-sized silver.

Electrum —Mixture of gold and silver.

Emergency Script —Paper money issued by states, cities, towns, or private business concerns in times of depression or tight money conditions.

Escudo —Portugal. 100 centavos.

Exergue —Portion of a coin beneath the device, usually used for the date.

F

Face —The flat surface of a coin.

Fair —Term describing condition of coin—much worn but date and lettering visible.

Fanam —Small coin of India.

Farthing —England and some English colonies. ¼ penny of copper or bronze.

Field —Portion of coin not used for device or inscription.

Filler —Hungary. Copper. 1/100 krone.

Fillet Head —Head of Liberty on United States coin, with hair tied with a band.

Fine —Term describing condition of a coin—in very good condition, everything showing.

Fineness —Purity of gold or silver.

Flan —Piece of metal on which a coin is made.

Fleur-de-Coin—Uncirculated, mint state.

Florin —Originally a gold coin of Florence, Italy. English two shillings, formerly silver. Netherlands 100 cents.

Flowing Hair —Hair of Liberty on United States coins—flowing, not confined with band as it is on fillet head.

Follis —Late Roman bronze introduced by Diocletian, third century A.D.

Franc —France. 100 centimes. Also Switzerland.

Fun —Mongolia. Copper coin.

G

Good —Term describing condition—worn, but date and lettering visible.

Gourde —Haiti. Unit of currency.

Graining —Milled edge of coins.

Groat —Originally an English silver worth about fourpence. Later used in other countries: gros (France); grosso (Italy); groschen (Germany).

Guinea —English gold coin of 21 shillings.

Gun Money —Ireland. Issued by King James II in 1689 from metal in old cannon.

H

Half Eagle —United States. $5 gold.
Heller —Austria. Copper 1/100 krone.
Hemidrachm —Greece. Half drachma.
Hemiobol —Greece. Half obol.
Hidalgo —Mexico. Gold. 10 pesos.

I

Imperial —Russia (old). Gold. 15 rubles.
Incuse —Intaglio. Sunken impression of a design on coin, in contrast to usual raised type.
Inscription —Legend or lettering on coin.

J

Jeton *or* Jetton —Small medal, counter, or token.
Joachimthaler—Silver dollar-size coin. So-called from being coined in St. Joachim's Dale (or Valley), Bohemia, in early sixteenth century. The name later contracted to thaler, daler, etc.

K

Kopek —Russia. Copper. 1/100 rouble.
Korvanetz —Russia. Gold coin.
Kran —Persia. Monetary unit.
Kreutzer —Austria. 2 hellers.
Krona —Crown. Sweden: 100 ore. Iceland: 100 aur.
Krone —Austria: 100 hellers. Denmark and Norway: 100 ore.

L

Laureated —Crowned head on coin.
Legend —Wording on a coin.
Lepta —Greece. 1/100 drachms.
Leu —Roumania. 100 bani. Plural: lei.
Lettered Edge—Inscription around edge of coin. Example: some old United States half dollars and old European crowns.
Lev. —Bulgaria. 100 stotinki.
Lira —Italy. 100 centesimi.
Litra —Greece and Sicily. Minor coin.
Louis d'Or —France. Gold. 20 francs.
Lulab —Bundle of palm branches shown on Jewish shekels.

M

Maravedi —Old Spanish coin worth ⅖ cent.
Maundy Money —Small English coins especially struck for distribution by the reigning monarch on Holy Thursday, consisting of 4, 3, 2, and 1 pence.
Media Decimo —Chile. 5 cents.
Mil —Copper coin of Palestine.
Milling —Fluted edge of a coin.
Milreis —Brazil. Unit of 1000 reis.
Mint Mark —Letter on coin to show mint at which issued. Sometimes shown by other symbols such as crescent, fleur-de-lis, etc.
Miskal —Mohammedan weight. Silver 10 dirhem coin of Morocco.
Module —Diameter of a coin.
Moneyer —An authorized mintmaster or coiner, as in medieval England.

Mule —A coin struck from dies not intended to be used together.

Mutilated —Refers to a coin with holes not intended to be there, cuts, excessive scratches, and nicks.

N

Napoleon —France. Gold. 20 francs.

Nickel —United States. 5 cents.

Noble —England. Gold coin introduced by Edward III.

Nomisma —Byzantine gold coin.

Notgeld —Germany. Pewter, lead, or aluminum postwar coins (World War I), notgeld paper money, postwar emergency script.

O

Obol —Greece. Silver coin.

Obole —Half a denier.

Obsidional Coins —Coins issued during siege. Money of necessity.

Obverse —Front or face of coin, commonly called "heads."

Octodrachm —Eight drachms.

Or —Latin. Gold.

Ore —Denmark, Norway, and Sweden. 1/100 krone.

Overstrike —A new impression made on an old coin after the old one is wholly or partially obliterated.

P

Pagoda —India. 42 fanams, equal to about 2 dollars United States money.

Para —Turkey and Egypt. 1/40 piastre.

Patina —Green covering found on many ancient copper coins, caused by oxidation.

Pattern —Experimental or trial coins, some of which are finally selected as regular currency, while others are discarded.

Penni —Finland. Cent. 1/100 markka. Plural: pennia.

Penny —England and colonies. Bronze coin, originally silver, patterned after denarius.

Peseta —Spain. 1/100 centavos.

Peso —Spain, Mexico, and several Central and South American countries. Usually dollar-size coin.

Piastre —Turkey and Egypt. 40 paras. An old dollar-size silver coin.

Pice —India. ¼ anna.

Pieces of Eight —Spanish milled dollar, used in all parts of North and South America by Spanish colonists, and later by English colonists. The direct ancestor of the United States dollar. Such coins were cut in eight pieces for small change in the West Indies, the resultant pieces being called "bit," worth 12½ cents. Also, later a small nickel coin of Danish West Indies.

Planchet —Blank piece of metal on which coin is stamped.

Pound —England. 20 shillings.

Premium —Price paid for a coin over face value.

Proof —Coins with a bright surface especially struck for collecting purposes.

Q

Quadrans —Roman. ¼ of an as.

Quarter —United States. 25 cents.

Quarter Eagle—United States. Gold. 2½ dollars.

Quetzal —Unit of Guatemala. Named in honor of the quetzal, a beautiful long-feathered bird of the parrot family.

Quinarius —Roman. Half denarius.

R

Reeded Edge —Coins with roughened edges, such as present United States silver coins.
Reichsmark —Germany. 10 pfennig.
Reis —Brazil and Portugal. 1/1000 milreis.
Restrike —Coins from original dies struck at a later date than the original.
Reverse —Back of coin, commonly called "tails."
Rial —Morocco, Persia, and Zanzibar. Unit of currency.
Rin —Japan. 1/10 sen. One of the smallest copper coins.
Rixdaler —Netherlands. 2½ gulden.
Riyal —Saudi Arabia. Unit of currency.
Rose Noble —England. Gold coin introduced by Edward IV.
Ruble *or* Rouble —Russia. 100 kopecks.
Rupee —India. 16 annas.
Ryal —Old Scottish coin. Later, coins of Muscat, Oman, and Yemen.

S

Satang —Siam. 1/100 tical.
S.C. —A common legend on Roman bronze coins, meaning "with the consent of the senate" (*Senatus Consulto*). The emperors reserved for themselves the right to coin gold and silver coins, while the Senate had authority over bronze coinage.
Sceat —An Anglo-Saxon silver coin.
Scudo —Gold or silver coin in use in Italy and the Papal States between the seventeenth and nineteenth centuries.
Semis —Roman. ½ as.
Sen —Japan. 1/100 yen.
Sestertius —Roman. Large bronze of the early Empire. Four asses.

Sextans	—Roman. 1/6 as.
Shekel	—Silver coin of Judea. Originally a weight of Eastern countries.
Shilling	—England. 12 pence. Formerly silver.
Shinplaster	—Slang term for early United States paper money.
Siege Pieces	—Coins struck during siege, also called obsidional coins or money of necessity.
Siglos	—Persia. Silver coin.
Siliqua	—Roman silver coin.
Skilling	—Small silver or copper coin of Denmark, Norway, and Sweden.
Sol	—Peru. Unit of currency.
Solidus	—Roman. Gold coin which succeeded the aureus.
Sou	—France. 1/20 franc or 5 centimes.
Sovereign	—England. Gold coin introduced by Henry VII.
Stater	—Greece. Unit of currency in silver or gold.
Sterling	—English silver pennies.
Stotinka	—Bulgaria. 1/100 lev.
Sucre	—Ecuador. Unit of currency.
Symbol	—Secondary device on coin, generally in the field.

T

Teston	—France. Silver coin. England: a silver coin of 12 pence, forerunner of the shilling. Italy: the testone.
Tetradrachm	—Greece. 4 drachmas.
Tetrobol	—Greece. Four obols.
Thaler	—Silver dollar or crown.
Tical	—Siam. 100 satang.
Trade Dollar	—Silver dollar issued especially for trade with a foreign country. In the United States, trade dollars were first issued in 1873 to stimulate trade with the Orient. Other countries have also issued trade dollars.

Triens —Roman. ⅓ as.
Trime —United States. Silver. 3-cent piece.
Triobol —Greece. 3 obols.
Type —Design of a coin.

U

Uncia —Roman. 1/12 as (ounce).
Uncirculated —Mint condition. A coin entirely unused.

W

Warn —Korea. Gold coin.

Y

Yang —Korea. Copper coin.
Yen —Japan. Unit of 100 sen.
Yuan —China. Silver dollar, or 100 fen.

Z

Zecchino —Gold coin of Venice and Papal States, similar to a ducat.
Zloty —Poland. Unit of currency.

ABBREVIATIONS

AV—Gold
AR—Silver
AE—Copper
B—Brass
Br—Bronze
C—Copper
Unc.—Uncirculated
F.D. C— "
V.F.—Very fine
F—Fine
G—Good

L—Left (In looking at a coin, the viewer's left)
R—Right
Laur.—Laureated
MM—Mint mark, or, in the case of medals, millimeters.
N—Nickel
Obv.—Obverse
Rx or Rev.—Reverse
Diad.—Diademed
R—Rare; RR—very rare; RRR—extremely rare; RRRR—of greatest rarity.

Numismatic Periodicals

Bulletin of the South Australia Numismatic Society, P.O. Box 3644, Sydney, New South Wales, Australia.

Canadian Numismatic Journal (monthly). Canadian Numismatic Association.

Coin and Medal Bulletin (monthly). B. A. Seaby, Ltd., 65 Great Portland St., London, W.1, England.

Coins and Medals, Link House Publications, Ltd., 10-12 South Crescent, Store Street, London, W.C. 1, England.

Coins Magazine, Iola, Wisconsin 54945

Coin World, Sidney News Bldg., Sidney, Ohio 45365

Numismatic Chronicle and Journal of the Royal Numismatic Society. London, England.

Numismatic Circular (monthly). Spink & Son, Ltd., 5-7 King St., St. James, London, S.W.1, England.

Numismatic News, Iola, Wisconsin 54945

Numismatic Scrapbook Magazine (monthly). Hewitt Brothers, 7320 Milwaukee Ave., Chicago, Ill. 60648

The Numismatist (monthly journal of the American Numismatic Assn.). Jack R. Koch, Executive Director, P.O. Box 2366, Colorado Springs, Colo. 80901

Whitman Numismatic Journal, Racine, Wisconsin 53404

World Coins, Sidney News Bldg., Sidney, Ohio 45365

Clubs and Organizations

Following is a list of coin clubs and organizations in this country and Canada. Since names and addresses of officers change at least yearly, street addresses are not shown. However, the official journal of the American Numismatic Association, *The Numismatist,* regularly lists all clubs affiliated with that organization, together with names and addresses of officers.

United States

American Numismatic Association. Jack R. Koch, Executive Director, P.O. Box 2366, Colorado Springs, Colo. 80901

American Numismatic Society. Broadway at 156 St., New York 32, N.Y.

American Vecturist Association. Wm. E. Eisenberg, Secy., 2717 W. Carson St., Pittsburgh 4, Pa.

California State Numismatic Association. Thos. W. Ward, Secy., Route 1, Box 85, Fallbrook, Calif.

Central States Numismatic Society. Early C. Brown, Secy., 7005 S. Normal Blvd., Chicago 21, Ill.

Empire State Numismatic Association. Jacob Cheris, Secy., 214 State St., Albany, N.Y.

Middle Atlantic Numismatic Association, Inc. Eldridge G. Jones, Secy., P.O. Box 6266, Washington 15, D.C.

New England Numismatic Association. Edna Czerwonk, Secy., 111 Shores St., Taunton, Mass.

Alabama —Birmingham Coin Club

Arizona —Phoenix Coin Club
Tucson Coin Club

Arkansas —Albert Pike Numismatic Society (Fort Smith)
Arkansas Numismatic Society (Little Rock)
White River Valley Coin & Stamp Club (Newport)

California —Orange County Coin Club (Brea)
West Valley Coin Club (Chatsworth)
Hanford Coin Club
Douglas Numismatic Society (Long Beach)
Long Beach Coin Club
Los Angeles Coin Club
Merced Coin Club
East Bay Coin Club (Oakland)
Pasadena Coin Club
San Bernardino County Coin Club (San Bernardino)
Convair Coin Club (San Diego)
San Diego Numismatic Society
Pacific Coast Numismatic Society (San Francisco)
Bay Cities Coin Club (Santa Monica)
Redwood Empire Coin Club (Santa Rosa)
Vallejo Numismatic Society
San Fernando Valley Coin Club (Van Nuys)

Colorado —Pikes Peak Coin Club (Colorado Springs)

Rocky Mountain Numismatic Society (Denver)
Greeley Coin Club

Connecticut —Fairfield County Numismatic Association (Stratford)
Hartford Numismatic Society
Meriden Coin Club
Naugatuck Valley Numismatic Association (Naugatuck)
New Haven Numismatic Society
Norwalk Coin Club
Waterbury Numismatic Society

District of Columbia —Washington Numismatic Society, Inc.

Florida —Clearwater Coin and Stamp Club
Daytona Beach Numismatic Club
Jacksonville Coin Club
Key West Coin Club
Lakeland Coin Club
Miami Coin Club, Inc.
Central Florida Coin Club (Orlando)
Pasadena Coin Club (St. Petersburg)
St. Petersburg Coin Club
Tampa Coin Club

Georgia —Atlanta Coin Club

Illinois —Corn Belt Coin Club (Bloomington)
Blackhawk Coin & Stamp Club (Byron)
Champaign-Urbana Coin Club (Champaign)
Chicago Coin Club
Hawthorne Coin Club (Chicago)
De Kalb County Coin Club (De Kalb)
Freeport Coin and Stamp Club
Western Illinois Coin Club (Galesburg)
Tri-City Coin Club (Moline)
Oak Park Coin Club

Peoria District Coin Club
Quincy Coin Club
Central Illinois Numismatic Society (Springfield)
Illinois Valley Coin Club (Streator)
Lake County Coin Club (Waukegan)

Indiana —Calumet Numismatic Club (East Chicago)
Indianapolis Coin Club
Logansport Coin Club
South Bend Coin Club

Iowa —Burlington Coin Club
Cedar Rapids Coin Club
Des Moines Coin Club
Fort Madison Coin Club
Iowa Numismatic Association (New London)
Ottumwa Coin Club
Waterloo Coin Club

Kansas —Coffeyville Coin Club
Great Bend Coin Club
Pratt Coin Club
Salina Coin Club
Topeka Coin Club
Wichita Coin Club

Kentucky —Frankfort Coin Club
Louisville Coin Club

Maryland —Baltimore Coin Club, Inc.
Maryland Numismatic Association (Baltimore)
Western Maryland Coin Club (Cumberland)
Numismatic Society of Frederick, Md.

Massachusetts —Boston Numismatic Society
Chicopee Coin Club

	Franklin County Coin Club (Greenfield)
	Carnegie Coin Club (Northampton)
	Springfield Coin Club
	Worcester County Numismatic Society (Worcester)
Michigan	—Detroit Coin Club
	Flint Stamp & Coin Club
	Grand Rapids Coin Club
	Royal Oak Coin Club
	Saginaw Valley Coin Club (Saginaw)
Minnesota	—Northwest Coin Club (St. Paul)
	Winona Coin Club
Mississippi	—Jackson-Mississippi Coin Club
Missouri	—Joplin Coin Club
	Heart of America Numismatic Association (Kansas City)
	Missouri Numismatic Society (St. Louis)
	Ozarks Coin Club (Springfield)
Montana	—Electric City Coin Club (Great Falls)
Nebraska	—Lincoln Coin Club
	Omaha Coin Club
New Hampshire	—New Hampshire Collectors' Club (Concord)
	Cheshire County Numismatic Society (Keene)
New Jersey	—Camden County Coin Club (Camden)
	Pingry School Coin Club (Elizabeth)
	Jersey City Coin Club
	Newark Coin Club
	New Jersey Numismatic Society (Newark)
	Paterson County Numismatic Club (Paterson)
	South Jersey Coin Club (Penns Grove)
	Trenton Numismatic Club

	Delaware Valley Coin Club of New Jersey (Woodbury)
New Mexico	—New Mexico Coin Club (Albuquerque)
New York	—Albany Numismatic Society
	Brooklyn Coin Club
	Bison City Coin Club (Buffalo)
	Long Island Coin Club (Floral Park)
	Oswego County Coin Club (Fulton)
	Westchester County Coin Club (New Rochelle)
	Bronx Coin Club
	New York Numismatic Club
	Finger Lakes Numismatic Association (Penn Yan)
	Rochester Numismatic Association
	Syracuse Numismatic Association
North Carolina	—Asheville Coin Club
	Charlotte Coin Club
	Gaston Coin Club (Gastonia)
	Greensboro Coin Club
	Eagle Coin Club (Lexington)
	Daniel Boone Coin Club (Salisbury)
North Dakota	—North Dakota Coin Club (Bismarck)
	Red River Valley Coin Club (Fargo)
Ohio	—Akron Coin Club
	Ashland Stamp & Coin Club
	Canton Coin Club
	Cincinnati Numismatic Association
	Cleveland Coin Club
	Columbus Numismatic Association
	Dayton Coin Club
	East Liverpool Coin Club
	Hamilton Coin Club
	Cedar City Coin Club (Lebanon)
	Allen County Coin Club (Lima)

	Mansfield Stamp & Coin Club
	Mt. Vernon Numismatic Society
	Toledo Coin Club
	Warren Coin Club
	Wayne County Coin Club (Wooster)
	Youngstown Coin Club
Oklahoma	—Miami Coin Club
	Oklahoma City Coin Club
	Osage Coin Club (Pawhuska)
	Tulsa Coin Club
Oregon	—Coos County Coin Club (Coos Bay)
	Eugene Coin Club
	Oregon Numismatic Society (Portland)
	Salem Numismatic Society
Pennsylvania	—Main Line Coin Club (Ardmore)
	Bradford Coin Club
	Butler Coin Club
	Delaware County Coin & Stamp Club (Chester)
	Schuylkill Valley Coin Club (Conshohocken)
	Cloister Coin Club (Ephrata)
	Shenango Valley Coin Club (Farrell)
	Greenville Coin Club
	Harrisburg Coin Club
	Johnstown Numismatic Club
	Lehigh Valley Coin Club
	New Castle Coin Club
	Numismatic & Antiquarian Society of Philadelphia
	Philadelphia Coin Club
	Brookline Coin Club (Pittsburgh)
	Pittsburgh Numismatic Society
	Reading Coin Club
	Scranton Numismatic Association

	Monroe County Coin Club (Stroudsburg)
	Susquehanna Valley Coin Club (Sunbury)
	Wilkes-Barre Coin Club
	York Coin Club (York)
Rhode Island	—Coin Club of Rhode Island
South Carolina	—Palmetto Coin Club (Columbia)
	Greenville Coin Club
	Spartanburg Coin Club
South Dakota	—So. Dakota Coin & Stamp Club (Aberdeen)
Tennessee	—Chattanooga Coin Club
	Cleveland Coin Club
	West Tennessee Numismatic Society (Jackson)
	Smoky Mountain Coin Club (Knoxville)
	Memphis Coin Club
	Nashville Coin Club
Texas	—Amarillo Coin Club
	Austin Coin Club
	Beaumont Coin Club
	Corpus Christi Coin Club
	Dallas Coin Club
	Fort Worth Coin Club
	Greater Houston Coin Club
	San Antonio Coin Club
	Waco Heart O'Texas Coin Club
Utah	—Utah Numismatic Society (Salt Lake City)
Vermont	—Chittenden County Coin Club (Burlington)
Virginia	—Monticello Coin Club (Charlottesville)
	Tidewater Coin Club (Norfolk)
	Richmond Coin Club
	Stamp & Coin Club of Roanoke

Washington	—Bellingham Coin Club Puget Sound Numismatic Society (Bremerton) Seattle Coin Club Inland Empire Coin Club (Spokane)
West Virginia	—Kanawha Valley Coin Club (Charleston) Huntington Coin Club
Wisconsin	—Rock River Valley Coin Club (Beloit) Madison Coin Club Milwaukee Numismatic Society Racine Numismatic Society

Canada

Toronto	—Toronto Coin Club
Montreal	—Antiquarian and Numismatic Society of Montreal Montreal Coin Club
Vancouver	—Vancouver Coin Club